PRAISE

"*Elsie's Story: Chasing a Family Mystery*" *is a labor of love. Doris Green was twelve when her beloved Aunt Elsie died in a small apartment above a tavern in northern Wisconsin. As an adult, Green sets out to discover the full story behind the tragic event. The author leaves no stone unturned in detailing her exhaustive search for the truth about why and how Elsie died and who was responsible, creating a roadmap for genealogically minded readers to follow in the pursuit of the past. The book is a testimony to the author's determination and familial loyalty.*

— Patricia Skalka,
author of the Dave Cubiak Door County Mystery series

Doris Green tells the story of her long journey to solve the mystery of her Aunt Elsie Green Woodson's death. She displays the tenacity, determination, and resourcefulness of a sleuth as she sifts through the bits and pieces of Aunt Elsie's life, interviews family members, scours and re-scours newspapers and public records, and even explores hypnosis and astrology looking for answers. She weaves the meticulous details she has gathered into a story that gives voice to Aunt Elsie, solves the mystery of her death, and illuminates the culture and lifestyles of the World War II era.

— Marshall J. Cook, professor emeritus,
University of Wisconsin-Madison

Doris Green has written a book that could be quite helpful to genealogists, be they professional or amateur, because she not only cites where she looked for info, but also raises and discusses questions that arise in the course of her research. In solving this family mystery, she also tells how she experienced the enigmatic circumstances unfold as a twelve-year-old child, and contrasts that with her understanding as an adult.

— Genevieve Davis, artist, filmmaker,
and author of *Secret Life, Secret Death*

ELSIE'S STORY

CHASING A FAMILY MYSTERY

Other books by Doris Green:

Wisconsin Underground: A Guide to Caves, Mines, and Tunnels in and around the Badger State

Minnesota Underground and the Best of the Black Hills

Explore Wisconsin Rivers

ELSIE'S STORY

CHASING A FAMILY MYSTERY

Doris Green

Doris Green

HenschelHAUS Publishing, Inc.
Milwaukee, Wisconsin

Published by HenschelHAUS Publishing, Inc.
2625 S. Greeley St. Suite 201
Milwaukee, WI 53207
www.henschelHAUSbooks.com

Cover design by Lisa Imhoff

ISBN: 9781595985583
E-ISBN: 9781595985590
LCCN: 2017948156

Publisher's Cataloging-In-Publication Data
(Prepared by The Donohue Group, Inc.)

Names: Green, Doris (Doris M.)
Title: Elsie's story : chasing a family mystery / Doris Green.
Description: Milwaukee, Wisconsin : HenschelHAUS Publishing, Inc., [2017]
Identifiers: ISBN 9781595985583 | ISBN 9781595985590 (ebook)
Subjects: LCSH: Green, Doris (Doris M.)--Family. | Aunts--Death. | Wisconsin--Genealogy. | Cold cases (Criminal investigation)--Wisconsin. | Family secrets--Wisconsin.
Classification: LCC F580 .G74 2017 (print) | LCC F580 (ebook) | DDC 920.0775--dc23

Printed in the United States of America.

To the memory of
Cecelia and Andrew Green, Sr.

GREEN FAMILY PRINCIPALS

- Andreas (Andrew) Peter Green (1876 – 1950) married **Cecilia Petrine Kirstine Petersen** (1878 – 1965) in 1896. Andrew and Cecelia Green left their native Denmark with their four oldest children, arriving in Racine, Wisconsin, in October 1903. Their children:

    - George (John) Petersen Green (1897 – 1962) married **Inez Neitzel** (1900 – 1994) in 1930, had one son, and lived in Burlington, Wisconsin.

    - Peter (Pete) Petersen Green (1898 – 1988) married **Edna Gonsky** (1898 – 1984) in 1921, had four children, and farmed in Racine County.

    - Carl Marinus Petersen Green (1900 – 1982) married **Glenys (Peg) Peck** (1905 – 1997) in 1923, had two children, and resided in Aurora, Illinois.

    - Martin Petersen Green 1903 – 1985) first married **Frances Reimann** (1899 – 1957) in 1927 and after her death married **Maria Pantaja Andrale** in Mexico. Martin had two daughters from Frances' first marriage, one son with Frances, and two adopted sons from his second marriage.

    - Laura Petersen Green (1905 – 1989) married **Berthold (Bert) Olsen** (1900 – 1964) in 1923 and they had three daughters. Following their divorce, Laura married **Reuben (Rube, Rudy) Larsen** (1901 – 1990) in 1949, whom she also later divorced.

    - Andrew Petersen Green (1909 – 1972) married **Adeline Bickel** (1908 – 1976) in 1937 and they had seven children and farmed in Marinette, Wisconsin.

    - Elsie Christina Petersen Green (1912 – 1960) married **Roy Woodson** (1901 – 1988) in 1938 and died in Mattoon, Wisconsin, on July 31, 1960. They were childless.

    - Herman Petersen Green (1914 – 1981) married **Marjorie (Margie) Makovsky** (1914 – 2015) in 1944. They had two daughters and lived in Racine, Wisconsin.

    - Clara Louisa Petersen Green (1920 – 1997) married **Roy Miller** in 1941. They had four children and lived in Racine.

TABLE OF CONTENTS

PART THREE

PART ONE

1

QUESTIONS

The summer I turned twelve, my Aunt Elsie died in a cramped apartment above the tavern she ran with Uncle Roy in northern Wisconsin. Other aunts and uncles had no words for it, certainly no closure: Something suspicious was going on up there in remote, small-town Mattoon.

Only days before she died, Elsie had phoned our house in Racine, asking my dad to come get her, but he had to work and put her off. Yet even I knew the story of her death began earlier, when she moved to Mattoon with Roy the year before. Or maybe it began when Elsie married Roy, a divorced man with a mysterious, if not questionable, past.

Officially, Elsie died from an overdose of Nembutal. From the first frantic phone call the bartender made to my Uncle Pete, our family was left with growing suspicions and unanswered questions, among them:

Why had Elsie been drinking in the tavern with the local undertaker the Sunday morning of her death?

Where was Roy that morning?

Why did Roy decide to have a quick burial in Mattoon without informing Elsie's family?

Could the undertaker have spiked Elsie's drink?

The more the family learned, the more questions they had. Elsie had said she was not feeling well and retreated to the upstairs apartment. Soon after, the bartender and undertaker heard a thump overhead. They rushed upstairs to find Elsie lying unconscious on the floor. They never called an ambulance. Why not? Why was there no suicide note, no autopsy, no inquest?

As an adult, I took up the search sporadically, picking through the detritus left behind in my parents' home. I poked into cramped cubbyholes and stretched to reach boxes pushed to the back of closets. I sifted through shoeboxes of Cracker Jack prizes, jacks, and small plastic cowboys packed away long ago. I peeled away bits of rubber that once banded old letters, peeling away the rust of decades.

Nostalgia pulled at my sleeve and dusted my hair as scraps of meaning tumbled from drawers and escaped from rickety wardrobes. Finding a World War I postcard, World's Fair souvenir, or 1922 silver dollar was reward enough, though their market value mattered little. What counted were the memories they evoked and the meanings that wafted from lives long completed.

A red plastic coin purse glinted in the corner of yet another dusty box, standing out among the packets of old Christmas cards, paid invoices, and World War II ration coupon books. Stamped in silver letters were the words: "Flamingo Inn, Roy Woodson, Prop., Mattoon, Wis." I unsnapped the black metal button and peered inside.

Empty, except for a dime and four pennies minted in the 1940s.

A penny for your thoughts. Three more for your memories. And a dime for a token on a journey seeking answers to a childhood mystery.

Lord knows, I tried for years. I interviewed aunts, uncles, and cousins. I searched newspapers and public records—censuses, births, marriages, divorces, and property transactions—following good leads and slim leads. When there were no leads, I consulted astrology, hypnosis, and imagination.

Family history matters to some more than to others. Growing up, our vacationing family stopped at every farm implement museum where Dad would reminisce about walking plows and old threshers. About crazy times and crazier people.

Or maybe my interest in family history began during confirmation studies when, in the midst of reading the ever boring book of Numbers and its begets, our pastor assigned our class to draw our family trees. A few months later, after interviewing Grandma Cecelia Green and hearing her vivid memories of the Old Country, I proudly contributed ancestor names to a family tree begun by an older cousin.

The family tree assignment came only months after Elsie's death stopped me cold as a snowmobiler crashing through rotten ice. The impact marked the beginning of adulthood and its lure of new destinations. Decades later memories of Elsie would still create the path, leading to journeys into genealogy, regional history, and criminology.

There are people who no doubt remember the events surrounding Elsie's death differently. My husband Michael and I once attended a writing workshop at which author Ben Logan said that after *The Land Remembers* was published, his brothers voiced disagreement with some of his depictions of growing up on a Southwest Wisconsin farm. No two people share the same experience. I'm not claiming to be right about my family's history, only aiming to give voice to Elsie, who died decades too soon.

FIRST CALL: COME TONIGHT

*E*yes tracking the TV screen, I stuck an arm into a pajama sleeve. Hunkered cross-legged on the floor, back against an overstuffed chair, I followed the action while getting ready for bed.

A rifle poked from a bush halfway up the steep hill bordering the trail to the left. Marshal Wyatt Earp caught the movement and drew up his horse as a shot exploded overhead. The bullet struck the ground ahead of him. The marshal slipped from his horse in an instant, dodging right and sheltering behind a low rise. Wyatt Earp drew his gun.

I drew a breath, holding it close.

That summer I was twelve, still busy with 4-H baking and sewing projects (shorts and a sleeveless blouse) for the upcoming Racine County Fair. Television in our house was still black and white, though color was on the way. Also on the way were the first televised debates between presidential candidates and in a few months time people would be talking about John Kennedy's youth and how bad Richard Nixon had looked and his refusal to wear unmanly makeup for the camera. But that July night I had eyes only for Marshal Earp and those ominous outlaws.

Suddenly a bell jangled from the hallway beyond the television. Jerked to the here and now, I watched Mom pick up the phone and turn away from the TV. She cupped her hand over her free ear. From my angle she appeared to be wearing half a set of earmuffs, a strange sight in the heat of summer. "Yeah, he's here." Mom dropped her hand and waved to Dad.

He rose from his swivel rocker, eyes fixed on Earp's ambush all the way to the hallway.

Mom turned down the sound on the TV and plopped on the couch next to my younger sister Diane. We all strained to simultaneously hear the television and Dad.

"What? I can't hear you." The crease dividing Dad's eyebrows deepened as if carved with my penknife. "You want me to do what? Now?"

Beyond the TV hum, Dad listened for a long minute.

"Who is it?" I whispered.

Mom shook her head, tuned to whatever Dad would say next.

Onscreen, Wyatt Earp stuck his hat above the low rise, and the desperado shot it out of the marshal's hand. The shooter stood up to look for Earp. Big mistake. The marshal fired a perfect hit to the bad guy's gun arm.

"Not tonight," Dad was saying. "I've got to work in the morning."

The bad guy screamed and staggered from behind the bush.

In our hallway there was another long silence from Dad.

Before my eyes, Wyatt Earp snapped handcuffs on the scowling crook.

"Look," Dad finally said, "I can come on Saturday. Can't you hold on until then? If you still want me to come, call me Friday night and I'll drive up Saturday."

Dad listened some more. "Okay, I'll wait to hear." With that, he replaced the receiver.

Sometimes polite words like "hello," "goodbye," and "you're welcome" aren't necessary when talking with a person you know well.

I looked at Dad, then at the television.

Wyatt Earp pushed the crook ahead of him toward his ever patient horse. Another murderous attempt thwarted.

"Elsie wants me to drive Up North and bring her back to Racine," Dad said in a low voice to Mom.

"We were there less than two weeks ago. She seemed okay then," Mom whispered back.

"Does Aunt Elsie want to come stay with us?" I piped up. Of all Dad's brothers and sisters, Aunt Elsie was the only one we'd ever taken trips with—to places like the Cave of the Mounds and Wisconsin Dells—I figured that was because she and Uncle Roy had no children of their own. Lucky for us.

Mom frowned down at me. "We're not sure."

She turned to Dad. "Elsie could call one of your brothers, Pete or John, or even Clara."

"Clara! Elsie and Clara haven't got along for years." Dad picked up the receiver and set it down again. "It would be crazy to drive off in the middle of the night."

"I could drive up there tomorrow," Mom glanced at Diane. "The girls could stay at my sister's."

Dad shook his head. "I don't want you driving to Mattoon alone. Roy can be a reckless sonofabitch." He took a step toward the bathroom. "Who knows what's going on? Elsie can wait. I'm going to bed."

Mom sighed and went to the kitchen to make Dad's lunch for the next day.

I turned off the television, the show was over. What'll happen on Saturday? Wonder if Dad will be able to sleep tonight.

An hour later, I lay awake and still in my single bed. Every move brought a creak or scream from the springs, though there was no one to disturb unless Mom, too, was restless. Across the room, Diane slept like a log, and Dad's rumbling train snores sounded throughout the house as loud as ever.

3

AUNTS, UNCLES, AND COUSINS GALORE

G randpa and Grandma Green walk through my early memories and wave from long-ago dreams. I see Grandpa puffing on his pipe and, later, shrouded in a white-sheeted hospital bed. I glimpse Grandma orchestrating the details of a meal around the big kitchen table in their little gray house in Franksville. There's the white-painted wooden stool where I perched atop a stack of catalogs.

Back then my secure world revolved around aunts, uncles, and cousins too numerous to count. Our family regularly visited the homes of both Mom's siblings and Dad's brothers and sisters, where I played with Lincoln Logs®, climbed trees, picked sour apples, and enjoyed stomach-busting meals with cousins and cousins once removed.

On weekends, our parents joined throngs of relatives at one house or another to laugh and connect over brimming favorite dishes. It was a world where everyone depended on everyone else. After Grandpa Green died, we took our turn at cutting the grass at Grandma's house and taking her to our house for dinner every week.

In the early 1950s, most of Dad's siblings still lived in and around Racine, although Aunt Laura, after years of dreaming about it, would move to Alaska in 1953. The exception was Uncle Carl and Aunt Peg, who had moved to Aurora, Illinois, about 1926. Visits to Aurora were memorable, day-long excursions usually involving a big dinner at noon and a late "lunch" around four o'clock before the drive home.

By the time I came along, Carl and Peg were already empty nesters with time to pitch horseshoes and knit sweaters, as well as act the jovial hosts. On at least one early visit when I was perhaps four years old we stayed overnight, with me tucked safely in a double bed between Mom and Dad. On those early visits, I looked forward to playing with Peg's magnetic Scottie dogs. With a touch of a finger, I could make the little metal terriers—one black, one white—chase each other around the living room floor.

We weren't the only overnight guests to enjoy Carl and Peg's happy hospitality. Mom told me about one visit that must have occurred in the mid 1930s. Uncle Andrew chauffeured Aunt Elsie and her friend Ann Litzkow to Aurora for a dance and a weekend visit. Elsie had been close to Andrew, as well as Dad, especially before Andrew's 1937 marriage to Aunt Adeline. (Years later I would find several birthday and Christmas cards sent by Elsie to Andrew, squirreled away in Mom's house. I have no idea how the missives landed there, but they testified to the close relationship.) As Mom relayed the story, I could easily envision the scene in Carl and Peg's cozy home—with only a few imagined embellishments.

"I don't remember when I've been so relaxed," Elsie said, as the five adults gathered around a card table. "I'm so comfortable here."

"That's the idea," Peg said. "We figure if you have a good time, you'll come down more often." She shuffled a deck and dealt the cards, placing the rest of the pack face down in the middle of the table.

Andrew picked up the hand he'd been dealt. "Then, we'd have more chances to beat you at schafkopf."

"You wish," Carl grinned at his brother.

Elsie's eyes roved about the room. "You've added a new sofa since we were here last. I hope Roy and I can have a place this nice."

"So has Roy asked you to marry him, then?" Peg frowned at her cards and set them face down before her.

"He hasn't but I can feel that he wants to." Elsie turned to pick up the Scottie dogs from a low shelf and set them down a few inches apart on the tabletop. They immediately slid together, hitting with a soft tap.

"Hmmm," Carl said.

"You've always had good instincts," Peg said. "If you feel that Roy's going to ask you, he's probably planning on it. Have you met Roy's family yet?"

Elsie rearranged the cards in her hand. "He has two older sisters living in Kenosha and his parents live in Racine."

"He seems a little mysterious," Ann said. "You don't know his family or who his friends are or where he grew up."

"I know enough." Elsie thumbed her cards and glanced around the table. "Besides a house, we've talked about traveling. We'd both like to see lots of places."

11

"You sound like Laura," Carl said. "She keeps talking about going to Alaska." He drew a card from the overturned deck. "I'll raise you five cents."

Five hands later, Elsie stretched her arms over her head. "I wouldn't be any good at another game. I'm ready for bed."

"It is late," Ann agreed, "and we need to be off early in the morning."

Carl looked at their piles of pennies. "Andrew, you're the big winner."

Andrew eyed the copper piles. "Yeah, I must've won at least fifty cents. I'll pay you for a nightcap."

"No need to pay for it here."

"I'll walk you two upstairs," Peg pushed back her chair and stood.

Carl picked up the scattered cards. "I'll say goodnight then. Sleep well and don't worry if you hear anything unusual. Sometimes there are odd noises in this old house at night."

"I'm too tired to be bothered by even the headless horseman," Elsie said.

The women climbed the stairs, with Peg leading the way to the guest room. Twin beds, a dresser, and two pressed-back chairs all but filled the inviting room. She pointed out the extra blankets in the closet and moved to draw the curtains over the room's single window.

"Please, leave it open," Ann said. "I love to have the moonlight coming into the room."

Elsie nodded agreement. A three-quarter moon shone between two wispy clouds, sending a luminous ray across both beds.

Ann and Elsie quickly donned pajamas and slipped between sheets that had dried on Peg's clothesline and smelled of all outdoors.

"I could live like this every day," Ann whispered.

"So, could I," Elsie said. "It would be wonderful to be a guest in someone else's house forever."

As the young women were beginning to drift off, a soft scraping sounded near Elsie's bed.

"What was that?" Ann asked.

"Remember what Carl said about odd noises. It's probably nothing."

Before Ann could respond, the sound came again. "It's something, alright, but what?"

"It sounds a little like Pa's rocking chair scraping against the porch floor."

A sound like sandpaper rubbing on hardwood punctuated her words. Then the chair near Elsie's bed seemed to give a little start. Both women jerked to sit upright and stared at each other in the moonlight.

"I think it's this chair," Elsie said. The chair rattled against the hardwood floor, as if in assent.

Ann swung her feet to the floor. "I'm getting out of here!"

The chair rattled once more and then lurched forward before crashing to the floor.

By now, Elsie was on her feet and reaching for her robe. "I'm with you."

The chair clattered from its new position, and the two friends rushed to the door. They flung it open and ran down the hallway, as the chair continued its tantrum behind them.

Downstairs in the kitchen, Peg was putting the dishes, drained and dried since dinner, into the cupboard. Carl and Andrew were seated at the table, eating large pieces of chocolate cake.

"Do you want a glass of m...?" Carl reached for the bottle.

"Your house is haunted!" Ann blurted out.

"One of the chairs in our room rattled and jumped on its own," Elsie explained.

"Then it fell over," Ann added.

Peg raised a hand to her mouth and retreated to the broom closet.

Andrew sat back, crossed his legs, and eyed the two young women.

The corners of Carl's eyes crinkled. "We've sometimes heard noises at night. But are you sure the chair really moved?"

Elsie stepped back and looked closely at her brother. "What sorts of noises have you heard?"

Carl's lips twitched. "Oh, just odd noises," he said, dropping his eyes to his half-eaten cake.

Suddenly, Elsie rushed at him, grabbing his arm. "You tricked us! You rigged that chair to move!"

"Not me."

"Then, why do you look like you've taken a big gulp of Pa's hard cider?"

Andrew broke into a laugh, "She's on to you—the jig is up!"

Carl grinned at Elsie and repeated, "Not me."

Above them, an object bumped against the floor.

14

"There!" Ann said. "Did you hear that?"

All eyes moved to the ceiling as if they possessed Superman's x-ray vision.

From the corner of her eye Elsie noticed a movement behind the partially open closet door, and again the chair bumped overhead. "What are you doing in that broom closet?"

Peg giggled and stepped back into the kitchen. "It was Carl's idea. I wish I'd taken a picture of your faces when you came running in here."

Elsie peered into the closet. A heavy string hung from a crack between two ceiling boards.

Peg followed her gaze. "That string is attached to the leg of the chair in your room. I was afraid you'd see it, but I'm glad you didn't." She went back into the closet and tugged on the string, initiating a series of bumps on the floor above.

"You're cruel, both of you," Elsie shook her head. "Peg, I can't believe you went along with this trick."

PEG AND ELSIE — NOT TO MENTION Carl and Andrew — were always up for fun. I almost wished I'd grown up with them, instead of a generation later. On rainy days, I would look at old family photos and became particularly fond of an image of Elsie and Carl. She held tightly to his waist as they stood and posed cheek to cheek, his fedora perched jauntily on her head. Carl leaned down to Elsie, one arm draped around her shoulder like a warm shawl and the other stuck casually in a pants pocket. His double-breasted jacket hung open; his dark tie drooped

Elsie Green with her brother, Carl Green, about 1936

Elsie Green with her brother, Andrew Green, Jr., about 1932

against his white shirt. In another blurred snapshot Elsie and Carl's wife, Peg, appeared dressed as men, their hats pushed far back on their heads and cigars firmly in hand.

I'd seen a parallel pose among Mom's family photos. A picture of Mom's sister, my Aunt Pat, depicted her standing on my maternal grandparents' porch in male attire. Mom had explained that Pat had worn their brother's suit just for fun.

These comparable photos were taken in the 1930s. Women had probably always cross-dressed, but was doing so for a joke a Depression-era trend? Was there an undercurrent pointing toward women's rising independence?

Like Elsie and Roy, Pat and my Uncle Jim had no children of their own and they visited us often. Once when they came for dinner, Dad tried out one of several joke gifts that Roy and Elsie had supplied. This particular item, which reminded me of the apparently self-propelled chair in Aurora, consisted of a silver-dollar-sized inflatable rubber pouch with a narrow tube attached and a bulb on the other end.

After I set the table, Dad carefully placed the pouch beneath Pat's placemat. When we had been eating for several minutes, he surreptitiously squeezed the bulb. Aunt Pat's plate lurched a bit to the left. But she had just then looked up and didn't see the movement. I stifled a giggle and quickly looked down at my own plate as if there were nothing more interesting in all the universe

17

than chicken, mashed potatoes, gravy, and peas and carrots.

Pat returned her gaze to the table and must have noted the slightly changed position of her plate, because she readjusted it before lifting another bite onto her fork. Dad squeezed the bulb again and once more the plate jumped left.

This time, Pat saw the movement. Startled, she looked up round-eyed but said nothing when we all managed to remain poker-faced. Pat put the forkful into her mouth, chewed, swallowed, and looked down to pick up another bite.

Dad pinched the bulb and the plate bounced again.

"What was that?!" Pat lifted her plate and peered underneath but, of course, could see nothing.

At first, Dad looked sober enough, but when Pat cocked her head and looked closely into his eyes, he smiled and then burst out laughing. The rest of us joined in and soon the joke was revealed.

"You had me fooled," Pat admitted. "I didn't know what to think—I even wondered if a baby mouse could have gotten trapped beneath my plate!"

PAGING THROUGH FAMILY ALBUMS, I'd always stop at photos of dogs—Mom with Shep, Dad with his favorite dog (I forget his name) on a leash, or, one time, a dog on a sled. I loved our own Smokey (followed by Queenie, Pepper, and another Smokey) and stories about dogs captivated me, even if they lacked a happy ending.

One time, Roy accidentally backed his car over a dog belonging to one of Clara's sons, killing the dog. The incident had wounded Roy doubly: he had both killed an innocent dog and hurt my cousin. Roy subsequently brought my cousin another dog that then lived with Clara's family for many years.

I didn't need the tale of my cousin's dog to know that Roy and Elsie cared—about dogs, kids, and the lives of most everyone else in their world. One other story stuck deep in my mind.

For years, Elsie and Roy lived next door to Clara's family, the two houses an easy pitch from each other on Charles Street. Sharing DNA, a Danish heritage, and husbands both named Roy (Woodson and Miller) the two sisters embraced much in common and always had each other's back when the chips were down.

Yet their personalities were as different as Milwaukee and Amarillo. Elsie was likable and radiated rock-like loyalty. Clara was talkative, mercurial, and often the lively heart of the party. Where Clara could be combative, Elsie was simply stubborn. Locked in loving sisterhood, their relationship was at best unpredictable. So when Clara's daughter ran away to hide out at Elsie and Roy's house, the move threatened relationships on all sides.

One night, the daughter slipped out of Clara's house to take refuge in the back seat of Elsie and Roy's car. When they found her huddled there, Elsie and Roy hustled her into their kitchen. Torn between caring for their niece and loyalty to Clara, Elsie and Roy fretted over what to do.

The next day, they drove into our driveway to seek advice from Dad and Mom.

I was playing in a neighborhood softball game and missed most of the conversation. By the time the game ended and I ran home, Elsie and Roy were preparing to leave, finishing their conversation with Mom and Dad in our front yard. After they drove off, Dad drifted into the garage and I asked Mom what was going on. She explained that my cousin had run away, hidden in Elsie and Roy's car, and asked to stay with them.

"Does Aunt Clara know she's there?" I wanted to know.

"She may suspect," Mom said. "And she's bound to ask Elsie and Roy if they've seen her."

"What are they going to do?"

Mom turned toward our back door. "Your father said they should go to the police."

I followed Mom into the kitchen. "What did Aunt Elsie say?"

"Elsie wanted to keep her at their house for a while, until Clara simmers down."

Even then, I understood that Clara might need simmering-down time. Like a tornado or blinding downpour, she was a force to be reckoned with.

"What did Uncle Roy say?"

"When Roy was growing up his cousin Helen lived with his family for a while and she got along real well with him and his sisters. Roy felt as if he had another sister, so now he would like Clara's daughter to live with them."

"What are Aunt Elsie and Uncle Roy going to do?"

"Elsie worried that calling in the police might make the problem bigger."

"It already sounds like a big problem."

"The longer they put off dealing with it, the bigger the problem will get."

I envisioned Clara erupting like Vesuvius, a volcano I'd recently read about, and didn't want to be there when that happened. "Could Aunt Clara think that Aunt Elsie and Uncle Roy kidnapped her?"

"I hope not!" Mom ran hot water into the sink to wash four cocktail glasses and dessert plates.

Grabbing a dish towel, I looked at the dirty dishes. "Did you serve them my jelly-filled cookies?"

"Yes, they turned out real good."

But thoughts of my cousin lingered. "Will she stay with Aunt Elsie and Uncle Roy?"

"That's the sixty-four-thousand-dollar question. If both Clara and Elsie agree, it might work."

"Could Dad call Aunt Clara and tell her what happened? Then Aunt Elsie and Uncle Roy wouldn't need to go to the police."

"Your father doesn't want to get in the middle of those two. Clara would think he was sticking his nose where it doesn't belong. And she'd be right." Mom handed me a clean dessert plate.

"So, what happens now? Are Aunt Elsie and Uncle Roy going to the police?"

Mom focused on the dishes in the sink. "I don't know."

4

CAVE OF THE MOUNDS

Visiting the Cave of the Mounds was Aunt Elsie's idea. On a summer Saturday soon after my eighth birthday, she and Uncle Roy arrived at our house ready to set out in our two-car caravan toward Southwest Wisconsin.

But, first, there were gifts. Carrying her purse and a wrapped package, Elsie climbed the short set of steps leading from our back door, through the cubicle where the milkman delivered glass half-gallon milk bottles, and into the kitchen. Roy trailed behind, bearing a second gift-wrapped box.

"This is a late birthday gift for Doris," Elsie said, handing me one of the identically shaped packages.

The rectangular box might contain a book, maybe the latest *Hardy Boys* adventure, though Aunt Elsie, who even for this excursion wore lipstick and a flower-print dress, had never encouraged my tomboy tendencies.

"We couldn't resist getting a present for Diane, too," she said, offering the other bright box to my little sister.

CHILDLESS, ELSIE AND ROY GAVE us more presents than any other aunts and uncles and not only at birthdays and holidays. Surely no other gifts were more welcome, though I also appreciated Uncle Martin's offerings.

Whenever he visited, Uncle Martin, who was over six feet tall, would duck his head beneath the archway to our living room, walk to me and touch his right hand to my left ear. Suddenly astonished, he would hold out his hand to reveal what he had found there: a half dollar, which I'd take from him with a grin. No longer a surprise, the much anticipated trick always cheered me.

Martin was the only uncle who gave me cash; I understood then that he had more money and just as much kindness as my other uncles, who more often demonstrated their affection through teasing and tall stories involving cowboys, grizzly bears, or chocolate milk from Brown Swiss cows.

Elsie and Roy gave us humor and good times, often in the form of funny animal gifts. Diane and I each received six-foot-long stuffed snakes that we wound around ourselves in bed at night. We also got stuffed turtles, big as chair cushions, with heads that squeaked when you squeezed them—or accidentally sat on them. Roy enjoyed these gifts almost as much as we did; he squeezed a turtle's head before we barely had it out of the box.

We happily received other unusual gifts that none of our friends had. Many came from a toy store in Kenosha, Wisconsin, bought on trips to visit one of Roy's sisters. I'd never met his sisters, but imagined Kenosha to be like Disneyland, opened just two years earlier. Once Roy and

Elsie gave me a wind-up music-box that doubled as a purse. Topped with faded fabric flowers in a clear plastic bubble and sporting a white plastic handle, that purse still plays a joy-filled melody when I turn the key.

Discovered years later, the red coin purse, its white letters proclaiming, *"Flamingo Inn, Roy Woodson, Prop., Mattoon, Wis."* seems to hum a different tune. It's the only keepsake from Elsie and Roy that carries a shadow of sadness. It's also the only memento that's a mini mystery, since their tavern was never called "Flamingo Inn." It was just "Roy and Elsie's"—never anything more pretentious.

My aunt and uncle did vacation more than once in Florida, so maybe they first envisioned this bar as "Flamingo Inn," before realizing that the name could never suit a small-town, Up-North tavern decorated with mounted fish and beer signs.

ON THAT SUMMER DAY, DIANE and I tore off the wrapping paper and opened the boxes to discover matching t-shirts of brilliant yellow printed with an illustration of a skunk across the chest and the words, "I'm a Little Stinker!"

Diane, who could not yet read, laughed at her gift and ran to put it on.

I smiled and remembered to say, "Thank you!"

Still, I had mixed feelings about this present. On the one hand, I was too grown up and dignified for this message and too embarrassed to ever wear the shirt among my friends. On the other hand, the words, "I'm a Little Stinker," were absolutely true in the case of my little sister, the bane of my existence. At least the gift wasn't a girly necklace or frilly top. In the end, I overlooked the message and focused on the bright new shirt, a rarity in my closet filled with hand-me-downs from a cousin and Goodwill purchases. I was not about to look this gift horse in the mouth, as Mom might have said.

What Mom did say was, "Why don't you put on your new shirt." It wasn't a question, so I headed to our bedroom to change.

Soon, Diane and I were ensconced like two bright bumblebees trapped together in the back of our Ford two-door, as Dad drove out of the yard behind Elsie and Roy's dark sedan. As usual, Roy wanted to lead the way.

We passed familiar Racine County sights—my country school, built back in the 1880s when the area was known as Skunk Grove, and Uncle Pete's Farm—to soon reach unfamiliar fields and fencerows. Each held their own highlights, from Holsteins to Herefords, alfalfa to rye, oats, and wheat. The familiar geography beckoned like an old friend; flat fields, marked by only an occasional stream, dip, or roll in the landscape, drew us ever toward the western horizon.

As we drove west on State Highway 20, I read every billboard advertising everything from ice cream shops to car dealerships. "Is that the kind of new car we're getting?" I asked.

"Yes," Mom looked back at us. "We'll buy a Fairlane in the fall when the price comes down."

Slowly the landscape changed, now rising and falling, rolling away from the highway in waves of woodland and rock-pocked pastures. A sign marked the still expanding southern unit of the Kettle Moraine State Forest, as the Wisconsin Conservation Commission continued to buy up adjacent parcels from private landowners and enlarge the forest established back in 1936.

A page from a classroom science book flashed into my head and I remembered that kettle-like holes were left in the land at the edge of the glaciers that had once covered this part of the state. Also left behind were moraines, or mounds and ridges of rock, gravel, and sand now covered with topsoil and plants. Because the mile-high glaciers crushed everything in their path, caves more often occurred in areas that the glaciers had missed, including Southwest Wisconsin.

We drove through a tiny town that had a grocery, drugstore, tavern, and church on its main street, but only a single traffic light. When Dad stopped on red behind Elsie and Roy, Aunt Elsie turned around and waved at us.

Dad nodded, and Mom, Diane, and I waved back.

When we drove over a river, the land flattened again, but soon lifted and folded into steeper hills and valleys. We had reached unglaciated Southwest Wisconsin and the Driftless Region, spared from the ravages of the glaciers and their debris, left like gray snow drifts melting in March.

I spotted a small sign for Eagle Cave. "Is that where we're going?"

"No, though your dad once visited that one." Mom patted his shoulder.

I glanced at Dad, but he remained silent, eyes fixed on the road and the sedan ahead.

"The Cave of the Mounds is supposed to be prettier than Eagle Cave. I can't believe we've never made this trip before, so I'm glad Elsie suggested it," Mom said. "The Cave of the Mounds is only a two-and-a-half-hour drive from home. Eagle Cave is another hour farther west."

I asked to see the state map and Mom handed it over the seatback. Following our route with my finger, I could see we were getting close to the cave. Around us, the land buckled and lurched. Rocks protruded from every pasture and road cuts revealed the broken edges of their unhealed wounds. The Driftless Region continued into Minnesota and Iowa where there were even bigger caves and I wondered whether I could convince Mom and Dad to visit them.

"There's a pheasant," Dad nodded toward the shoulder where a red-necked male ignored our passing.

Woodlands replaced more and more of the cultivated fields, and a solitary deer crossed the road in front of Elsie and Roy's car. Even though Dad said there were no bears in this part of the state, I searched the forests and pictured a bear watching us from behind every clump of shrubs.

Early promotional brochure

The closer we got to the cave, the more billboards directed us to the natural marvel, with words like "marvelous" and "breathtaking." Finally, we reached a rock entrance sign and Dad followed Roy along the drive and into the gravel parking lot. Dad pushed the transmission into park and Mom and Dad stepped out.

Keyed up for adventure, I shoved the front seat forward, sprang from the back, and headed toward the visitor center, built of mortared boulders.

"Wait!" Mom handed Diane and me our summer jackets and slipped a sweater around her shoulders. "It'll be cool in the cave. The brochure says 'forty-eight degrees'."

Tickets purchased (adults—85 cents; children up to age twelve—40 cents), Elsie and Roy, Mom and Dad, and Diane and I joined a group of a dozen other visitors to follow a teenage guide into the cave. He led us on a constructed path into the blackness, sporadically illumined to show off the cave's many features. Our guide easily named these dripping spaces—Gem Room, Cathedral Room, Dream River—and pointed to formations that resembled various animals, bacon and eggs, and other fanciful features.

Mom, Dad, and Diane walked ahead, with Elsie and Roy behind me. They were in a jovial mood, happy to be on a day trip away from their everyday world.

"Great air conditioning!" Roy whispered, as I heard him zip his cotton jacket.

I turned to look up at him and Roy winked back at me. "A scientist has a plan to pipe this cool air into the State Capitol building in Madison. All the politicians there are full of hot air and really need to cool off."

Elsie elbowed Roy. "Shhh!"

I turned back to follow Dad and Mom at the end of the ragged line of tourists. Soon, Roy was again whispering to Elsie: "Do you remember when this cave was discovered?"

"How could I forget?" she murmured back. "We'd only been married a year when quarry workers blasted into it. We were eager to see it, because it had been hidden and protected from people who wanted to write their names on the walls or break off and take home a stalagmite."

I looked back at her. "It would be fun to have a piece of the cave sitting on my desk at home," I said, keeping my voice low.

"Exactly." Elsie patted my shoulder. "Thousands of people came when the cave was first opened to visitors. You sometimes had to wait over an hour to get inside. If everyone who came here left a message or broke off a piece, it wouldn't be so lovely today."

All around us cave, formations loomed like nothing on earth. In a booming voice (*was he practicing to become an actor one day?*), our guide explained that the Cave of the Mounds was discovered less than twenty years ago and had never been vandalized. Its formations, created by surface water dripping through the limestone, were still growing. Stalactites (they held tight to the ceiling) and stalagmites (they might grow to the ceiling one day) continued to elongate and might grow an inch in a hundred years.

The play of light and shadow from electric bulbs placed strategically along the walkway revealed a shifting panorama of stalactites, stalagmites, and columns. One stalagmite towered seventeen feet high.

I stopped behind Mom and Dad as the guide paused to point out key formations like the Painted Waterfall and the Cathedral Room, which, as the billboard had promised, took my breath away. Rows and clusters of stalactites were welded together like organ pipes, and more than one engaged couple had opted to be married here.

Shivering in the chill space, I looked up at the twinkling lights and into the dark voids beyond. This underground universe seemed as immeasurable as the night sky. *What could be more frightening than infinity?*

Halted behind me, Elsie murmured, "The cave was not so well lit when it first opened. Imagine what it would be like if all the lights went out."

Suddenly overcome by the vast depths, I took a sharp breath and swayed on the uneven floor. Tears sprang to my eyes and, completely unbidden, my mouth opened in a loud sob.

"I'm sorry," Elsie bent down, looked into my eyes, and handed me her scented handkerchief.

The tour guide called an abrupt halt. All turned to me as I wiped my eyes and managed to stop the flow of tears.

Elsie stood and spoke above my head to Dad, repeating her words about the lights going out and adding, "I almost said, 'What if we were trapped?' but then thought better of it."

Dad nodded, but I shook my head. *That wasn't it. How to explain to grownups that the underground space swallowed us like the heavens at midnight?* I settled for, "I'm okay."

Elsie smoothed my hair, and Roy put his arm around her waist. Mom, who held Diane's hand at the head of our little group, smiled encouragingly. Dad nodded again. And the guard waved us forward.

Cave draperies hung heavy from the walls and flowstone appeared like glassy pools in the mist. A single actual pool lay beneath a vast dome, and the Dream River twisted around stalagmites, eventually disappearing into its stone stanchion. The underground universe mirrored the mountains and rivers and seas above ground and the limitless, heavenly Milky Way. I felt as if I were in church on Easter morning, during the hush before the final hymn rings out.

As we trekked onward, winding among the spot-lighted formations, I walked in a dreamscape, awed anew at every step by the changing speleothems, fossils, and rooms ranging in size from those in my dollhouse to our church reception hall.

Finally, the walkway turned upward and we climbed slowly back to the visitor center. Ignoring the displays of post cards, key chains, and other mementoes for sale, I went outside where I stripped off my jacket to let the sun warm my bare arms. The others followed me, and Diane followed my example, handing her jacket to Mom, who draped it through the handle of her straw bag. There we stood in our yellow shirts, two bees hovering in the breeze that flowed along the limestone ridge top.

The sunlight glinted off Roy's glasses when he looked at me. "What did you think of the tour?"

Elsie nudged him, shaking her head and doubtless remembering my tears.

But Roy kept smiling down at me.

"I liked it! I wish we had a cave in our backyard!"

"You could have wonderful parties there, any time of year. Rain or snow wouldn't be a problem and there'd be room for lots of people." Roy took a pair of sunglasses from his pocket and slipped them on. "And think of all the games we could invent down there."

Elsie smiled. "You never know what you'll find underground. The farm your dad grew up on was very close to a farm where they dug up a few mammoth bones."

"Really?"

"Besides being good farmland, all those peat fields in Kenosha County preserved several wooly mammoth bones. Who knows? Maybe one day they'll find a whole skeleton."

Dad groaned. "Now, she'll be digging up the garden."

I shook my head. *Adults could be so dense.*

Little did I know then that digging up the past was exactly what I would do one day, nor the skeletons I would find.

5

BREAKDOWN

Whenever we visited Aunt Elsie and Uncle Roy's house, I dressed up, exchanging jeans for a dress even in winter. One New Year's, Eve we climbed into our 1957 starlight-blue Ford for an early dinner at their white-sided bungalow. Their snug home sparkled with holiday lights inside and out, the exterior bulbs casting colored cones on the crystal snow. Indoors, unlike our real Christmas tree that sucked up quarts of water and shed piles of needles, their tree stood forever silver, perfectly straight and unfazed by the home's heat and lack of humidity.

Like Ed Sullivan, Roy served as master of ceremonies, eagerly welcoming us into the warm home that smelled like roast beef and sounded like Christmas, with carols playing in the background. "Come on in out of the cold, folks. Marge, let me take your coat." He hung our heavy coats in the front closet and ushered us into the living-dining room.

Elsie waved from the kitchen, separated from the living-dining area by a half wall topped with shelves full of knick-knacks. "Make yourselves comfortable. Dinner will be ready soon." Mom scooted around the half wall into the kitchen to help.

Roy and Dad dropped into chairs near the tree. Diane and I settled on the modern, black-and-white couch.

Speaking above the carols and Mom and Elsie's murmured conversation, Roy said, "Elsie's outdone herself tonight—besides the beef, there's garlic mashed potatoes, and just for you, Herman, buttered parsnips."

Roy must have caught my look of distaste. "You'll like these parsnips; they're specially seasoned. Even if you don't like parsnips, you'll like the three-layer cake we're having for dessert. There's a raspberry crème filling between the layers."

I smiled. I could deal with parsnips for that kind of reward.

Diane had been glancing around as if looking for something. Finally, she asked, "Where's your dog?"

"Lucky's in the basement," Roy said. "If he was up here, he'd jump on the table to get to the roast. He'd also want to sit in your lap, and he's a big dog."

I pictured the white Alaskan husky bouncing onto the couch between Diane and me. We'd have welcomed him with hugs and belly rubs.

"Last week I thought we might lose him," Roy went on. "He ran into a problem with the Christmas tree."

"Did he try to eat a glass ornament?" I asked.

"No, though that would've been bad. He did knock a few off the tree with his tail, so we moved all the glass ornaments higher on the tree."

We all looked at the tree. Why hadn't I noticed? The bottom two feet contained only tinsel garlands.

Roy stretched his long legs straight out toward me. "The big problem was that Lucky chomped the cord to the Christmas tree and the shock threw him right into the air. I pulled the cord from the socket, but the jolt must have knocked him off the cord right away."

"You picked the right name for that dog," Dad said.

"He seems no worse for the shock, though he won't go near the tree anymore. We could put strings of popcorn on it, and he wouldn't touch them."

"In a way, you're as lucky as the dog," Dad said.

"You mean because we now have a well-trained dog? At your house, I suppose the dog wouldn't be in the living room."

"He wouldn't be white either."

Roy peered over his glasses at Dad. "Why not? He'd get too muddy outside after a rain?"

"He'd shed white fur; it would show up on our dark floors."

Roy pushed up his glasses and glared at Dad. "We have different priorities. Your old man never let dogs in the house at all."

"We had working dogs that slept in the barn and helped drive the cows in for milking. They helped with hunting, too."

"Elsie and I live different here."

"I can see that." Dad's eyes roamed the well-appointed room.

In the dining area, the gleaming table extended from its hiding place in the hutch for what seemed like twenty feet into the room. Whenever Elsie and Roy had company for dinner, they opened the doors in the lower half of the hutch and unfolded the table from its storage space. When not in use, the table leaves, folded in half, also rested inside the blonde hutch.

The dining table hutch fascinated me. I had seen Murphy beds, but no one I knew had a pull-out table. Tonight it was covered with a dark blue tablecloth. Elsie's gold-painted Meito dinnerware shone like patches of sunlight on the frozen Root River.

During the meal, I focused on my plate—or, plates, since each setting featured bread and salad plates, as well as the dinner plate. The adult conversation wafted about me. At one point Elsie asked Mom if she missed not working at Western Printing.

Mom glanced at Dad and set down her fork. "I miss the group I worked with; we had a lot of fun together."

"I worked there, too, for a while, you know," Elsie said. "Sometimes I think about going back to work."

"After Diane is older, maybe I'll think about it," Mom said. "But I'd want to be home to cook dinner and in the summer, I'd want to be there for the girls. Besides, taking care of our big garden is practically a full-time job."

"There's no need for either of you to work," Roy said. "Right, Herman?"

Mouth full, Dad nodded, for once in agreement with Roy.

Following the memorable meal—well, I remembered that cake—we carried the dishes and leftovers to the kitchen. From there, we walked through to the den at the back of the house.

"I'll do the dishes later," Elsie said when Mom offered to help.

Restless, I walked to the window to peer into the backyard, softly illuminated by light cascading from the windows. "It's snowing!"

Elsie came to stand beside me. "We'll have clean white snow for New Year's Day. It's a good beginning for the New Year."

We settled on couches and chairs surrounding a polished coffee table. Figurines of every ilk—birds, elephants, heads of ladies wearing extravagant hats— covered its top and lower shelf. Dusting Elsie's knick-knacks looked like a full-time job.

Roy seemed to read my thoughts. He gestured toward the tabletop. "We don't let Lucky into this room, though I've suggested to Elsie that the dog could dust these with his tail."

"He's gotten in here a few times though. Once brushed this bird off the table." Aunt Elsie picked up a large parrot. "But it landed on the carpet and didn't break."

"Lucky again," Dad said.

Full of cake, I must have dozed for a few minutes. Thinking back on the scene now, the conversation that followed feels like a dream, except it wasn't.

Suddenly Roy leaped up and headed to the kitchen. "Be right back. There's something we want you to try."

We heard the refrigerator door bang shut and a few minutes later a mysterious churning, followed by the sound of breaking glass.

Elsie flinched. "Sometimes Roy gets carried away in the kitchen, but we hope you'll like his latest invention."

He returned with six punch cups on a Florida souvenir tray. Two cups held cinnamon sticks and he handed these to Diane and me. "Special drinks for special girls."

After we all had our drinks, Roy offered a toast, "To a New Year that's better than the old year."

We clinked cups together and sipped the spicy eggnog.

"It's the perfect amount of brandy," Dad said.

"Glad you like it," Roy said. "It has a secret ingredient."

"What?"

"Egg shells."

We all looked at Roy.

"Of course, I wash the eggs first and then dump them whole into the Osterizer along with the spices and brandy."

"These are those organic eggs from that farm on Highway 31?" Mom asked.

"Yup, twelve dollars for a dozen and they're worth every penny," Roy said. "These have more vitamins than store-bought eggs, especially when you throw in the shells. They're good for you!"

I stared at him, thinking about how I routinely walked the half mile from our house to a nearby farm, avoided its collie guardian, and paid the farmer's wife fifty cents for a dozen eggs. Fifty cents wouldn't buy one of Roy's eggs.

"We raised chickens up until three years ago, and I can't see how there'd be a difference in these eggs that would be worth a dollar each," said Dad, who ate two eggs for breakfast six days a week. On Saturdays, Mom changed the routine with oatmeal or cream of wheat.

"You'd be surprised," Roy said.

"Yeah, I would be," Dad said. "We fed our chickens feed from Klema's Mill in Franksville, and all that feed was ground from grain grown right around here."

An image of the flower-printed feed sacks popped into my head. After they'd been emptied, Mom used the material to sew aprons as Christmas or birthday gifts for Grandma.

Roy walked to the kitchen and returned with a carton of eggs. He opened it and held out an egg for Dad to see. "This may not look different, but the chicken that produced this egg was fed more vegetable matter and nutrients than any feed Klema's Mill could produce."

Unconvinced, Dad only frowned.

Mom held up her cup. "No matter what the chickens ate, you sure can't taste the shells. This is good!"

"Let me make up another batch." Roy carried the eggs back to the kitchen. We heard a glass clink and then he coughed, as if he'd swallowed something the wrong way.

"Let me know if you need any help in there," Elsie called out, before turning to Mom. "He's been doing more cooking and puttering around the house since his hours were cut at the plant."

"I heard that!" Roy's voice called from the kitchen. If he said anything else it was drowned out by the noise of the Osterizer.

"I know Massey-Ferguson laid off a bunch of men, but I thought that Roy's job as a foreman would be safe," Mom said. "He's been there a long time."

"Except for a year during the Depression, Roy worked for Massey-Harris for almost thirty years. Now that it's Massey-Ferguson, the plant's not the same." Elsie set her empty cup on a coaster that matched the Florida tray. "Still, he's not likely to be laid off."

"No, they won't lay me off." Roy's voice flowed in from the kitchen. A few minutes later, he reappeared in the doorway of the den. Stepping forward, Roy's foot caught on the edge of the carpet and he stumbled but caught himself.

Elsie jumped up and took the tray from him, distributing the fresh drinks.

Roy slumped into his chair. "Massey-Ferguson won't lay me off," he growled. "But they won't do my any favors either. I'm working fewer hours. There's no overtime now. I used to earn twenty percent of my wages in overtime."

Dad nodded his understanding. "Yeah, our shop is slow, too. While I'm happy not to work eleven-hour days in the summer, when there's grass to cut and a garden to cultivate, I wouldn't mind working overtime now."

Roy took a big swallow of his eggnog. "The lack of overtime isn't the worst of it. You probably heard they demoted me from foreman to machinist."

Dad and Mom exchanged a glance. Mom opened her mouth to speak, but Roy rolled on.

"I'm a good foreman and make sure all the guys do good work." Roy took another gulp, then used both hands to set the cup carefully on the table, He rubbed one hand across his eyes.

"The plant manager said that so many men have been laid off that Massey-Ferguson doesn't need me to be a foreman anymore. He said I'm a good machinist and hopes I'll stay because the company still needs a few experienced men."

"That's great news," Mom said. "It does sound like your job is safe."

"Sounds like is right! The truth is a different thing!" Roy leaned forward on his elbows cupping his face in both hands. "Any time a guy quits, there's cake and a going-away party. There's less and less work every week and the company wants a few more guys to leave. Never mind what the manager says. Every day he hands me more work than one guy can do and then criticizes me when I can't keep up. The truth is he'd like me to quit." Sudden tears flowed from Roy's eyes to stream down his flushed cheeks.

Elsie leaned forward. "It's stressful. You know Roy was in the hospital a few days last month?"

I stared at Roy, who sobbed openly. Dad never cried.

"They think I'm too old!" he cried. "Too old to be a good foreman, or a good machinist. Too old to be good for anything!"

Roy pulled a white handkerchief from his pocket and wiped it across his red face. He leaned forward, elbows on his knees and cradled his head in his hands.

"Honey," Elsie rose. "I'm going to get a couple of those pills you got in the hospital. They might make you feel better."

Roy nodded. "Good idea." He lifted his head and picked up his almost empty cup but then set it down without drinking. "Bring a glass of water, too."

Dad got to his feet and stood next to Elsie. "It's time for us to go."

"Let me make you coffee before you leave."

"It's way past the girls' bedtime." Mom stood and turned to rouse a sleepy Diane.

"We need to be leaving," Dad insisted. He led the way back through the kitchen to the coat closet. The last thing I wanted to do was put on my heavy coat in the hot, suffocating house.

Once outside, I took deep breaths of the cold air, numbing my lungs. I wished it could numb my mind.

On the way home, Diane fell asleep on the other side of the back seat. But my mind circled around a track, the image of Roy sobbing always before me, like a rabbit leading a racing greyhound. I'd never known anyone who had a nervous breakdown.

When my other uncles had hard times, they attacked the problems. Whether threatened by unemployment, death, injury, or illness, they battled until—win or lose—the fight was over. Troubles didn't keep my other uncles from joking and laughing at weekend *Schafskopf* (Sheepshead) games or from pulling my leg with stories of the grizzlies they'd killed. That night was the first time I saw a grown man cry. Dad would never cry.

WHEN ROY ANNOUNCED SOON after the New Year's dinner that he and Elsie were moving Up North, I didn't at first put the pieces together. After all, they weren't the first of Dad's siblings to move Up North.

Aunt Laura had moved to Alaska, in search of adventure and a land similar to the Denmark my grandparents left behind in 1903. Uncle Andrew and had moved his family to a rocky, swampy farm near Marinette, Wisconsin, in 1954. Dad and Andrew remained close and Diane and I loved our summer vacations at the farm, where we observed the hand milking, drank unpasteurized milk, cavorted in the haymow, and hung out with our favorite cousins.

After his wife died in 1957, Uncle Martin, a manager at John Oster Manufacturing Company in Milwaukee, moved to Mexico City in order to establish a plant there. He soon remarried and lived the rest of his life with his new family south of the border. Writing to Dad and Mom in June 1958, Martin gloried in his new world: "I have never felt better in my life than I do now. The weather is really nice here all the time, winter or summer, flowers, green grass and trees all the time."

He wrote again in September, describing his new country home near the mountains and urging Dad and Mom to visit: "I know you would like it here [because it's] nice and peaceful [and] I really like it here in Mexico, more as time goes by ... it is more peaceful than back home."

When I reread Martin's words years later, my eyebrows rose. I'd seen photos of Martin's home in Mexico—complete with iron-barred windows—and wondered whether Martin had viewed Mexico through the same glasses that Laura had worn when looking at Alaska, which barely resembled Denmark.

Not for the first time, I wondered what Elsie had thought about moving to Mattoon—and what my grandparents had believed about their move to the New Country. Idealists all? (This might have been a good time for me to reconsider the rainbow of a quest I was chasing, but I wasn't any more ready to give up this journey than Laura or Martin had been to abandon their adventures.)

Carl had moved south, too, relocating about 1925 in Aurora, Illinois, an easy two-hour drive from Racine. Back-and-forth visits were frequent in the late 1950s;

when our family visited Aurora, Diane and I raced around the backyard with Carl's grandkids. In Dad's family, staying put in Racine seemed the anomaly. Of the nine siblings, only the two oldest and the two youngest (John and Pete, Dad and Clara) remained in Racine County after 1959.

Yet despite all the role models for moving on—not the least of which was my grandparents' immigration—Elsie always struck me as a homebody. If not for Roy and his problems, would she have ever left Racine, Grandma Green, and the rest of the clan, never mind good friends like Ann Litzkow? Had Elsie ever had any regrets about marrying Roy? Had she had other suitors?

A postcard Elsie sent to Mom, Dad, my sister, and me suggested she might have been happy rooted in Racine, so long as there were opportunities to travel. Postmarked from Tarpon Springs, Florida, on July 9, 1956, it read:

> *We got to Port Richey Fri. We have been on the go ever since. There is just so much to see. Will tell you all about it when we get home. I hope Ma has been getting her cards. I have sent her one each day, except Sat. Enjoying every bit of our trip.*
> *Love, Elsie & Roy*

Even on vacation, Elsie took the time to write to Grandma Green back in Racine every day.

6

LETTERS FROM ALASKA

A unt Laura's letters brought to life images of the Wild West, minus the cowboys. She lived in the untamed past, in a wilderness cabin near a lake beneath the Northern Lights of pre-statehood Alaska. Laura was Grandpa and Grandma's firstborn in the United States. She grew up hearing tall tales of Denmark and yearned for her own distant explorations. So strong was Laura's desire, Uncle Pete once said, that she divorced her first husband because he didn't share her Alaskan dream.

Laura found a man who shared her vision and married Reuben Larsen (aka Rube, Rudy, or Rude) in 1949; they set out for that final U.S. frontier in 1953 with the youngest of Laura's three daughters, age sixteen. Reuben was fifty-two, Laura forty-eight—the same age as Elsie when she died. What adventures might Elsie have had, if she had lived longer?

I had scant early memories of Laura and must have been in high school when she returned for a visit to Wisconsin. What I remember most about that visit was the pet raccoon Laura had on a leash. She did not expect Dad to let her bring the coon into the house, and Dad didn't disappoint. Laura, Reuben, Mom, and Dad stood around talking in the front yard while the coon explored the evergreen bushes surrounding our porch.

Mom saved Laura's frontier reports, which I found years later stashed in a cigar box inside an unheated cubbyhole of our house in Racine. At first, Aunt Laura's letters seemed to offer little help in my search for information about Aunt Elsie, yet as I read on, clues emerged, along with a new perspective on Elsie's personality and behavior.

Laura seemingly feared nothing—certainly not divorce or the dangers of rugged travel—offering a strong example for Elsie, seven years younger.

Excerpts from Laura's letters attest to her courage and forthrightness:

June 28, 1953
Palmer, Alaska

Dear Herman & Margie,
I guess if we had realized how far away Alaska was, we might not have had the guts to start out in the first place. It sure was one long, rough trip. With the exception of a ten-mile stretch in North Dakota, we had wonderful roads as far as Edmonton, Canada, then the fun began. From there to Dawson Creek where the Alaska Highway begins, is 500 miles of the roughest, hardest, dustiest road you ever did see. There is not so much scenery here either to compensate for the bumps you take. The only thing that kept us in good spirits was the thought of

getting on [the Alaska Highway.] The prices on everything are terrific.... We paid as high as 70 cents a gallon for gas. That is a stiff price to pay anywhere but up here it's worse because you can't get mileage on those rough roads and the steep mountains that you have to climb. It sure runs up the cost of your trip. ...

It is an expensive trip but it is worth every cent.... It is like riding day after day through parks, one right after the other. There is no use trying to describe it, it can't be done. You have to see it yourself to appreciate it. Those mountains are really something to look at even if they are a little stiff to climb at times. Steamboat Mountain was the highest, but Trutch Mountain was the steepest. Our poor little 60-horse-power motor groaned and smelled like it was going to melt but we made it....

I guess I'll have to cut your letter short and get at the other [letters] although I could write a book....

As ever, affectionately,
Laura & Rube

October 7, 1953
Palmer, Alaska

Dear Herman & Margie—
We have been having such wonderful weather that we want to be out enjoying it every single day if possible. When we are not hunting we are logging, getting in our winter supply of fuel.

The hunting up here is really wonderful. This little lake right below our house is just lousy with ducks. We hike over to *the other side of the lake to get them, about a ten-minute walk [to] where the lake comes to a point [and] flows into the creek.*

We have two big picture windows overlooking the lake and when we are sitting around home we always keep one eye on what goes on outside. At breakfast time is when we see the most ducks. We are always dressed for hunting and when we see a flock fly over and then swoop down we drop our forks and run for the guns and out we go. Is it ever exciting. I've got three [ducks] in the oven right now and they've been in just long enough to smell so darn good ....

I've got so much to say I couldn't tell all of it even if I scribbled a whole pack of paper so I'll quit right here. Anyway, the ducks are done and Rube will be home in about ten minutes. Good-bye for now.

    Love,

    Laura & Rube

Laura and Rube traveled across Alaska, finding adventure on short trips to remote villages and longer stays in larger towns where they found work for a season or two. They lived frugally, putting all available time and money and energy toward clearing and owning their own wild homestead. Sometimes they lived apart—working in turn on the homestead or at a job that paid the bills. In the end, Laura's happiness seemed to come not from fulfilling her dream but from the effort expended in gaining it.

March 21, 1954
Palmer, Alaska

Dear Herman & Margie—
Boy, is it ever hot this afternoon. I have a table by the big front window for writing and I had to close the drapes to keep cool. The snow and ice is melting off the roof and dripping like rain. We can expect the break-up any day now. ... We are going to pack up and leave this place before it comes because we would really be sewed up here. A person can always make it over a few snow banks on foot, but I don't relish the thought of plowing through thick, gooshy mud that goes over my boot tops.

[W]e are going down to Homer and from there to the Fox River Valley.... We have talked to quite a few people who have been down there and they sure rave about it. It is on the shore line, so we will get to see the ocean—always thought it was the Pacific, but it's the Bering Sea. I finally got around to buying a big wall map and have all kinds of fun picking out places to go and see. Dawgonnit, it makes me mad when I think what a fool I've been all my life—I wish I had started out 30 years ago and kept on going. I couldn't think of a better way to spend my life than just picking up bag and baggage anytime I feel like it and moving on to the next stop. I knew all the time I was right, but somehow or other I always let myself get talked out of it ...
    Love,
    Laura & R.

December 15, 1954
Palmer, Alaska

Dear Herman & Margie—
How have you been anyway? I was beginning to think
everybody dropped dead, or something, and then I happened to
think maybe it's me. Boy, am I lazy lately, especially when it
comes to writing.

I just finished a letter to Elsie and after it was all sealed
up I remembered something. Tell her to let me know how much
the postage was on that [hair] clipper. I was so excited about
opening the package that I tore the wrapper off and put it in the
stove without looking for it. Tell her I'll send it as soon as I hear
from her.

I'll bet you would get a kick out of watching me use
that clipper. We don't have electricity—we use a small power
plant and it sure sounds funny to hear that thing popping away
while I cut hair.

We don't go out and cut our wood this year and bring
them out of the woods end over end—we have three oil barrels,
side by side. It sure takes the romance out of frontier living
even if is handy and keeps a nice even heat.

Have a Merry Christmas,
Love, Laura & Rude

January 10, 1956
Palmer, Alaska

Dear Margie & Herman and Ma
I am here in Palmer for the holidays and about this time I'm
getting homesick for the old homestead. We have been having
some pretty rough weather—lots of snow, high winds and …
30 below here in Palmer, down to 40 below on the Palmer
Anchorage highway and 57 below at Portage on the Sterling
Hwy.—our route to Homer. Down at Homer it never gets that
cold … I should have gone back before this but there have been
snow slides on the highway [and] Rudy has been too busy to
take time off from his job to go back with me. I can't go alone
because we bought a new radio and a chain saw and he has to
help me get them out to our place. Besides, he's got to show me
how to operate that chain saw. … They say you can do in 15
minutes what it would take 3 or more hours to do by hand. My
goodness—what will I do with all that spare time?!
You have no idea what winds we get here in the
Matanusha Valley. One time it knocked Rudy down twice on
his way home from work, a distance of about two blocks. I saved
myself several times by flattening myself against the buildings
and once I grabbed a fence and hung there until the gust blew
over. It's blowing like that now and it's about 25 below. We
have a pretty cozy one-room apartment so it's not bothering us
too much. I like this little place—it's small but everything is
there for comfort & convenience, it's all yellow, even the floor,
with a white ceiling. We have 3 chairs, a table that folds up on
the wall and a daveno, that opens up into a bed. It's ideal for
Rudy when I'm in Homer—not too much housework …

I hope Ma had a nice Christmas—I suppose one of the kids took care of that—and I hope Santa took care of all of you.

Love,

Laura & Rudy

June 15, 1956

Homer, Alaska

Dear Margie & Herman—

Thanks for the pleasant surprise—I really owed you a letter, you know and for a pretty long time, too. I'm getting to be quite an expert at stocking up excuses for not writing but lately I have had a few legitimate ones—punishment maybe. I went on a clam digging excursion across the Bay and coming home I was taking a sack of clams from the dinghy to load them in the car and I fell and landed with my shin on the sharp edge of a steel girder. ... I had that almost healed up and then I hurt the other shin.

I was driving home one night and met a dirty so-and-so who needed all the road. To avoid a head-on collision, I drove into a swamp, or mud hole. There was a 4 or 5 foot drop right there and no one could figure out how I made it without turning over. I must have leaped because there were tire tracks on the shoulder and tracks where I landed and none at all in between for a distance of about 5 feet. Anyway, I ... put a nice big goose egg on my forehead and a lump on my shin right below the knee. It was the funniest looking sight I ever saw. From the side it looked like I had two knees. ...

We had a cold spring here, too but it sure has been nice this week. Rudy came down from Palmer with a friend and we went out to the homestead and knocked down a few more trees. It's going to be a mighty big summer for us — we have to have our clearing done by August in order to secure a patent on our land. The cannery will be going full swing in another week [and I'll be working there again this season], so Rudy will have to work alone [at the homestead].

We bought a trailer to live in near town when we can't make it back to the homestead in one day. We are still parked in a friend's yard but when we find a home site we'll move it out.

Speaking of moving reminds me — we have some things stored at Elsie's house. Would you pick them up and when you have time would you ship them up? There is a Nesco roaster, don't send it, you can have that or give it away, suit yourself. It needs a small part that costs around $2.50.

There is a spinning wheel and a sewing cabinet with all my photographs, etc. They should be crated for shipping but there is no particular hurry — you can do it any time. I'd sure [appreciate] it and I'll pay all the cost for crating and shipping. ... I'm sorry to bother you with this but I don't know what else to do. Elsie's gone off on one of her wing-dings and there is no use asking her. When Elsie wants to get mad — she gets mad — she doesn't have to have a reason. ...

In your next letter, will you tell me if Ma got her packages or her birthday, Easter & Mother's Day [cards] and did she get the pictures?

Love,

Laura & Rudy

When I reread this letter in 2015, the lines about Elsie's "wing-dings" surprised me on two counts. First, because I couldn't remember Elsie ever getting angry, even though other relatives had mentioned that Elsie had not always gotten along well with her younger sister, Clara; but, then, a number of people hadn't always seen eye-to-eye with outspoken Clara.

Second, because I had not rightly understood how Laura's spinning wheel and other possessions had come to rest in our attic and assumed that she had simply been unable to carry them all when she moved to Alaska. The fact that they'd come from Elsie's house was news to me. Perhaps Elsie's anger had been justified. Maybe Laura had promised to send money to have her belongings shipped as soon as she and Reuben had gotten settled in Alaska; maybe the items were in the way at Elsie and Roy's house.

I lacked Elsie's—much less Roy's—side of the story. Might Elsie and Roy already have been thinking about emptying their house and moving from Racine three years before they actually did so? This seemed unlikely, but it was possible.

December 22, 1956
Palmer, Alaska

[Note on back of a Christmas card]

Dear Herman & Margie—
Well, I'm off the "boon docks" back to civilization— electricity,
oil heat, running water, inside outhouse and all the other stuff
that helps make a person fat and lazy. I'll be glad to get out to
our homestead and stay there for a change ... We've had lots of
[rough weather], below zero almost every day and those
howling winds. They whistle around the gables and make it
sound like we're living in a pipe organ.
>   *Love,*
>   *Laura & Rudy*

November 10, 1958
Seward, Alaska

Dear Herman & Margie—and Ma
I haven't heard from you for so long it's almost like writing to
strangers. How have you been anyway? ...
>   *Have you still got my Nesco roaster in your attic? If*
you have, will you ship it to me please? I'd like to have it in
time for Christmas because our oven here is no good. [The
Nesco] needs a new part.... I wish you would get that fixed
before you ship it because up here you always have to pay six
prices for every little thing you have done. Send me the bill and

I will repay you for that and also the cost of shipping. I hate to bother you but will you get it as soon as possible? I'm hungry for a nice big goose for Christmas.

> *Love,*
> *Laura*

P.S. How is Ma getting along? Give her my love and hilsen [greetings and best regards].

December 22, 1958
Seward, Alaska

[Note in a Christmas card]

Dear Herman & Margie
I have the roaster now—many thanks for the trouble. I'll send the money in January.

> *Love,*
> *Laura*

July 9, 1959
Seward, Alaska

Dear Herman and Margie:

I'm sorry I made you wait so long for this money but I just plumb forgot about it. ...

The homestead is all ours now but I wonder if we'll ever get a real house on it and improve it—it takes so darn much money and there is none to be made in Homer. So we keep running around the country working everywhere else and the homestead always has to wait. ...

Love,
Laura

November 28, 1959
Seward, Alaska

[Note in a Christmas card]

Hi Kids—

I sure wish we could have made it home for the holidays. We are going to have a rather quiet Thanksgiving tomorrow. Rudy is in Palmer and won't be able to make it. The radio has been announcing bad driving conditions with two bad accidents. It's nearly always bad on the Portage Pass—they have those white-outs. You can't see a thing—it's like driving up against a giant sheet. I made that trip once in my Jeep and it took me 12 hours to drive 185 miles. I had to dig myself out 3 times when I ran off the road and plowed into snow over the top of the little thing....

> Love,
>
> Laura

I stacked Laura's letters in chronological order and placed them in a manila folder. For all her brave words about wanting to travel ("picking up bag and baggage anytime I feel like it and moving on to the next stop"), she sure tried hard to develop their wilderness homestead.

Though Laura eventually failed at the endeavor—and divorced Reuben Larsen—she never regretted the move north. Eventually Laura moved to Arizona before returning to Wisconsin, where she died in 1989; she is buried near her first husband, Bert Olsen, in Graceland Cemetery, Racine.

7

MATTOON

*E*lsie and Roy's move to Mattoon came fast as a twister in Tornado Alley. Despite a sluggish economy, they had sold their Racine house by the end of May 1959 and bought a northern Wisconsin, small-town tavern. Strictly speaking, Mattoon, which lay just south of State Highway 64, was not quite Up North, but to our family in far southern Wisconsin, it sounded like the Arctic Circle.

We had never heard of Mattoon. Located in northern Shawano County, the village (population: 435) lay about three miles west of Menominee County (largely coterminous with the Menominee Indian Reservation). How had Elsie and Roy chosen this place?

In the frenzy of planning and packing, there was no time for a going-away party and, anyway, not every family member celebrated Elsie's leave taking. I came home from school one day to find Mom rearranging our kitchen cupboards, making room for three boxes full of plates, cups, saucers, and serving pieces.

"Elsie gave us her set of Meito," she explained. "They won't have room for it in their new place."

My aunt and uncle jettisoned other prized possessions to follow what had become Roy's primary mission—if not obsession. They gave up much in order to shoehorn their houseful of trendy goods into the tiny apartment above the tavern. Clara received several items, and her family helped with the move, driving a load north. There was no need for a moving company: Roy and Elsie had to drive there anyway, and Clara wanted to see their new home.

Our family first visited Mattoon later that summer during the regular shutdown and mandatory vacation at Dad's plant.

After a visit with Uncle Andrew's family in Marinette, Dad took the long way to Matoon, detouring through a corner of the Menominee Reservation, most of which had officially become Menominee County in 1954. The forest threatened to engulf the ill-kept roads, and I wondered whether we'd get lost. Through breaks in the trees, dirt yards and rundown homesteads occasionally appeared, a few corralled children at play, though I saw no bikes or trikes, balls or bats. The houses were sometimes only tarpaper shacks—they had to be cold as heck in the winter. Why had we come this way? Nestled in our newish car, I felt embarrassed to be seen by the Menominee children. At the same time, I wished we could live so close to the earth. It would be like camping out every day.

FINALLY OUR BLUE, TWO-TONE '57 Ford swept into Mattoon like a one-float parade. Our car stood out against the line of faded storefronts. *This town hasn't gotten the news,* I thought, *the world has moved to Technicolor.*

I set my *Hardy Boys* book on the hot car seat between Diane and me. *Mattoon would make a good murder scene.* I scanned the street for suspicious characters, but it lay empty and still, like an island lost in an inland sea of cutover, rock-strewn pastures, and new-growth wood-lots.

Mom took stock of the weathered buildings on the main street: three taverns, no churches. She had suspect-ed that Mattoon would look like this.

Where were the people, the cars? Through the open window, I strained to hear any engine running other than our own, the call of a bird, or the bark of a dog; but quiet permeated the town.

A sign heralded *Roy and Elsie's* and the tavern, sided with brown-gray asphalt meant to look like brick, loomed from the gloom. A doorway angled into a corner, deep in shadow.

Dad pulled to the curb and turned off the ignition. We stared at the tavern for a long minute. Then Dad twisted around, hooking an elbow over the seatback. "I've got an idea." He looked at Diane, hot and sticky in shorts and a sleeveless blouse. "We'll surprise them. You go in, walk up to the bar, and ask for a beer."

Even Mom smiled at the thought of the joke.

I felt my eyebrows crawl up my forehead.

Diane listened, laughed, and reached for the door handle. Her bare thighs made a smacking noise when she clambered off the sticky seat.

The rest of us climbed out and hesitated on the sidewalk, while Diane walked to the tavern, opened the screen door, and disappeared inside. In a moment, we heard her announce, "I want a beer."

"Sure, honey, coming up." Roy's voice sounded matter-of-fact through the open doorway, like he served five-year-olds every day.

"You want peanuts with that?" Elsie's voice bubbled like a spring and overflowed into laughter.

"Damn!" Dad swung open the door. Mom caught it on the fly and held it for me.

"You don't sound surprised," Dad grumped as we stood behind Diane, perched on a bar stool.

"You can't fool your big sister," Elsie said. "I was upstairs near the bathroom window when you pulled up. You gave me plenty of time to run down here and warn Roy that we had guests."

"Next time, I'll park down the street," Dad grumbled.

"I can hear a car coming a mile away," Elsie said. "But you did catch me fixing my hair." She patted the yellow towel that turned her head into a sunflower. "I'll run up and comb out these waves. Be back in a minute." She smoothed a hand over Diane's long hair and disappeared into the shadows. A moment later, her feet sounded on the stairs.

I climbed onto the stool next to Diane. On the back wall, liquor bottles glimmered like stalagmites beneath a spotlight at the Cave of the Mounds. Waxed wood flowed along the bar and across the scattered tables. Behind the bar the light reflected from Roy's glasses.

He turned and the reflection disappeared. Roy's brown eyes focused on a glass and he pulled a Pabst for Dad before digging bottles from a cooler—7-Up for Mom and a grape soda for me. Diane was already drinking an orange soda.

I spun back and forth on the red vinyl-topped stool and waited for one of us to say something.

Roy pushed up his glasses.

"We would've been here earlier but we got behind two tractors pulling hay wagons." Mom tasted her drink

"Got to make hay while the sun shines." Roy glanced out the window to the shadowed street.

Dad crooked an eyebrow and glanced about the room. I followed his gaze around the empty tables. If I squinted, I could imagine three Old West cowboys playing poker at the darkest table in the back corner. But that would have been Deadwood; this was Mattoon. Here, the gamblers would've been lumbermen in checked shirts and high laced boots—more like Paul Bunyan than Pecos Bill.

I sipped my grape soda. Diane was halfway through her orange. I jumped when a clatter broke the silence and rattled the stairway at the back of the building.

But it was only Elsie bouncing into the room again. Blonde hair in smooth waves, she wore a spring green blouse, a skirt of many colors, and a big grin. She draped an arm over Dad's shoulder. "You didn't have any trouble finding this place?"

"Nope." He looked up. "We stayed at Andrew's farm for a few days and drove over from there."

"How is our favorite brother?"

"The same—always ready to have a good time."

"I worried when he and Adeline and their brood pulled stakes to move Up North, but now look at us!" Elsie laughed and snitched a sip of Dad's beer. "I guess their move worked out okay."

"Their farm is awful poor. The hayfields are full of rocks and the pasture is a swamp. If you step wrong, the mud will suck your boot off."

Savoring my soda, I remembered the farm with its unpainted barn, outhouse, and photo of the Dionne quintuplets in an upstairs bedroom of the uninsulated house. I missed it already. Diane, and I had climbed trees with our cousins, eaten green apples, and watched the milking, which Andrew and my older cousins did by hand. Best of all, we swung from a rope high in the barn loft, dropping into mounds of piled hay, scratchy against our bare legs.

"Are they glad they moved?" Aunt Elsie asked.

"If you're going to be poor, be poor on a farm. They hunt and fish year-round and have a big garden." Dad leaned an elbow on the bar and said, "It's more peaceful

Up North. There's more space and no one tells you what to do."

"We're glad we moved," Roy said. He waved an arm around the room. "I've got no job stress, only one employee, and no boss to report to—except for Elsie," he winked. "We have our regular customers and we have good times here."

Elsie grinned at him. "You have a good time."

"And so do you."

"I miss Racine." Elsie moved around the bar and helped herself to a Pabst.

"Can't you come for a visit?" Mom asked. "We have an extra bed."

"We have a bartender who helps out, but even with her help, we're as tied down as if we had a farm and cows to milk." Elsie held her glass up to the light streaming in from the window.

I looked at the golden glassful and the glint in Elsie's eye. As if she knew I saw it, she rubbed the glint away. Had it been a tear about to drop?

Elsie nodded to Mom. "Come upstairs. I'll show you our apartment. I wish we had space for an extra bed or two, so that you could stay here." Elsie lifted Diane off her stool, as I slid down and Mom stood.

Mom laid a hand on Dad's arm. "You coming?"

"You go ahead," Dad said, as Roy refilled Dad's glass and slid it, like a table shuffleboard puck, along the bar into his waiting hand.

WHEN ELSIE OPENED THE DOOR to the tiny kitchen, I thought we were entering a Disney fairyland. Glass knickknacks glittered on the windowsills like dew-adorned daisies and sunlight reflected off the yellow enameled table. Outside, the sun peeked out from behind a cloud, sending streams of light into the apartment. Like Alice, I stood in sparkling wonder—in this bright space I could do or be whatever I wanted.

Mom led us inside and laid an envelope on the table. She pulled out a chair. "I brought pictures from the reunion."

We all settled on the yellow vinyl and chrome chairs.

Elsie picked up the Kodak packet and glanced at each black-and-white snapshot before laying it flat on the table like a game of solitaire, so we could all see the shots of Grandma, aunts and uncles, and myriads of cousins.

"I sure wanted to go home to Racine for that reunion," she said.

"Pete's family is sure to organize a reunion next year or the year after," Mom said. "Let Roy manage the tavern. We'll come get you."

"Ma looks just like she did fifteen years ago, but the children grow so fast." Elsie dealt photo after photo, laying each down on the tabletop. "It's hard to believe I'm over forty, almost fifty, really."

"When you're young, you think nothing ever happens after you turn forty." Mom smiled at Diane and me. "But Andrew was forty-four when he moved his family Up North, and Laura was almost fifty when she moved to Alaska."

Elsie looked closely at a color photo of a beaming woman standing next to a Jeep in a blue expanse of wildflowers. "Was Laura at the reunion?"

"Now how did that get in this envelope?" Mom took the remaining stack from Elsie and shuffled through it. She removed three other pictures. "Oh, I remember. Laura sent these and I added them to the reunion pictures because I thought you'd want to see them."

"Laura seems to love Alaska." Elsie scanned the four photos. "We Greens all get wanderlust in middle age. You better keep hold of Herman or he'll soon be moving you to Canada."

"I'd like to move to Canada," I offered in the long pause. "I'd like to see moose and bears and live in a log cabin. Did you know that a bear once broke into Aunt Laura's cabin?"

"You can have adventures anywhere," Aunt Elsie said.

"Do you have adventures here?" I gazed around the room, looking for hints among the china elephants and other bric-a-brac.

"You'd be surprised. There's lots of wildlife here."

"What kind of wildlife?"

"Oh, deer and possums and coons and weasels—lots of weasels hereabouts," Elsie winked at Mom. "If you drive around the back roads at dusk, you'll see deer. We saw a doe with two fawns this spring."

71

"Herman would probably like to drive around these country roads." Mom slipped the packet of photos into her purse. "We can do that tonight."

After we returned to the bar, we perched on stools to Dad's right and watched the customers dribble in. A few farmers in overalls sat hunched over the small tables, and two men lined up along the bar on the other side of Dad. I sipped another grape soda. My stomach swelled and my feet developed a mind of their own, kicking nonstop against the legs of the barstool.

"Don't let Roy fool you," said the old man sitting next to Dad. "Roy knows what he's doing with this place. He has the gift of gab to get a crowd, but he knows when to keep quiet, if you know what I mean."

"Roy knows how to keep a secret." The younger guy to the left of the old man reached across him to nab the last cigarette from the pack on the bar in front of Dad.

The gray-haired man laughed. "Roy knows what not to tell your wife when she calls looking for you, Butch."

"My wife wonders why she always seems to call just after I've left."

"How about this?" Roy polished his glasses on a bar rag. "I'll tell her that a hot air balloon landed in the wayside and you took a ride in it."

"Talk about hot air!" the old man jeered.

Butch brightened. "I've always wanted to go up in a balloon! My wife would believe that."

Elsie set an unopened pack of cigarettes in front of Dad, who nodded his thanks. "Roy's a card-carrying member of the Burlington Liars Club, but I can always tell when he's pulling my leg."

She looked across the bar to Butch. "Why don't you bring your wife here sometime? Roy won't bite and she might have a good time."

"Oh, she wouldn't be afraid of Roy," Butch said.

"But maybe you should be," the old man said. "I've heard stories."

Elsie shot him a sharp glance and then remembered me. She smiled and pointed to my chin. I rubbed away a spot of soda.

Next to me, Diane dug into a bag of potato chips.

Mom eyed us and then turned to Elsie, "You'll have to excuse us. We should take the girls to dinner. There was a café we noticed driving in."

"You'll get a good home-cooked meal there. I wish I could invite you for dinner here, but we'll soon get busy."

I slid off the barstool. Eating out was a rare occasion. Mom and Dad usually ordered roast beef sandwiches, while I opted for a hamburger and the added treat of chocolate milk.

Afterward, we drove around the county but didn't see any deer or any other wild animals. Dad dropped us at the motel while he went back to the tavern.

WHEN DAD FINALLY RETURNED TO our room, I feigned sleep in the bed I shared with Diane, who had zonked out an hour before.

"I've been thinking," Dad said. "We should move Up North or even to Alaska. Laura seems to be doing okay there."

"Your sister paid a big price when she moved."

"You mean Reuben?"

"Her first husband was worth more than a cabin in the middle of nowhere, and she hasn't seen her older daughters in ages."

"Laura always was bull-headed, like all of my sisters," Dad said.

Like the whole family, I thought, except for Elsie. I imagined Mom's eyes rolling, but she remained quiet.

"At least, Laura managed to grab her dream, like Ma and Pa moving from Denmark," Dad went on. "Then Andrew bought that farm. Now Elsie has moved up here. I'd be happier too in a place where there's more space and a guy can do what he wants."

"I'd miss our relatives and neighbors," Mom said. "In Racine, there's always someone to call when the car breaks down, the power goes out, or we need someone to stay with the girls."

"Your relatives are in Racine. Mine are driving away like they were on a drag strip."

"How would you make a living?"

"I'd find something," Dad said. "Roy and Elsie seem to be doing all right."

"I'm not so sure. The bar wasn't all that crowded tonight and three bars in one small town seems like two more than it needs."

"Farmers come from miles around."

"I bet farmers don't come from miles around in the dead of winter with snow coming every other day. It probably takes days to plow all the back roads."

Coins and keys jingled as Dad emptied his pockets.

"Think about what it must be like in the winter," Mom persisted. "Who do Elsie and Roy talk to, except for the customers? What is there to do, besides drink? Elsie used to entertain and knit, and bake fancy desserts, but she has no time here for anything outside the tavern. And who is there to entertain?"

"Slide over." The bedsprings creaked. "Elsie talked about winter tonight. When the tavern is doing better, she wants to shut down every February and take a vacation in Florida—the Sunshine State."

"More like the state of dreams."

"That's where I'm heading." Dad's rhythmic snoring soon lulled me to sleep, a scratchy record needle stuck in a worn-out groove.

OVER THE WINTER I WROTE TO Elsie and received a rose-embellished thank-you note in her perfect handwriting:

Dear Doris —

I sure enjoyed your letters. I am sorry I don't have more time to write to you. We want to thank you and Diane for the Christmas presents and also for the nice Valentines you sent us.

Our winter up here has been very mild. We only have had 2 days below zero. The only heavy snow we had was

*Christmas Day, since then we have had only a few snowflakes.
We are really lucky. When you had your snow storms we didn't
get any.*

*Roy and I have both been sick with the flu. I have had a
cold since before Christmas. But we are both better now.*

*Say hello to my Mother and I am glad she liked the rug
we sent her for her birthday.*

*Tell your Mom and Dad we say hello and write again,
Doris.*

*Love
Elsie & Roy*

I must have answered this note, though when searching
many years later, I found no other correspondence from
Elsie.

8

SECOND VISIT, SECOND CALL

O ur family repeated our Up North pilgrimage in early July 1960, circling through the Dells, stopping by Andrew's Marinette County farm, and spending a week at a cottage on Pickerel Lake before returning to Mattoon. If anything, Roy and Aunt Elsie's tavern seemed livelier now and brighter, with all lights blazing and winking beer signs aglitter.

"Herman! Marge! And the girls! We wondered when you'd get here," Elsie ran from behind the bar to greet us when we all trooped in on a hot afternoon.

"We got an early start this morning," Mom said, "and had a quick lunch at a wayside."

"It was quick because even at high noon the mosquitoes were awful," Dad said.

Diane held out her arms, covered in red welts.

"The mosquitoes love her," Mom said.

"We all love her." Elsie swung Diane onto a high stool. "What'll you have? An orange soda?"

An older man moved down the bar, so that we had four stools in a row. Dad nodded to him. "Still helping them make a go of this place?"

"Someone has to." He played a tattoo on the bar with the fingers of his left hand, then reached for a peanut from a glass bowl. "Without me around, Roy here would give the place away. At least he'd give free drinks to anyone he liked the looks of."

"Bones," Roy said to the grizzled fellow, "you know better than to tell tales about me. I just want to be everybody's favorite bartender and make a go of this place. A free drink now and then is good advertising."

"You can never be everybody's favorite," Bones said.

"'Bones' is Bill Johnson, our undertaker," Elsie said. "He always gets the last word."

"Except when you do," the older man said.

Roy laughed and wiggled his eyebrows at Bones. I recalled the Uncle Wiggly books I'd read as a kid of nine or ten. Not that Roy looked like a rabbit. But now it seemed I had my own Uncle Wiggly.

"He always gets you in the end," Uncle Wiggly-Roy pointed a finger at Bones.

"I might get the last word, but you're the guy in charge," Bones said. "People know not to cross you."

Roy's smile suddenly reversed into a frown. "Right. I do give drinks to customers I like, but I draw a line. People need to know a bartender means business or they'll walk all over you." His right hand shot beneath the bar. When his hand came up, it clenched a club. I'd thought he was going to pull out a six-shooter like John Wayne, but, no, Roy clutched a club exactly like a street patrolman on *Dragnet*.

I stopped kicking the stool. Diane set her soda bottle on the bar.

"Maybe you noticed the sign on the door?" Roy pointed the club at the entrance. "'No Indians' means '*No Indians.*' They can't handle their liquor and when they drink, they fight."

"The Menominee Reservation is what—two miles from here?" Dad asked.

"As the crow flies. It's maybe three miles by car." Roy rapped the club on the bar. "The Indians go to that tavern down the street," he pointed with the club. "That guy takes their money and turns the other way when they get riled up. Sometimes one of them will take a poke at a guy. Next thing you know, there's a regular riot. That'll never happen here." Roy slammed the club into his open hand and glared around the room.

The men at the bar looked at their drinks. I looked at Diane's feet, then my own, encased in the moccasins Dad bought us in the Dells.

Our summer travels often took us to Wisconsin Dells, and I sometimes wished I could be an Indian there. We explored the attractions of the day, like Storybook Gardens, Fort Dells, and Enchanted Forest and Prehistoric Land, where Diane and I posed for photos atop a cement stegosaurus. Once we took a boat tour through the dells of the Wisconsin River and once we took in the Ho-Chunk's Stand Rock Indian Ceremonial. But we never rode the amphibious Wisconsin Ducks, my big disappointment.

Too bad the ceremonial was just another show, a staged performance little different from Paul Bunyan's Cook Shack, where we gorged on all the pancakes we could eat. Though the dancers mesmerized us with color and movement, I wondered what their life was like and where they slept at night.

"ELSIE AND I RUN A SAFE PLACE," Roy was saying. "We have a good time and there's no fighting." He pointed the club at Bones. "Our regular customers have become our friends. We got what we want here."

Our aunt noticed Dad's empty glass. "You want another beer?" Before he could answer, Elsie swept the glass away and refilled it, touching his hand when she set the foaming glass back on the bar. Then Elsie came out from behind the bar and moved to a group of farmers gathered around a corner table to take orders for drink refills.

Roy still stood behind the bar, watching her. The club had disappeared.

WE'D BEEN HOME A WEEK OR SO when Elsie called that evening to ask Dad to come get her. I'd wondered then whether he would be driving to Mattoon on Saturday. *Would Dad take me with him?* Probably not, I decided, though I'd have gone along in a heartbeat.

Caught up in my summer routine of garden chores, ballgames with the neighbor kids, and 4-H cooking and sewing projects, I soon forgot about Elsie's appeal. On

Friday night we played kick the can in a neighbor's backyard, stopping only after full dark. After the game a friend and I lay on the grass staring upward, and I shivered at seeing the infinite swath of the Milky Way. It was impossible to grasp: in all this universe, how had I come to be here?

Saturday came and Dad cultivated the vegetable and flower gardens. Sunday we attended the morning service at the white clapboard, nineteenth-century church that now served our new Mount Pleasant Lutheran congregation, which in turn served a burgeoning population west of Racine.

The call finally came that evening, though it wasn't the call we were waiting for. This time the telephone rang in the middle of a *Maverick* rerun.

I liked Westerns—especially the horses, the adventure, and the security of knowing the good guys always won. But that phone call thrust me into dark anxiety—to the point in the plot when the villain gets the upper hand and turmoil ranges across the trackless plains.

When the phone jangled, Dad jumped in his chair as if he'd been shot, even though Bret and Bart were only sitting around their campfire. Dad picked up the receiver and Mom came in from the kitchen. She'd been packing the raspberries we grew into plastic bags that stood open inside small cardboard boxes lined up on the counter, almost ready for the freezer. She froze strawberries, too, plus vegetables, day-old bread from Kappus Bakery, and half a steer we bought for a year of steaks and burgers.

"Pete, I thought you might be Elsie calling." Dad stood at the phone, not bothering to sit in the diminutive chair next to the telephone stand.

Uncle Pete had somehow become the family patriarch after Grandpa died. Dad's oldest brother, John, had gone off to World War I and then taken a job selling a livestock feed additive for a company in Burlington, Wisconsin, where he settled down and served as alderman. Fifteen months younger than John, Pete had also been drafted into the U.S. Army, but he got only as far as training camp before the war ended. Pete returned home, married Aunt Edna in 1921, and soon purchased his farm.

On the TV screen, brothers Bret and Bart sipped coffee from metal cups. A movement in the brush behind Bart caught my eye.

"Oh, no!" Dad groaned.

Mom had sunk onto the couch between Diane and me and now she tensed at Dad's words. She absently tapped my arm with a raspberry-stained spoon.

I rubbed the red smudge.

"Elsie called here Tuesday night and wanted me to drive up there and get her, but I told her that I had to work in the morning and to call me Friday if she still wanted me to get her on Saturday," Dad said in a whoosh of breath. "But she never called back."

Bret stirred the campfire. The camera swung to capture a black shape creeping toward the brothers.

"It makes no sense. She was fine when we were up there, and Carl and Peg visited her a week after that. They had a great time."

Bret cocked his head and turned toward the brush.

"I hear you. How did it happen?" Dad asked. He leaned back against the wall. For many long minutes he said nothing.

We listened and waited. Onscreen the black shape morphed into the silhouette of a man, now just outside the circle of campfire light. He brandished a pistol in his right hand.

"Okay," Dad finally said. "I can do that. Talk to you after you get back."

After he hung up, Mom pointed her red-stained spoon at the TV and Dad switched it off. He faced us, where we sat like a row of limp dolls on our scratchy old couch.

"Elsie died this morning. At least Pete thinks it happened this morning." Dad sat down heavily in his rocker and swiveled toward us.

"How? And what do you mean, 'Pete *thinks* it happened this morning?" Mom asked.

"Pete's not sure. Elsie was drinking in the tavern with the town undertaker—remember, we met him when we were up there?"

We nodded.

"The tavern was open on Sunday morning?" Mom questioned.

Dad shrugged. "I guess so. The bartender was there, too. All of a sudden, Elsie wasn't feeling well and went upstairs. The next thing, the bartender and the undertaker heard a thump. They went upstairs and found Elsie on the floor. She was still alive.

"They thought Elsie had taken some pills, so they tried to force mustard down her throat to make her throw up." Dad rubbed a hand across his face. "But it was too late, and she died."

"They thought Elsie had taken pills?" Mom tapped the spoon against the palm of her hand. "If she was only half conscious, I wonder that she didn't choke on the mustard."

"Pete didn't know much about how it happened or how it could have happened in the first place. He and John are leaving for Mattoon as soon as John can pack and get to Pete's house."

"Roy wasn't there when it happened?"

Dad shook his head. "He had driven into Antigo."

"What reason would he have to drive there on a Sunday morning? It's not like he ever went to church!"

"Pete didn't know. When Roy came back and found Elsie dead, he wasn't going to call anyone in Racine. He and the undertaker were planning to bury her up there."

"But then Roy came to his senses and called Pete," Mom interrupted.

"No!" Dad glowered at us. "The bartender thought Elsie's family should know what happened. Pete's number was on a pad by the phone, so she called him. Then Pete asked to talk to Roy and the bartender called him to the phone. That's when Roy told Pete the funeral would be in Mattoon. But Pete wants to bring Elsie's body back to Racine."

"Why wouldn't Roy call you or Pete? It makes no sense."

"Maybe Pete and John will come back with some answers." Dad swiveled away from us and then back again to look at Mom. "Whatever happened, Roy is the key to it."

"Elsie should never have moved up there."

I squirmed into a new position and faced Mom. "Aunt Elsie wasn't old."

Mom looked at Diane and me. "She was forty-eight, a little older than your father but way too young to die."

Mom turned back to Dad. "Your mother will be beside herself when she learns that one of her children died before her. And Elsie was her favorite."

Dad started. "Pete wants me to go and tell her. You'll have to come with me."

Mom straightened and shook her head. "You have five brothers and two other sisters. It's not up to me to go with you."

"They don't all live in Racine."

"You'll have to ask Clara."

Dad scowled, stood, and went back to the phone. But he got a reprieve. Grandma had gone to Clara's house for dinner. When Pete called Clara, Grandma overheard the conversation and knew right away Elsie was in trouble. After the call, Clara told her the details—such as they were.

9

FUNERAL

*I*n those days, no one in our family cried before, during, or after a funeral, maybe because both Mom and Dad had grown up on farms, where birth and death marked the daily routine—from new calves to hog butchering to accident and disease.

Matter-of-factly, Mom selected her black-and-white print dress and a silk hat to wear to Elsie's funeral. She helped Diane choose a dress, while I wore the striped navy skirt I'd made in 4-H. We wore white shoes. Funeral or no, summer meant white shoes and purses for us and a straw fedora for Dad.

An hour before the 10 a.m. funeral service on Thursday, August 4, Dad parked next to Pete and Edna's car in the almost empty lot at Immanuel Danish Lutheran Church where Elsie had once been a member. Built in 1890, the brick, Gothic Revival church stood tall and austere, with its tower and pointed, arched windows pointing to heaven.

We walked without speaking through the colonnaded entrance, wide enough to accommodate a bridal party—or a casket and pallbearers. Deep carpeting silenced our steps and ranks of flowers scented the room.

I waved my hand in a useless attempt to brush away the fumes; I hated the cloying smell of funeral flowers.

Voices drew us to the basement. Dad and Mom, Diane at her side, approached a knot of aunts and uncles standing in the center of the room. I trailed behind, circling to where Grandma Green sat by herself on a straight-backed chair.

Grandma wore her best navy dress, its hem eddying about her ankles. Even in summer, she wore three-quarter-length sleeves that would've been perfect on a cool fall day. Her eyes, watery and red-rimmed as usual, looked up at me. She pulled out the white handkerchief stuck inside the fabric belt at her waist.

"I wish I hadn't lived to see this," Grandma said in her heavily accented English. After emigrating from Denmark as a twenty-five-year-old, along with Grandpa and their four oldest boys in 1903, Grandma had eventually learned English. She learned it mostly from John, who was old enough to enroll in Racine's Howell School and young and social enough to pick up the new language quickly.

I don't remember Grandpa's voice, though he must have learned English largely on the job at the J. I. Case Company. I do recall visiting him in the hospital before his death, the white room, and the white sheets covering my white grandpa. It was the last time I saw him. I was two-and-a-half years old and he was a month shy of his seventy-fourth birthday when a heart attack felled him following prostate surgery. His death seemed like a huge tree falling in the forest, a thundering death for a man larger than life.

Now it was Elsie's turn to leave this world. So unforeseen, her death crashed even louder in my life and I could not imagine how Grandma must feel. *What else to say?*

"I'm sorry," I squeaked. "I'll miss Aunt Elsie." But it didn't matter what I said. Grandma lived in her own world, seemingly centuries removed from the place I occupied.

We sat in silence until Pete approached. He smiled at me, stooped, and held out his arm for Grandma to take. "It's time to go," he said, leading the way upstairs. I trailed behind as Pete guided Grandma to a front row seat before the casket, where she dropped her hold, to sink, sighing, into the chair, like a spent balloon coming to rest.

I entered the second row of pews to sit behind Grandma. I'd seen caskets before and prepared to see the wax-like figure of Elsie, looking like a doll in a playroom. But her casket was closed. When I glanced away, it still stood hard and shiny in my mind.

Standing in the aisle at the end of my row, Mom crooked her finger to me. "The girls and I are going to look at the flowers," she told Dad, who moved to stand with Clara and my uncles, Pete, John, and Carl. They stood in a line to the right of the casket, ready to greet a growing queue of mourners.

Mom led Diane and me to the tier of vases standing sentinel around the casket.

I pictured Aunt Elsie lying inside. Could she see us? Could she tell us what happened the day she died?

Mom bent to read the card stuck into the first bouquet. "Here's the arrangement we ordered." She pointed to the spray of yellow and purple irises.

We paused at each colorful arrangement of mums, gladiolas, lilies, daisies, and more. I wondered, How did people decide which flowers to buy?

"Elsie liked yellow," Mom said, as if I'd spoken aloud.

"Look at the big arrangement from Uncle Roy." I pointed to the blanket of yellow roses cascading over the casket. A white heart on top contained one word, "Wife."

Mom must not have heard me. She continued piloting Diane along the ranks of bouquets, reading off the cards. After the final one, signed by a long list of adult cousins, Mom led us to the second row of chairs where I had left an open hymnal behind. I reclaimed my seat.

"Elsie always knew just what to say," a strange woman was telling Grandma, still seated in the first pew. "I can never find the right words."

"Yah, yah," Grandma nodded.

In a flash I was back in the Cave of the Mounds with Elsie, Roy, and our family. I remembered how Elsie thought she didn't have the right words and had said the wrong thing just before I burst into tears. But Elsie had said nothing wrong. Overwhelmed by the underground infinity that echoed the Milky Way above, I had cried. The emotion had no place else to go.

Tears again pricked my eyes, as I watched the queue ever so slowly advance and the people one-by-one greet Dad and the others. Missing from the greeting line-up were Laura, still in Alaska; Andrew, presumably tied to his farm in Marinette, and Martin in Mexico City, who, as a widower, had remarried a woman twenty years his junior.

Age hadn't mattered in Elsie's marriage either, as Roy was eleven years her senior. Or had it? I wondered, *Would Aunt Elsie have been happier if, like Mom and Dad, she had married someone her own age?* Age mattered to me, and I couldn't imagine what I'd be doing in eleven years as a twenty-three-year-old adult. *Maybe working in a library or teaching school?*

I craned my neck to one side and then the other. *Where was Roy?* Finally I spotted him standing with the Mattoon funeral director, Bill Johnson, or "Bones." They were conferring with the pastor at the back of the church.

Soon, the pastor in his flowing robe made his way to the front of the church and conducted a short service of liturgy and prayer. I wish I could remember what he said. *But what could he have said? What words could possibly have given peace to my family following Elsie's demise under such strange circumstances—especially with Roy looking on?*

I supposed then that Roy was grieving, too, though his grief was not the family's biggest worry: Always, the family's biggest concern was for the comfort of Grandma Green.

Afterward, we filed into the narthex, where Mom picked up a folded, four-page mini card with the heading, *In Loving Memory*, and stuck it in her straw purse. I took a card for myself and studied the pink and gray image on the cover: the garden scene depicted a bench where someone had discarded a cape and left a book, presumably to follow a center path leading toward fields and woods enveloped in pink clouds. Inside, a poem, *In My Father's House,"* by Robert Freeman, did little to dispel my grief:

> *No, not cold beneath the grasses,*
> *Not close-walled within the tomb;*
> *Rather, in my Father's mansion,*
> *Living in another room ...*
>
> *Shall I blame my Father's wisdom?*
> *Shall I sit enswathed in gloom,*
> *When I know my loves are happy,*
> *Waiting in the other room?*

I hoped that Aunt Elsie was happy and wondered whether she could see me from the place where she now lived.

On the facing page, the dates of Aunt Elsie's birth (May 16, 1912) and death (July 31, 1960) appeared, along with the note that the Reverend Cornelius Hanson officiated at her funeral service. Arrangements were by the Johnson Funeral Home, Mattoon, Wisconsin. The back of my neck tingled: *Had Bones gotten Elsie in the end?*

EMBEDDED NEAR THE MIDDLE OF the funeral cortege, we drove west along Washington Avenue to West Lawn Memorial Park. Founded in 1929, it already held the flat, in-ground bronze plaque and flower vase marking the grave of Grandpa Green. Clara and Roy Miller owned several adjacent plots. They never expected to sell one of them to Roy Woodson for Elsie's final resting place, though that's what happened—a fact I learned years later on a visit to the West Lawn office.

Our family stood to the back of the crowd gathered at the gravesite. The day was perfect—if there ever was a perfect day for a funeral—the temperature would rise to seventy-five later that afternoon and not a raindrop threatened. I heard the slow words of the minister while staring at the backs of my aunts and uncles. I imagined Grandma Green at the front of the group, twisting her handkerchief and wiping her eyes as the pastor droned on.

For both Grandma and Elsie, the move to Mattoon had been traumatic, but for Grandma, Elsie's death seemed unique and unfathomably sad. I wanted to ease her pain but didn't know how. Listening to the whispers of the adults conversing above my head, I wondered why Pete or John had not contacted the police with their questions about how Elsie had died. They must have had a good reason for remaining silent.

Years later, Pete talked with me about the family's emigration from the Old Country. When Grandma Cecelia left Denmark, her mother stood on the Danish shore wailing and waving goodbye to her only child. Both mother and daughter knew it would be the last glimpse they'd ever have of one another. Burying Elsie must have been like that.

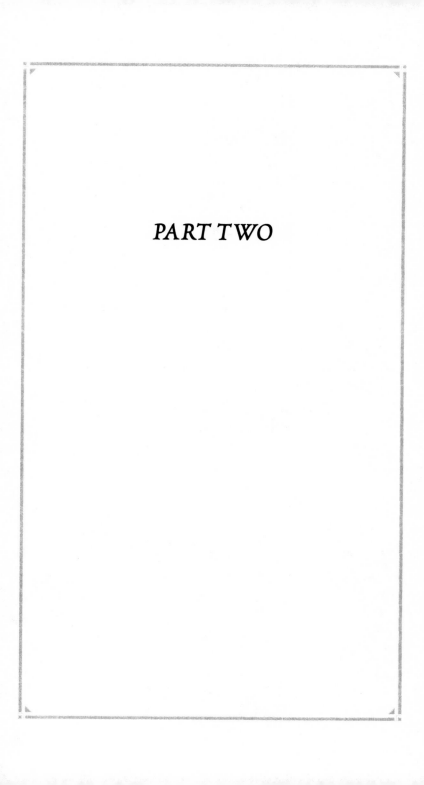

PART TWO

10

GENEALOGY 101

In the fall of 1960, I began two years of confirmation classes on Saturday mornings at Mount Pleasant Lutheran Church, then located at the intersection of state highways 20 and 31. Following the enthusiastic lead of Pastor Louis Piehl, we focused on the Bible that first year, saving Luther's Catechism and all things liturgical for the second year.

Pastor Piehl would call out Bible verses for us to look up, and I'd whip through my King James' version, usually being the first to find the passage, stand, and read it aloud. The other students pointed out that I had an unfair advantage: My Bible had thumb cuts at the beginning of each New and Old Testament book, though I protested that I never used them. Pausing to read the first three letters of the book inscribed on each thumb cut would have slowed me down.

We didn't read the entire Bible that year but did review sizable chunks of it, with extended reading assignments each week. The class breezed through Genesis and Exodus, made it through Leviticus, and then bogged down in Numbers before we could dive into Deuteronomy's powerful stories of Moses, the Ten

Commandments, and Joshua's crossing of the Jordan River and entrance into Canaan. In an effort to make the book of the "begats" (Numbers) come alive, Pastor Piehl gave an additional assignment—to create our own family tree.

I had occasionally asked Grandma Green about her life in the Old Country, but she had shared little, possibly hampered by her knowledge of English and her desire to spare me the details of a demanding life and arduous voyage. Now I was determined to get solid answers to questions about her—and my—lineage.

One Thursday evening after the dinner dishes had been washed, dried, and put away, we sat at the kitchen table. Grandma had a cup of coffee before her, and I had a blank sheet of paper, ruler, and pencil. I printed my name at the top of the tree (whether this was the assignment or my twelve-year-old's self-centered understanding, I no longer remember) and cast my mother and father's lines downward on the page.

"Who were your parents?" I began.

"John Petersen and Maren Jepsen." Grandma scooped a sugar cube from the bowl that Mom kept just for her and tucked the hard lump into her mouth. I waited until she had taken a sip of coffee, sucking the hot liquid through the cube.

"Do you know the names of Grandpa's parents?"

"Yah, yah," she readily replied, "Peter Grøn and Karen Bramsen, and the name of Karen's father was Peter Bramsen."

But when I asked the names of her own grandparents, Grandma Green could supply only the names of her paternal grandparents, Peter and Elsie Petersen. *How could anyone not know their grandparents' names?* I wondered, little understanding that in nineteenth-century Europe people did not routinely live to three score and ten, much less Methusaleh's 969 years.

IN THOSE DAYS TRACKING THE births and deaths—not to mention the marriages and whereabouts—of Dad's extended family was like deer hunting: It required patience and often the assistance of other family members.

No one did more than Gladys, who married Pete's son Riley. Gladys and Riley organized family reunions at their Union Grove farm, a locale large enough to accommodate the Green clan, which by the 1960s encompassed my Grandma Cecilia Green, her six boys (including my father) and three girls (including Elsie, her favorite middle daughter), and a growing legion of in-laws, children, and grandchildren.

Riley and Gladys provided Dixie Cup ice cream and sodas, orchestrated the potluck dinner, and directed the placement outdoors of chairs for the elders and buffet tables that stretched end-to-end beyond the farmhouse back door.

These much anticipated gatherings gave me the opportunity to get to know cousins' personalities, explore the barns with cousins once removed, and look into the eyes of my Uncle John. Mom made a point of introducing me to John, who had served in World War I and shared my June 17 birthday. That connecting link overcame the years between us; his birth year of 1897 reached back to nineteenth-century Denmark and linked me to ancestors unknown. It seemed to me then that placing my hand in his was like reaching back and touching the Dark Ages.

Long before I'd heard of astrology, shared birthdates offered meaning and commonality in a world of differences. I had a cousin born on the Fourth of July, but the only other family member to share a birthday with anyone I knew was Dad. He took pride in the fact that he had been born exactly thirty-eight years after former President Herbert Hoover, who came into this world on August 10, 1876.

Dad also shared a birthday with Roy Woodson, born thirteen years before him on August 10, 1901, though this fact was seldom mentioned. I wondered, *Did the shared day give them a special bond? Did Dad better understand Roy's moods and decisions than many of the rest of us?*

If so, he may have had another good reason. After Elsie's death, Dad's job soon became as stressful as Roy's had been, albeit for the opposite reason. While Massey-Ferguson had been shrinking its Racine footprint, Oster Manufacturing Company in Milwaukee continued to expand.

By now an experienced machinist, set-up man, and foreman at Oster, Dad continually refused a promotion into mid-management. The refusal eventually led to the loss of his job, and he spent the summer of 1961 unemployed.

Dad looked for a new job closer to home and worked briefly at a farm cooperative feed mill. "No one wants to hire a guy over forty-five," he said during his stint at the feed mill, where he labored lifting sacks of grain and sweated away ten pounds or more. Arriving home on those hot nights, Dad would head directly to the cool basement, where he'd change, wiping himself off, and dropping his sweat-soaked clothes into the washing machine.

Within a few weeks, however, he found a job at a meat-wrapping machine company in Franksville that soon became a division of Reliance Electric Company. He started out "at the bench," but eventually became one of two testers, taking a half day to thoroughly test each machine, which automatically wrapped plastic around trays of meat, before the machines were shipped to grocery stores.

THOUGH I LOVED THE SUMMERTIME Green family reunions, I began to dread the month of July. Two years after Aunt Elsie left this earth, my Uncle John died suddenly at home at age sixty-five on July 3. Again, Grandma Green attended the funeral of one of her children, hearing the final service for her firstborn at Plymouth Congregational Church in Burlington and watching him lowered into his grave at Burlington Cemetery.

Now eighty-four, Grandma was slowing down, age and tragedy taking their toll. A few short years later, no longer able to properly care for herself, Grandma moved to a nursing home, where she died on August 6, 1965, the year I began my senior year of high school.

Back then, I didn't know that Dad, too, would die in the summertime, another July casualty, yet I wondered all the same, *Why did so many of my relatives die in the warmth of a beautiful Wisconsin summer?*

I COUNTED MY COMING OF AGE at nineteen, the summer I spent working at a northern Wisconsin resort between the end of my sophomore year of college at the University of Wisconsin campus in Racine and the start of my junior year at the Madison campus.

It was the first time I had lived away from home, walked along a lakeshore alone, and socialized with a wide mix of waiters and other resort staff. It was the first time I earned my way (sort of—$300 for the summer) in the world.

I reveled in the casual vacation lifestyle but nevertheless dressed up to receive a phone call from a U.S. Navy medic I had met a month earlier. Then stationed at Great Lakes Naval Station, his purple hearts and Bronze Star had captivated me, and his stories introduced me to one perspective on a war that should never have been.

Madison's radical counterculture swarmed around me for the next several years, inviting me to create and voice my own opinions about the world. But I had cousins serving in Vietnam and sometimes didn't know what to believe about the reasons behind the deadly conflict replayed on the evening news each night.

One time, I crouched in a central green space, surrounded by the fortress of the university's Bascom Hall to save myself from the National Guard's tear gas wafting through the building on a day when my Shakespeare class met there.

The spring of my senior year, a student teaching assignment at Sauk Prairie High School, thirty miles north of Madison, saved me from the street riots that focused a state and a nation.

That same summer (of course, it was summer— August 24, to be exact), my apartment was close enough to the central campus to hear the 3:42 a.m. explosion that killed the young scientist, Robert Fassnacht, and injured three others. Leo Burt, David Fine, Karl and Dwight Armstrong blew up the Army Math Research Center at Sterling Hall, in protest of the war. The foursome split up and the latter three were all eventually captured, but Leo Burt was never found. Most people believe he died long ago.

Bob Dylan had come through Madison before he went to New York and became famous. Even before he wrote the songs that defined a generation, we all knew that change was "blowin' in the wind."

One song that Dylan wrote in 1963, three years after Elsie's death, connected in my brain to that pivotal event. *Who Killed Davey Moore* memorialized the death of a boxer who sustained brain damage during a fight with Sugar Ramos and sought to identify blame. In each stanza, a different party—the referee, the crowd, the manager, the gambling man, and Sugar Ramos—explained, *"It wasn't me that made him fall."* In my mind, Dylan's song became, *Who Killed Aunt Elsie*. My stanzas, in turn, blamed the bartender, the undertaker, Roy, an unknown assailant, and even Aunt Elsie herself. Yet the response for each was always the same, *"It was someone else who made her fall."*

During these years my black-and-white world turned more nuanced and finally evolved toward full color. How had it happened? Slowly—excruciatingly so at times—I grew up and the complications of adult life set in.

THE GREEN FAMILY REUNIONS WENT on as always. A quarter century before Ancestry.com, Gladys documented Elsie's death as she tracked births and deaths, made address changes in her Christmas card list, and updated her phone list. Every other year, she brought us happily together with a cheery smile and welcoming greeting. Without Gladys, our wandering clan would have lost the richness of relationships hardwired in DNA and embellished with Danish kringle and rhubarb pudding. There should be a Gladys in every family.

Following the reunions, Gladys and Riley Green's children would ask, "How is So-and-So related to us?" Their children asked the same questions that I had invariably asked Mom—"Who is the blond woman with the tight pin curls or that wild boy in the cowboy boots and how are they connected to me?"

Prompted by her children's questions, Gladys began a family history in 1975, requesting information and making notes at every family gathering. Six years later, with a rough outline complete, she wrote to individuals who might fill in missing details and plugged in many gaps with names, dates, and places. Laura contributed conversations she recalled with her grandmother, Karen Bramsen Green, adding the names of Karen's children who had died young.

The starting point for Gladys's family history was my great-great-grandfather, Peter Petersen Grøn, born in the hamlet of Sonder Stenderup, Jutland, in 1834. Even the barest outline of his life makes a stark statement about life expectancy in nineteenth-century Denmark and elsewhere, especially from infections of all types.

Peter's first wife, Swedish-born Bengta Monsdatter Luckner, died about 1859 at age twenty-six, possibly following childbirth, according to Gladys's record. The couple had one son, Jorgen, born in 1857.

After Bengta died, Peter married Karen Bramsen, who bore seven children. Five died young:

- Mary I died of tuberculosis as a young child not yet old enough to attend school.

- Lauritz died of cancer at age eighteen.

- Christian died of tuberculosis at eighteen or nineteen while in the Danish Army.

- Bendita died of tuberculosis at age eighteen.

- Christine died of tuberculosis as a young child not yet old enough to attend school.

IN 1882, PRUSSIAN PHYSICIAN Robert Koch published his research identifying the cause of tuberculosis as *Mycobacterium tuberculosis* and noting that one seventh of all deaths were then being attributed to it—more than the numbers who died from cholera and other plagues.

Though the toll was even higher in Peter and Karen Grøn's family, their two youngest children escaped both the disease and Denmark. My Grandpa Andrew and his younger sister, Mary II, (born and named after Mary I died) survived to adulthood and emigrated. Mary left Denmark first, with their half brother Jorgen, who had arrived in Racine, Wisconsin, in the late 1880s.

When Grandpa Andrew and Grandma Cecelia Grøn left Denmark in the fall of 1903, they already had four children—George (called John), age six; Peter, five; Carl, three, and Martin, six months. On arrival, they changed their name to Green as Jorgen and Mary had done before them, and they exchanged the open farmland of Denmark for the fenced fields and pastures of southeastern Wisconsin.

Seventeen years after Elsie's death, Gladys and Riley interviewed my Uncle Pete and wrote a short family account for a 1978 book compiled by the Racine County

Historical Museum, *The Grassroots History of Racine County*. As Gladys recorded it, Pete remembered:

> Andrew Green, Sr., twenty-six, and his wife Cecelia, twenty-five, with their four young sons ... set sail by cattle boat from Stenderup, Denmark. They landed in England and crossed England by train. They left Liverpool by boat for the United States. After landing in New York, they took the train by way of Canada to Racine, Wisconsin. It took four months to complete the trip.

The young family spent their first night in Racine at the home of Andrew's mother Karen and his half brother Jorgen, who located a rental home for them. Another Racine relation, Andrew's brother-in-law (Mary II's husband), Jess Winum, secured a job for Andrew at the Case Plow Works, where he labored ten hours a day, six days a week.

The family grew to include Laura (1905) and Andrew (1909), and moved three times before Elsie was born in 1912 and Herman (my dad) in 1914, on a farm in Paris Township, Kenosha County. The family was complete when Cecelia, age forty-four, gave birth to Clara in 1920 on yet another rented farm, located on State Highway 41, south of State Highway 20.

Five years after the publication of *Grassroots*, Gladys and Riley shared the family history they had compiled at a Green family reunion that Mom and I attended. A dozen legal-size pages recorded the generations of Peter

Petersen Grøn, who had died at age sixty back in Sonder Stenderup, Denmark. We were all in those closely typed pages: uncles, aunts, and cousins of various degrees, as well as descendants of Grandpa Green's half-brother Jorgen Green, who changed his name to John Green after immigrating to the United States.

This meant that I had a Great-uncle John, in addition to the Uncle John I had known. This also explained Dad's occasional references to "Uncle John" when telling stories about his boyhood.

I traced my finger through the pages. Organized in outline form, Gladys's "Green Family Tree" recorded each of Grandma and Grandpa's children, with the dates of their births, marriages, and deaths, as well as the

Cecelia and Andrew Green, Sr., in the 1940s with their nine children, from left: John, Herman, Andrew, Jr., Clara, Martin, Elsie, Carl, Laura, and Pete

causes of their deaths and similar information about their children and, in some instances, grandchildren.

Following a long section reporting on my Uncle Andrew and Aunt Adeline's seven children, came a very short section on Elsie. It noted her marriage to Roy on April 22, 1936, and her death on July 31, 1960, in Mattoon. No cause of death was listed.

Next, came a section documenting the lives of Dad, Mom, Diane, and me. A notation of Dad's death on July 27, 1981, just shy of his sixty-seventh birthday, reported his cause of death: heart attack. Though his death had come too soon and was a great shock, at the same time it had not been a complete surprise.

The last time I saw him, I had wondered whether it might be the last. It was a typical Racine weekend visit: I came home to catch up, eat Mom's comforting meals, and walk in the garden. What was atypical was that Dad and I strolled together through the rows of yellow and red raspberries, handing over the biggest and best berries for the other to try. Such intimacy would have been impossible in the past, but a part of Dad (ego maybe?) seemed to be already gone, only love remaining.

Later, I was grateful that my future husband, Michael, had come with me that weekend to meet my parents. I was glad Michael had met Dad and the two most important men in my life knew one another. Still, the sadness of Dad's passing never left: Suddenly he was gone and time was slipping away, out of reach forever.

Some memories remained vivid, like that long-ago catechism lesson about the book of Numbers and my childhood interview with Grandma Green. After the reunion, I contacted Gladys and shared what she had told me all those years ago, filling in the names of Cecelia's ancestors and a tiny portion of the information gap that stretched backward to—when, Genesis? Other relatives shared what they knew, and Gladys subsequently prepared and distributed every few years a new Green Family Tree Update. They last hosted a reunion at their farm on October 17, 1999.

Their work created a family touchstone. Even now, relatives at funerals and other infrequent gatherings will remark on a family connection and ask one another if they, too, still have a copy of Gladys's family history. All these years later, her work remains a beacon into the past and a signpost toward the future. These collected pages also bring to smiling life again Gladys herself, who died in 2000 at age seventy, leaving behind six children, twenty grandchildren, two great-grandchildren, and throngs of well-wishing church ladies, 4-H leaders, and fellow avid gardeners.

11

THE WAY PETE REMEMBERED IT

*T*wo years after Dad's death, I finally married Michael Holmes Knight, son of Gail Hinshaw and Oliver Holmes Knight, part of his family lore involving a link to Oliver Wendell Holmes—though that's another story. Together, we soon tackled a book project for the Swedish Historical Society of Rockford on that city's furniture manufacturing industry. As part of our research, I conducted oral history interviews with various former furniture workers and their descendants.

All these interviews convinced me to tape conversations with my own elders to learn more about my ancestors, especially Elsie. Almost a quarter century later, her death still shadowed my life like an occasional misty evening. While I wanted to know what had happened to her in Mattoon, I was afraid—unwilling to turn too quickly and see the ghost of truth staring back at me. What if it was murder?

Pete would likely know more about Elsie's death than almost anyone, and I interviewed him in December 1984, seven months after his wife's—my Aunt Edna's—death. He welcomed the opportunity to reflect on their life together and the events of his long lifetime.

We sat at a corner of his kitchen table, the room now more sparsely filled than when I was a child. Still spic-and-span, the kitchen seemed a skeleton of its former self, absent the cooling loaves of bread and the jewel-like jars of homemade jam—not to mention the rough laugh of energetic Edna.

I turned on my cassette tape recorder. "Can you state when you were born, and if you remember anything about Denmark—I think you were five years old when you left?"

"I was born September 15, 1898.

"As small as I was—I know it ain't no dream—I remember that we lived in a little bit of a house right at the road. It had straw for shingles and the floors was sand. The stove was built out of bricks."

"Like a fireplace?" I interrupted.

Pete nodded. "But there was a great big oven to bake bread."

"Did your father farm?"

"He worked on a farm. My mother did, too. She milked cows. They might have had two miles to walk to work. My brother John and I used to walk over there sometimes to see them. The people who owned the farm lived in the same building as their cows; each on one end of the building."

Pete's voice blasted like a foghorn through a rain-soaked night.

"There were no fences around the pastures. The farmers staked out the cows, chaining them to a stake that they drove into the ground. Three times a day, the farmers moved each cow to a fresh piece of pasture."

"So your parents came to the United States for better opportunities?"

"My folks and my Uncle John said that it would be much better for them here than in Denmark, but I don't know if they really had it better here or not. They had a job and got a little money anyway so they could live, but, God, it was tough."

"Your Uncle John [Andrew Green Sr.'s half brother Jorgen] left Denmark first, and then your folks followed him to Racine."

"We came over in 1903, in October, and it took at least a month to come over here. We left Denmark in a cattle boat to England."

"There were cows on the boat?"

"Yeah, it was a cheap way to get there. Then, we traveled across England to Liverpool."

"Did you cross England on a train?"

"Yeah, when we left Denmark, it was like a funeral. My mother was an only child and, of course, her mother was there to see us off, crying and waving."

"Do you remember crossing the Atlantic?"

"I don't know how the folks could do it—go that far with four small children." Pete's voice still grated, though it seemed higher and younger now, as a relived boyhood crept into his vocal cords. Grizzled Pete became age five again, traveling with Grandpa Andrew, Grandma Cecilia, and three of my other uncles—John, Carl, and Martin.

"There were two or three people who died on the way over, and they just threw them in the water," he went on. "Everybody got seasick from the boat rocking and there was nothing to do for it but to lie there and vomit. And the vomit just run back and forth across the floor."

"You were on the bottom of the ship?"

"Yeah, we were so darn poor, we had to stay down there. The water would hit one side and then the other of the boat, and you could hardly sleep. It was so rough, the plates were fastened to the table, because otherwise they would slide all over, and the coffee and milk would spill. It was an awful mess. I don't know how the folks could make it for that many days."

"After you finally landed, I think that you took a train across Canada to reach Wisconsin. Do you remember that train trip?"

"Only one thing. The train had stopped at a little town, and Pa went out, maybe to get something for us to eat. The train started out again, and he wasn't on it! Then we could see him through the window and he was running! But we thought we had lost him. God, we were crying! By gosh, he ran fast and just caught it!

"How frightening! You must have felt helpless, with the conductor and most others on the train not speaking Danish."

Pete nodded and shifted in the chair, using both hands to lift his right leg and cross it over the left.

"How did you all learn English?"

"Once we got to Racine, we all picked up some from Uncle John, and my brother John and I learned it on the streets and then in school. Pa learned it at the Case Company."

"How did he get that job?"

"A friend of Uncle John's worked at the Case Company, and they were looking for men to move pig iron."

"Move it how? In a wagon?"

"No, in wheelbarrows. Men pushed it to where they melted it."

"Sounds like hard work," I said, thinking it really sounded like labor in Dante's hell.

"It was an awful job, but Pa had to start some place and he'd try anything."

We were both quiet for a moment. I stretched my back and rotated one shoulder and then the other. "Where did you live?" I finally asked.

"For a time, we rented a house in Racine and Pa walked to work. We were crowded in that house, but we got out and went visiting every weekend."

"Who did you visit?"

"Sometimes, we went to Uncle John's or a friend's place."

"Did you visit anyone else regularly?"

"Some weekends, we went on the train to Milwaukee and visited Pa's cousin, Jess Jessen. Jess was real religious, and one time I went to church with him. I was so shocked when Jess threw a five-dollar bill into the collection plate! That was half of Pa's weekly wage!"

"I'm surprised you still remember that."

"He made an impression alright," Pete said. "But the person who really impressed me was Katrina."

"Wasn't she a friend of Grandma's?"

"She was a great friend. Katrina's husband worked for Jess and they would visit the Jessen home when we were there. The grown-ups would tell stories and have a high old time. But they wouldn't drink. No one drank at Jess Jessen's house.

"He was awfully religious and a good singer. For every meal—so many say a prayer before they eat—but he always sang it. And, that was really nice to hear him sing that."

"In Danish or English?"

"Oh, in Danish."

"Did you continue to visit Milwaukee some weekends after you moved to the first farm that your Pa rented?"

"Yeah, the North Shore tracks ran between the house and the fields."

"I'd heard that Grandma almost had an accident on those tracks."

"Ma was like your dad—a dreamer. One day she must have been thinking about something else when she started across the tracks to our garden.

"We had a big garden—Ma would hang the onions to dry and store the potatoes, carrots, and parsnips in the cellar. When she crossed the tracks that day, the blast of a whistle startled her. Just as she stepped off the tracks, the train whipped past, so close the wind blew her skirt."

"Sounds like a close call!"

We paused, envisioning the scene.

I picked up a dog-eared copy of Gladys's family history. "Laura, Andrew, and Elsie were born on this farm?"

"Elsie was born a year before we moved to a farm in Kenosha County that Pa rented from Racine Judge Roy Burgess. When we moved, the few cattle we had, we drove them in the road. There was no way to haul them then."

"How long did that take?"

"Two days. We had to find an empty barn that one night to put the cows in, and we did."

"After you moved, did you sometimes visit friends and relatives in Racine?"

"Yeah, it was an all-day chore. We'd leave six, seven o'clock in the morning and then come home, oh, six, seven, in the evening. And we didn't stay long in town either. We went with horses. One time we started out with a horse and a buggy and only got about half a mile when the damn horse got crazy and ran away. We all fell out of the buggy and the horse went with the buggy."

"Where did you find them?"

"The horse ran into a neighbor's yard and he kept it there. So, we didn't get to town that day. We got hurt—those buggies were high with no protection."

"No broken bones, just cuts and bruises?"

"No broken bones. There were really a lot of accidents with horses. People talk about cars, but the horses were worse."

"People weren't killed, but they were often injured?"

"They didn't get hurt too bad, but horses would run away. One time we had a team standing at home in the yard, and when I went out to get them, they were gone—two of them. An automobile wouldn't do that."

I laughed before realizing that Pete was calmly serious. "Dad used to say there was a lot of work involved in farming with horses."

Pete dipped his chin in agreement. "Nowadays, when you go out with a tractor, there ain't much work to get ready—you check the oil, put gas in—but at that time you had to brush and clean the horses, put the harness on. That's quite a job to harness up two horses and sometimes we had five-horse teams. You got to harness them up, put the fly nets on, and then hook them up—that's pretty near a half day's work."

"And then you had to take care of them when you came back to the barn."

"Yeah, when we came in for dinner, we had to separate them all and unhitch them, take them to the water tank, feed the horses, and then go in the house and eat our dinner. Then, we'd come out and had to [harness them all] over again. You wonder how we ever got anything done."

"A five-horse team was five across?"

"No, generally they had three ahead and two behind. And there were plenty of harnesses and lines to take a hold of."

"Must have been quite a job!"

Pete nodded. "I started behind a walking plow when I was nine or ten years old. When you hit a stone, the plow would jump. If you were a man, you'd be up above the handles, but if you were a kid, they'd hit you in the ribs or the head and sometimes near knock you out."

I tried to picture Pete as a boy. As a man, he was the shortest of the six brothers, taking after Grandma, in great contrast to the tallest brother, Martin, who stood well over six feet. What I said was, "Nine or ten seems awfully young to handle large animals like that."

"We didn't think nothing of it because that's the way we were brought up. It's all we knew. One time, I worked a month for a neighbor, and he gave my dad five dollars for it. My dad knew I wanted a watch pretty bad, so he gave me the five dollars and told me to buy a watch. And so I did. In those days, you didn't have no wristwatch. All you had were pocket watches. The very next day, I had it out, plowing with a walking plow and all of a sudden, I missed it. Oh, gee—did I feel bad!" Pete sucked in a deep breath at the memory.

"What happened?"

"I don't know what made me think of it—it ticked so loud. I thought that if I had plowed it under, if I crawled on my hands and knees…" Pete's voice trailed off.

"You could hear it?"

"And by God, I did! I didn't crawl very far. I must have lost it and missed it right away, because it was so heavy. I crawled along and I could hear it ticking. I dug in there, and there was the watch!"

"That's quite a story. Do you still have the watch?"

"Oh, yeah, it's in my dresser."

I remembered my own dad's pocket watch, kept in his top dresser drawer, and glanced surreptitiously at my wrist before returning to Gladys's family history. "The family must have moved to Paris Township around 1913?"

"Then in 1914, your dad was born on the Burgess place," Pete again rasped in his old-man's voice. "Six years after that, Clara was born. 'Course, I had left home by then. I was drafted in 1918, right before the war ended."

After Pete told how he had met and married Edna, I finally broached the topic of Elsie. "Later, when most of your brothers and sisters were married, how did it happen that Elsie and Clara lived next door to each other?"

"I don't even know." Even now Pete sounded surprised at the thought. "They should never have lived close together because they fought like hell. No, they should never have lived close together.

"Elsie and Roy built themselves a really nice house. Clara and Roy Miller's house is alright."

In my mind, I pictured the two homes, side by side facing a field across a narrow road. Both were small, though Elsie and Roy's home seemed neater on its broad corner lot.

One of the guys in May 1941: from left, John Green, Roy Woodson
(holding a beer with one hand and Carl Green's wrist with the other),
Carl Green, Martin Green

"It was a good thing when they moved apart because they fought all the time. Of course, Elsie didn't live long after she moved." Pete took a long breath.

Silently, I thanked him for facing the topic of Elsie without any prompting and waited, holding my own breath. *Would Pete reveal anything I didn't already know?*

"Elsie didn't live long enough. I don't know what she died of, but she died an awful death." Pete shook his head. "When she lived above that tavern, she went upstairs. Then, they heard a thump on the floor and they went up and she was lying on the floor, dead. They think that guy spiked her drink and killed her."

"The undertaker?"

"We should really have had..." Pete's voice faded away.

"An autopsy."

121

"Yeah, to see what really happened, though I suppose it wouldn't have done no good." Pete looked down at his gnarled hands, resting on the tabletop.

"You and John went to Mattoon and brought Elsie's body back to Racine," I prompted.

"The undertaker told me several times, he said, 'Don't think there's foul play; everything's alright.' But I think he was covering something up."

"Sounds like he didn't do a very good job."

"No, I'm telling you. I don't know how he could be that way and be an undertaker. But way Up North, I don't know."

"Maybe the rules were more lax Up North."

"I don't know. They never should have moved up there. Roy had a good job in town, but then he bought that tavern. Still, he seemed cut out for it. Roy knew how to handle the customers and make friends. I don't know if he's still living, or not."

"I'm not sure." I remained quiet, hoping Pete would offer more on Elsie, but he had other deaths on his mind.

"Martin … went to Mexico to start a new plant and build it up. Last week, his daughter told me that he's been in bed since September. From what she tells me, I don't know how he can be living yet. He has nurses around the clock, but there's nothing to do for him."

"He's had cancer a long time."

"Yeah, and Carl, he died of cancer, too, two years ago this month. Right before Christmas, it was, December 22." Pete lifted his hands, knotty and large from a lifetime of hard work, and placed them palm down on the table's edge.

"Have you kept in touch with Peg?"

Pete smiled. "After Carl died, she promised to come up here from Illinois and bring dinner. She said, 'I know what you like and don't like, so I'll bring just what you like.' She ain't showed up yet!"

"You'll have to remind her."

He grew serious again. "Now, we're all dying from cancer and heart attacks. Years ago, in Denmark, people mostly died from consumption."

"Tuberculosis."

"The folks always called it consumption."

I almost reached for his hand, but instead turned off the cassette recorder. "I wish we knew exactly how Elsie died."

"So do I."

PETE, THE LAST OF THE FAMILY'S six brothers, passed away from cancer four years after our interview, leaving behind three sons, one daughter, fourteen grandchildren, twenty-one great-grandchildren, and four great-great-grandchildren. While our conversation told me much about Dad and Elsie's childhood world, it shed little light on her death, though it certainly supported my suspicions.

12

PAPER TRAIL: TRACING A LIFE

A quarter century after Elsie's death, it still lay like an open wound, unhealed and seeping suspicion. The passage of time made some questions easier to ask, others more difficult. While concern for Grandma Green was no longer an issue, some information sources from the early 1960s had gone the way of the long extinct passenger pigeon. Still, the bald eagle was making a comeback from near extermination due to DDT, so maybe there was hope, too, for answers to questions surrounding Elsie's death.

I drove to the Racine County Courthouse on a blustery day, circling the downtown on a wave of nostalgia. The city's chameleon, Lake Michigan, had turned from a brilliant blue-green to a frothy gray. Breakers pounded against the shoreline and the spray leaped fifteen feet above the boulders. On the beach to the north, the waves hurled themselves far inland, chilling the sand. A damp coolness pooled across the city.

Battling the wind, I shivered and shoved open the door to the courthouse. Added to the National Register of Historic Places in 1980, the monolithic limestone building had always been a landmark on the drive downtown.

Inside, the 1930's Art Deco edifice looked like an old library, with dark corridors, high ceilings, and a hushed atmosphere.

The document I sought—a copy of Elsie and Roy's marriage certificate—seemed so personal and intimate as to be sacrosanct, and I imagined what Moses must have felt when approaching God on Mount Sinai. But the Register of Deeds assistant surprised me by explaining that copies of records could be had for only a small fee.

She led me into a windowless, claustrophobic room filled with old ledgers, some containing indexes by year, others filled with the certificates themselves. Within a half hour, I had located Roy and Elsie's marriage certificate. Thirty minutes later, I held an uncertified copy of the vital record—vital for them, more vital to me.

I carried the photocopy outside to view it in the daylight. Sitting in my Subaru, I cracked the windows. Outside, the wind had picked up and a woman clutched her purse to her chest as she hurried along the sidewalk. I inhaled a drag of the lake breeze and picked up Elsie and Roy's marriage certificate, wondering what clues it might offer.

The document recorded the date of the wedding as April 23, 1938. Oh, no—already another question! Gladys's family history had reported the date as April 21, 1936, two full years and two days earlier!

But maybe the discrepancy wasn't so surprising. After all, the "Green Family Tree" contained other errors as well—for instance, giving the family's year of emigration from Denmark as 1905 instead of 1903. As a writer and editor myself (then freelancing and working part time with Madison's WYOU Community Television), I knew how easily errors could creep in—despite, or sometimes because of, multiple rounds of editing.

The marriage certificate recorded the name of the minister, the Reverend Edwin Jaster (later, I'd learn he was affiliated with Epiphany Lutheran Church at 2921 Olive Street on Racine's south side); and the names of two witnesses: Elsie's friend, Anna Litzkow and my father, Herman Green. I hadn't known that Dad had stood up for Elsie at her wedding; here was another indication that their relationship was a close one.

But where were Roy's friends? Did he even have any, aside from Elsie? The certificate listed the names of Roy's parents (Charles Woodson and Nora Ferguson) and his place of birth (Peoria, Illinois). He worked as a "tool grinder," lived at 1116 Romayne Avenue on the city's north side, and was thirty-five years old.

Elsie, age twenty-five, resided on the south side at 811 Orchard Street. I had forgotten that Elsie was a full decade younger than Roy. But wait. Here was another discrepancy. Born in 1901, Roy was actually age thirty-six at the time of his marriage to Elsie.

Decades later, I stumbled across a photo taken on Elsie's wedding day and drove past the house where they were taken, which still looked the same, down to the shutters on the windows and even the shrubbery. The Colonial house at 811 Orchard Street became part of the

From left: Herman Green and Ann Litzkow,
with Roy and Elsie Woodson in front of the house at
811 Orchard Street on their wedding day

National and State Orchard Street Historic District in
2016. The forty-seven homes of various styles exhibited
"high quality design and construction," according to the
Wisconsin Historical Society release announcing the
designation:

> During the Great Depression, local companies
> such as Johnson Wax, Twin Disc, Western Print-
> ing, Oster Manufacturing, J.I. Case, Massey-
> Harris, Hamilton-Beach, Dumore, Modine
> Manufacturing, Andis Clippers, and Horlick Co.
> made conscientious efforts to maintain employ-
> ment of their workers and innovate to remain
> competitive. These efforts stimulated economic
> recovery into the 1940s. The unionizing of

Racine's workforce during this time, increased
wages and benefits and ultimately led to a high
number of blue collar homeowners. This in turn
led to an interesting mix of executives and
workers owning homes of this Historic District.

The historic registration property record revealed that the
811 Orchard Street residence had been designed by
Martin Nelson for George E. and Helen Cooke and built
in 1936, just two years before Elsie and Roy's marriage.

The father of two daughters, George Cooke was a
dentist and died thirty years later, according to a Racine
Journal Times obituary of May 31, 1966. Might Elsie have
worked for the family as a live-in housekeeper and/or
cook—or to help with the children, as Clara did as a
young woman for other families?

Neither the 1930 nor 1940 federal census reported a
housekeeper or cook living with the family. However, by
1940, a sister-in-law had joined the home: Mary Maning,
age thirty, was then living with the family.

Elsie and Roy's wedding photo in front of the
Orchard Street house suggested they had not had a big
church wedding: Elsie did not wear a bridal gown and
veil or even carry a bouquet, though she and Ann did
wear corsages and the guys sported boutonnieres.

I speculated on how and where Elsie had met Roy.
Later I'd discover that she had lived on Racine's north
side at a Geneva Street address around the time she and
Roy likely met. Maybe Elsie and Ann Litzkow had gone

together to a dance or a bar and struck up a conversation with him—the possibility seemed as likely as any.

Not only had Elsie wed an older man, she had also wed a divorced one, marrying Roy precisely one year and one day after his divorce from a "Beatrice Stewart" in Racine Municipal Court. After filing for the divorce in 1937, Roy had had to wait a full year before marrying Elsie.

I wondered what Grandma Green had thought about this fact—or had she even known? I wondered, too, what words Roy had used to tell Elsie that he had been married before, and when he had spoken them. Would he have bothered to file for divorce if he had not met Elsie?

Like his wedding to Elsie, Roy's first marriage had taken place in April, seven years earlier—on April 21, 1931, to be precise. Much later, I would learn that Roy also married his third wife almost on the anniversaries of his first and second weddings: April 20, 1962. Was the third week of April significant to Roy in some way? Did that really matter in the quest to understand what had happened to Elsie?

Growing up, I had understood, through overheard adult conversations, that Roy had been married when he met Elsie. Here was confirmation. But who was Beatrice Stewart and why had they divorced? Was she still living and might she talk to me?

I placed the certificate in a folder and climbed out of the Subaru. Returning to the Register of Deeds office, I asked about getting copies of divorce records. The assistant peered at the marriage certificate that I had placed on the counter. "We don't retain divorce records after fifty years," she said, handing the paper back to me.

"Where are they?"

"They're not here. I think they've all been destroyed."

Temporarily defeated yet satisfied with the information I did find, I left the dim interior of the courthouse for the outdoors, where the wind was dying and sun emerging from behind a line of clouds.

BACK IN MADISON, I CONTACTED the Wisconsin Bureau of Vital Statistics and eventually received an uncertified copy of Elsie's death certificate. I held the sheet gingerly, like a valuable treasure map to the past, and quickly skimmed the page, stopping at the listed cause of death— suicide!

"Oh!" I slapped a hand against my throat, startled to see the ominous word in black and white—a word that no one in my family had ever used.

According to her death certificate, Elsie died after "taking 12 tablets of Nembutal" and the "interval between onset and death" was a half hour. The informant of the suicide was Roy Woodson. The certificate was completed by two people with distinct handwriting.

Doubtless with help from the "informant," the Mattoon undertaker, William W. Johnson, filled in the blanks outlining Elsie's biographical information, including birth date and names of parents, as well as burial records. He noted her date of death as July 31, 1960, with burial at "Rest" Lawn Memorial Cemetery in Racine on August 4. (*Humph. He could at least have gotten the name of the cemetery right—West Lawn.*) In a different hand, Coroner L. E. Hoeff recorded the place of death, medical cause, and ruling.

At the bottom of the page, a third person, the registrar, had also signed the document, though the handwriting was undecipherable. I squinted at the seven-inch square sheet. The original registrar's signature, Mathilda Schwanz, though this name, too, was difficult to determine for certain, had been crossed out, with the new signature written beneath. The local registrar had received the death certificate on August 2, the same day it had been signed by Hoeff and two days before it was officially recorded in Shawano County.

The blurred, indistinct signatures were less important than other unanswered questions. Chief among them: What details of Elsie's death prompted the suicide ruling—was there a suicide note or conversation in the bar that indicated she was depressed? And if the ruling was suicide, the lack of an autopsy became more glaring than ever. Why was there no autopsy, no analysis of stomach contents, no inquest?

I couldn't stop thinking about autopsies. Scenes from *Quincy, M.E.*, other television shows and novels played in my head—not to mention the account I had read about an exhumation of President Abraham Lincoln. Could Elsie's body be examined? Could anything be learned from it twenty-five years after her death?

I picked up the phone, twisting the cord about my wrist. After a few referrals, I again connected with the Wisconsin Bureau of Vital Statistics and a helpful clerk detailed the requirements related to death registrations as outlined in State Statute Chapter 69.18.

There were two routes to disinterment: Elsie's remains could be exhumed at the request of a close family member or of a police or coroner's office as part of an investigation. If Elsie's next of kin (in 1985, that would have been Clara) were to request at exhumation, it could be done. The family, however, would need to pay for the cost, as well as the cost of analysis by the Wisconsin State Laboratory of Hygiene Forensic Toxicology Section, easily $1,000 or more.

If a police department or coroner's office made the request, the exhumation would be at taxpayer expense, but there would need to be evidence to warrant it. A judge would need to issue a court order, and the Racine County Medical Examiner would need to approve and handle the disinterment.

"What would you be looking for?" the clerk asked.

I outlined the circumstances of Elsie's death.

"If you suspect poisoning, you might not learn much from an exhumation after all this time," she cautioned. "Some substances, including arsenic, can leach into a casket from the surrounding soil." The clerk explained that an investigator would need to analyze the soil surrounding Elsie's grave as part of a thorough chemical analysis and compare the amount of arsenic and other chemicals in the soil to the amounts within the casket.

Yet, whether arsenic or Nembutal, it made little difference. I had no solid evidence to offer the police, nor money to pay for an exhumation; and I doubted that Clara would choose to investigate in this way, even if she did believe Elsie's death was suspicious. I untwisted the cord from my numb wrist, thanked the clerk, and ended the call.

But I wasn't ready to give up. One of the nation's best resources for genealogists and historians lay close at hand in Madison—the library of the Wisconsin Historical Society.

I holed up for hours in the stacks and microfilm room, gleaning what I could from federal censuses and Racine and Kenosha city directories. While these sources were far from foolproof and errors were commonplace, they nevertheless provided clues that—combined and doubled-checked against other clues—might lead to credible evidence.

The 1920 United States Federal Census recorded Roy, age eighteen, living at 873 Fremont Avenue, Kenosha, Wisconsin, with a sister, Velda, age twenty-three, and their parents, Charles and "Lanna." (Christened "Eleanor," Roy's mother alternately appeared in other documents as "Nora" and "Leona.") Charles and Lanna's niece, Helen, age eight, also lived with the family. All had been born in Illinois. Charles, Velda, and Roy worked in an "auto factory"—that would have been Nash Motors—with Charles listed as a foreman, Velda as a stock clerk, and Roy as an apprentice machinist.

The family next door was that of Fred and Elizabeth Stewart, including their seventeen-year-old daughter Sylvia. Might they be related to Beatrice Stewart, Roy's first wife? It seemed a long shot; Stewart was a common name.

A decade later, according to the 1930 census, Charles, Eleanor, and Roy were living together at 2614 West 20th Street, Racine. Velda was not listed. Father and son both worked as machinists at a tractor plant—probably either one of several J.I. Case plants in Racine or Massey-Harris.

I resisted the urge to rub my eyes, covered by hard contact lenses, and squinted at the blurry text. Roy's "age at first marriage" was twenty-one, so his first marriage would have taken place between August 1922 and August 1923—not in 1931, as recorded on Elsie's marriage certificate.

If Roy had married earlier, where was his wife when the census takers had come round? Why was Beatrice not living with the Woodson family or with Roy at a separate address? Either the census record or the marriage certificate was wrong; or both were wrong and Roy and Beatrice were married in some other year.

Since Charles and Roy worked full time, Eleanor likely responded to the knock of the census taker and provided Roy's "age at first marriage." If Eleanor reported his age accurately and the census taker recorded it exactly, Roy would have married eight or nine years before the 1931 date listed on the certificate of his marriage to Elsie.

Census records were notoriously incorrect for many reasons, with sometimes entire blocks of immigrants, for example, ignored in the count. The "age at first marriage" might represent a simple typo, although English was Eleanor's native language and the other information she provided seemed correct; so while possible, miscommunication between Eleanor and the census taker seemed the least likely explanation.

I wondered if Roy had any reason to lie about the date of his first marriage. Maybe he didn't want Elsie or her family to know that his first marriage had lasted not six years, but fourteen or fifteen years. *What difference could it make?* After all, if Roy and Beatrice had separated some years earlier, he may not have had any motivation to divorce her, until he met Elsie.

Only years later would I stumble upon another reason Roy might lie.

Dimly at first, another thought made its way into my consciousness. Even though Roy and Elsie's marriage certificate noted that he had one previous marriage, might Roy actually have been married twice before he wed Elsie? It was conceivable. Roy could have married his first wife about 1922 and then married Beatrice Stewart in 1931. My head pounded with the possibilities.

Clearly I needed to find Roy and Beatrice's marriage certificate.

On my second trip to the Racine County Courthouse, the archives felt familiar, less claustrophobic. I easily located the volume containing the lists of marriage performed during the early months of 1931 and heaved it onto a slanted reading counter. Flipping through the pages, I came to April and read every listing, but Roy Woodson's name did not appear on the handwritten register of newlyweds.

The census was right. I could feel it in the tingling along my spine. Roy had married sooner. I pulled out a 1930 ledger, then 1929. Still no Woodson listed. At least he had an uncommon name. Searching for Smith or Johnson would have been ever more tedious.

Slowly, I worked backwards, checking for any Woodson in 1928, 1927, and 1926. The room was stuffy, full of the smell of old paper. I stretched my arms over my head and did a chest-expanding yoga pose.

I stacked the volumes for 1925, 1924, 1923, 1922, and 1921 on the slanted counter, pulled over a stool, and went back to work. My eyes burned. Every few minutes, I pulled them away from the page and focused at the clock on the far wall. An hour passed. Then two. Not one Woodson to be found.

Time for a new tactic.

Again I called the Wisconsin Bureau of Vital Statistics and requested searches for a marriage between Roy and Beatrice in the adjoining Kenosha and Milwaukee counties. For a fee, the bureau would perform these searches on a county-by county-basis. I reasoned that Roy's family had lived in Kenosha before moving to Racine and remembered that Roy and Elsie used to visit his sister there. Or, since Milwaukee was the nearest big city, maybe he and Beatrice had opted to marry in the bigger town.

One week later, the answer arrived in the mail. Roy did not marry in Kenosha or Milwaukee counties anytime between 1921 and 1931. Was there anyplace else to look?

Wisconsin lacked a statewide database of all marriages during those years, and I lacked the funds to request searches in all seventy-two counties. Besides, without more evidence, it now seemed more likely that Roy and Beatrice might have married in Illinois, since the census listed Illinois as the birthplace of Roy and his family. But Illinois, too, lacked a statewide marriage database for the period.

To console myself, I headed to a local bakery for coffee and a cheese Danish. Had the search for Roy and Beatrice's marriage record reached a dead end? I took a bite of the Danish and pictured a cave passage pinching down to a tunnel that only a raccoon could squeeze through. Somewhere, I'd read that when exploring a cave, if a passage seems to end, you should search for any air current, to see that the cave still "goes."

Did this pathway still go? An image of a flickering candle, guttering in a breeze, swept into my mind.

I closed my eyes. A thought stirred just out of reach and I felt it struggling to surface. Suddenly the image of the candle returned, illuminating an open book. I recognized that book. It was a CD. A city directory.

GRATEFUL THAT ROY HAD LIVED in cities with published directories during the 1920s and 1930s and not the rural countryside, I returned to the Wisconsin Historical Society Library, housed in the Society's monolithic headquarters building at the foot of Bascom Hill on the University of Wisconsin-Madison campus. The fall semester had begun and even on this Saturday, students were everywhere, hurrying up Bascom Hill, catching a coffee at the union, playing Frisbee® on Library Mall.

Inside, oil portraits, pillars, and embellished ceilings looked like they had a century ago, though the marble stairways were now worn with dips and hollows from thousands of footsteps. A dozen floors of stacks bulged with old books, bound periodicals, directories, and government documents. I found the city directories on Level 7A; a few were also available on microfilm.

On a whim, I looked for the Woodson name in several early twentieth-century Peoria directories. In 1901, the year Roy was born, his father, Charles Woodson, appeared—listed as a machinist residing in Peoria Heights.

I conjured a mental image of a map depicting the Upper Midwest. During his lifetime, Roy had moved from Peoria to Kenosha to Racine, to northern Wisconsin, to Michigan's Upper Peninsula after Elsie's death. He kept moving north.

Did we all have an internal compass that pulled in one direction or another? I always headed for hilly terrain. Mountains were too steep, seashores too flat. Hills felt just right—sheltering without threatening.

MACHINIST CHARLES J. WOODSON first appeared in the Kenosha directory in 1908. In this and the 1910 directory, Charles was the only family member listed, but in 1912 "Leona" (Eleanor) also appeared, working as a stenographer at the Thomas B. Jeffery Company, an automobile and truck manufacturer that became Nash Motors.

Four years later, Roy's older sister Velda first appeared in the directory, working as a seamstress. Charles was still listed as a machinist and Leona as a stenographer. The family had moved to 258 Pleasant Street.

Roy first appeared in the 1920 Kenosha directory, also listed as a machinist. Velda now worked as a clerk, and the family had moved to 873 Fremont Street.

The 1921 and 1923 Kenosha directories listed only Charles J. and Eleanor Woodson, but not Roy. I jotted his absence in my notebook. My skin prickled. The fact might be insignificant. Publishers, as well as census takers, made mistakes. But a tingling rose along my spine. Where was Roy?

In 1921, Charles and Eleanor had moved to 221 Wisconsin Street. Charles still worked as a machinist, but

Eleanor was now the night cashier at Kappus Brothers bakery. These were probably useless facts, but who knew where any thread might lead?

A quick look at my copy of the 1920 census page reminded me that Velda would have then been about twenty-four and Roy twenty years old. Maybe Velda had married.

Roy reappeared in the 1925 Kenosha directory, as an autoworker living at 819 Drew Street—with his wife, Beatrice! I blinked at the page, but the words did not blur or melt away. Finally, confirmation of Beatrice's existence and her marriage to Roy!

Beatrice worked as a waitress at The Tea Shop. Quickly, I turned the pages to find The Tea Shop, 258 Church Street. It was owned by Esther Juliani. Could she be important?

I pulled out my photocopied page from the 1930 census. The record of Roy's age at first marriage as twenty-one was most likely correct, and the 1931 date on his marriage certificate to Elsie was likely wrong. Maybe Roy left home and lived and worked elsewhere, returning to Kenosha by 1925 with his new wife, Beatrice. And if Beatrice was his first wife, then Roy must have had only one previous marriage when he wed Elsie.

The 1927 Kenosha directory again listed Roy as an autoworker, though there was no mention of Beatrice's employment or of The Tea Shop. The couple now lived at 5819 Twenty-first Avenue.

By 1927, Charles and Eleanor had moved to Racine, appearing for the first time in that city's directory. They lived at 2614 Twentieth Street, and Charles now worked as a repairman at Nash Motors in Racine. The 1929 directory recorded the same home address, though Charles' employment was listed once more as "machinist."

Roy—but not Beatrice—appeared in both the 1929 Kenosha and Racine directories. The Kenosha directory provided a home address different from the one he last shared with Beatrice, 5514 Thirty-third Avenue, and listed his occupation as "assembler." I thought about the increasing likelihood that Roy had lied about the date of his first marriage on the certificate of his marriage to Elsie. *Might "dissembler" have been more accurate?* The Racine directory reported his occupation as "machinist" and that he resided with his parents at 2614 Twentieth Avenue.

My head throbbed. Could the date of Roy's first marriage as reported on his marriage certificate to Elsie have been a typo—1931 instead of 1922 or 1923? Or, was the date a conscious dissembling of the truth? If so, the question remained: Why might Roy want Elsie to believe that his first marriage was shorter than in fact it was? What did Roy tell Elsie about his first marriage?

Every question sparked yet more questions. What happened to Beatrice after she separated from Roy? Or, did he break up with her? If the couple stopped living together around 1928, why didn't they get a divorce then?

According to Elsie and Roy's marriage certificate, Beatrice and Roy had not divorced until 1937—if that date was even accurate.

I opened the 1931 Racine directory, which reported that Roy still lived with his parents and worked as a "lathe hand" at Massey-Harris, a tractor manufacturer where Charles now also worked as a repairman. Roy continued to live with his parents through much of the Great Depression and his employment seemed sporadic; in 1935, he worked as a machinist at Young Radiator Company.

For some reason, Roy did not appear in the 1933 directory. *Was he simply missed by the enumerator, or might he have found work elsewhere?*

The only year that Elsie Green appeared in the directory was 1937, when she lived on her own at 2110 Geneva Street on Racine's north side. This was also the address of Elsie's friend, Ann Litzkow, and her family. By then, Roy was back at his parents' home, again working at Massey-Harris.

This information was confirmed in 2003 when I ordered a copy of Roy's application for a Social Security number, dated November 27, 1936—just three days after U.S. post offices began to distribute the first application forms to employers. In addition to his residence and employment, the application recorded the names of Roy's parents as "Charlie Woodson" and "Nora Ferguson".

Racine did not publish a directory in 1938, but Elsie and Roy's marriage certificate reported that Roy worked as a tool grinder and lived at 1116 Romayne Avenue on the north side of town, while Elsie lived on the south side at 811 Orchard Street. The following year, they lived together at 2036 Hickory Grove Avenue, according to the Racine city directory, but by 1943, they had moved to a rural route address on Swamp Road. Later renamed as an extension of Charles Street, Swamp Road paralleled State Highway 32, running north from the city limits at the Three Mile Road to the Five and a Half Mile Road.

From 1939 through their departure to Mattoon in 1959, Roy worked as a toolmaker and then shipper at Massey-Harris, becoming a foreman by 1947. Ten years later, however, Roy's job had changed, and the 1957 Racine directory listed him simply as "factory worker." I considered—maybe the change in job title related to his eventual nervous breakdown. Or maybe it simply indicated a change in publishing format or a lazy canvasser.

Racine's 1950 directory was the only one to list employment for Elsie, reporting that she worked as a factory worker at Western Printing & Lithographing Company. During the post-war years, women—even childless ones—did not routinely work outside the home. When Mom re-entered the workforce around 1960, Dad at first objected, but Mom won out, explaining that she liked the social aspects of work in addition to the money, which she used to buy living room carpeting, drapes, and an electric sewing machine to replace our treadle-driven Wheeler Wilson.

Before her marriage, Mom had also worked at Western Printing in the 1930s and 1940s. I wondered whether Elsie loved the plant as much as Mom had. With her employer's blessing, Mom used to collect factory seconds of Whitman children's books and give them to some of my older cousins at Christmas. By the 1950s, Whitman books still lay around our house for me to find after I came along and grew into an enthusiastic reader. Yet for all the gifts received from Elsie, books were never among them.

13

BEFORE MEMORY FADES

I interviewed Mom twice in 1990, seven years after Dad died. The first time, we sat together in the garage-cabin they had built on forty acres near Tomahawk, a mile from the Wisconsin River. The cutover parcel boasted scrubby "popple" woods and a central clearing with a boarded-over well. Though unpromising as farmland, the parcel succeeded as pastureland for beef cattle owned by the family across the road and as hunting land for Dad and my uncles, especially after he retired in 1979.

Dad's retirement haven never seemed more than a remote, dismal garage to me, with an ever-hungry woodstove, the "facilities" out back, and a continual need to carry in water. The uneven land—pockmarked with deep, ankle-turning cattle hoof prints—made hiking a challenge, and one had to keep an eye out for the herd.

Nevertheless, the rough refuge took Mom and Dad back to their childhoods. They strung clotheslines indoors and hung sheets to mark off a "bedroom," they even used kerosene lamps, although the garage boasted a couple of light bulbs with electricity "borrowed" from the pole at the side of the road.

Eventually, Mom would sell this refuge, but for now, she still occasionally visited it, even without Dad, and energetically painted the exterior and washed the windows to keep up its appearance.

Mom and I sat at the oak table that had once served the Green family in the farmhouse outside of Franksville. The table bore the scars of heavy use, and silver bolts protruded from its legs—Dad's efforts to mend the failing joints in the glued-up stock. Warm sunlight filtered in through the small, high windows, illuminating two beds, kitchen cupboards, and the fishing boat parked at a right angle to the double set of overhead doors. I set the cassette recorder atop the oilcloth, switched it on, and asked Mom what she remembered about growing up on a Racine County farm.

The youngest of four children, she was born to Edward, Sr., and Agnes Makovsky on Nov. 19, 1914, in Caledonia, where her family had farmed along the Root River since emigrating from Bohemia in 1855. Mom described how Grandpa reveled in innovations and bought the first radio, one of the first cars (a Dort), and the first tractor in the neighborhood. "It made such a noise," she recalled. "The little kids would scream, 'He's going to start the tractor!'"

Mom remembered the dances held in their two-story garage and picnics in the pasture where the Governor of Wisconsin once spoke. She recalled the strawberries and other crops planted, hoed, and harvested; the beans and poppy seeds dried on the attic floor; and the mountains of cabbages, sugar beets, and apples stored after the fall harvests.

"Your dad used to be *amazed!* He'd go down to the cellar and see these shelves with all those apples. He'd say, 'Oh, my God!' because, you know, those apples kept pretty good there." Mom explained that when a customer came to buy a bushel or two, Grandpa would sort out the varieties wanted.

OUR SECOND INTERVIEW TOOK PLACE within the comfort of the kitchen in the Racine house, warmed by the yellow walls, cotton print curtains, and our steaming coffee mugs. Hanging on the wall above me, two decorative plates depicted the painted heads of a woman and of a man in nineteenth-century apparel. The name added beneath the male head read "Herman," and the other read "Margie."

Mom had known Dad and his extended family long before they finally married during World War II, and in late 1990, we talked about his side of the family. Unlike her stable childhood, Mom noted that Dad grew up on a series of farms in Kenosha and Racine counties, as Grandpa and Grandma Green first rented and then owned one farm after another.

"Your father was born in Paris Township, Kenosha County. When he was three years old, they moved to that big farm on County E—a little more than a mile west of Highway 41 …. The day they moved, when it was getting late and night came, Herman wanted to go home. He put his coat on. He thought his home was his old place."

I tried to imagine Dad at age three. I had seen photos of him as a boy of nine or ten, when he looked a little like me at that age, but I couldn't picture him as a toddler.

Mom went on, recalling the stories she had heard about Dad's youth from his family and from Dad himself. "On that big farm, they had cows and chickens, but they also raised cash crops on this peat ground. Carrots and parsnips grew real good there."

"This is the farm near where that mastodon was found?"

"Yeah, there were several mastodon bones found in that Kenosha County peat."

Stories that I had heard years ago came back now, and I asked: "Dad's friend Edwin lived nearby?"

"Edwin Hansen was Herman's age and an only child. He lived with his mother and dad in just a little shack. It wasn't anything, but his dad was such a jolly fellow, such a lot of fun. He never had a regular job, he just did odd jobs and made money where he could. "

"In those days the neighbors would sometimes visit each other's homes and play cards in the evenings?"

"They'd play cards and carom and have a little lunch." Mom looked through the window at a squirrel swinging from a feeder in her snow-blanketed backyard. "Edwin's family had a pot-bellied stove in the living room, and they would sometimes stick a big hunk of wood in and leave the top off because it wouldn't fit, and the place got all smoky." Mom laughed at the thought.

"You mean they didn't cut the log small enough to fit in the stove, so it stuck out the top?"

"Sometimes it would be gnarly and hard to split or saw, so they'd just leave it sticking out the top of the stove."

Glancing around Mom's bright kitchen, I envisioned smoke-blackened walls and windows and thought: *Who knew? Maybe Edwin's family had their values straight and knew to put fun above never-ending work.* I asked, "Weren't Edwin and Dad's farms near a schoolhouse?"

"No, your father's farm was about a mile from Three Oaks School. Not many kids went there, and they used to have to carry water from the farm of the student that lived closest. Each morning, the kids took turns carrying water, and they just had a dipper."

"The students used a metal dipper to get a drink from a bucket of water that they carried in?"

Mom sipped her coffee and nodded.

"And that's where Dad finished eighth grade?"

"Elsie, too. But I guess Andrew dropped out."

I scribbled a list of Dad's siblings in birth order and showed it to Mom. "The four older boys and Laura completed eighth grade before the family moved to County E, and Clara, six years younger than Dad, must have finished school after they moved to their next farm."

Mom traced a finger down the list. "None of them went to high school, but Pete took an agricultural course, and Grandpa Green paid for Carl to take a barbering course in Milwaukee. But then Carl changed his mind and went to work at the Barber Greene plant in Aurora [Illinois]."

My eyebrows raised at the thought that Carl might have at first misunderstood some celestial prompting toward "barber," but what came out of my mouth was, "Dad said Elsie suggested to Grandpa that Dad should go to high school, but nothing came of it. When the older boys and Laura were out on their own, how old was Dad when the rest of the family—Grandpa, Grandma, Andrew, Elsie, Dad, and Clara—moved to the next farm?"

"Herman must have been sixteen or seventeen when they moved to Highway 41. They didn't live there very long. There was a little building nearby on the highway where a guy was selling gas, and hamburgers and sandwiches. After a while, Herman would walk over and work there. He didn't have an actual job. Herman would pump gas and get tips, and he would put the tips in a sock. One time, he had pretty many coins in that sock he had."

"From there, the family moved to a farm near Franksville at the corner of County K and State Highway 38?"

"It's on K near where H runs from the south into K. They owned this house and they owned that land on the corner, but it was maybe a block or two from the house. That farm isn't there anymore, it was torn down years ago."

"If Dad was, say, eighteen, this would have been 1932," I jotted the year in my notebook. "Where were the older brothers and Laura living?"

"The older kids were gone away from home. Pete married so young, and John was long gone. John was in World War I, but he never got to fight because by the time his unit got to France, the war was over. Carl and Martin were on their own, and Laura got married young, too. By then, Andrew was working for different farms."

She continued. "Elsie got married when they were living on the farm on K. Just Herman and Clara still lived with their folks, but on Sunday, a whole bunch of them would come home. They'd have a big meal—Adeline [Andrew's wife] liked to cook meat and Elsie was real good at making desserts and fancy cakes. And they'd eat and fight and joke around and laugh."

I remembered what a cousin had told me. "This was before I was born, but my older cousins were there. They used to walk across the rafters in the barn hayloft."

"They all did crazy stuff. One time, Clara and Herman were sitting together when they were eating [cake]. Pretty soon, one of them slapped the other on the face with the frosting, and then somebody else slapped somebody, and it wound up that each person had frosting smeared all over their face. It was just craziness, and once in a while, Herman's dad would say, 'Oh, those crazy kids. If you're going to fool around, get out of the house!'" Mom laughed with the memory. "But he put up with it. No one was getting hurt. It was just crazy nonsense."

I laughed too. "By the 1940s, there could have been a lot of people around that table."

"Herman was almost twenty years younger than John, so by then, the older kids all had kids. Pete's oldest son, Roger, was only seven years younger than Herman and we went on a vacation to Door County once with him and his first wife, Jeannette."

"This is a complicated family tree."

"It's a big family, but when you know all these people, when you see them Sunday after Sunday, it's easy to keep them straight."

I said, "Gladys wrote that after the family moved to the farm on K, Grandpa started working at the Frank's Kraut factory when the factory polluted the creek that went past the farm. The cows drank from the creek, which tainted their milk; and when Grandpa complained, the kraut factory gave him a job. It was easier for the factory to give him a job than to end the pollution."

"Herman's dad had learned to make barrels in Denmark," Mom explained, "so they gave him a job making barrels in the basement of the factory. Then, after his dad started working there, of course, Herman started working there too. He got very fast at loading boxes full of cans into boxcars when other guys had trouble keeping up."

"When did Dad start working at the John Oster Manufacturing Company in Racine?" Launched in 1924, the company began producing hand-operated hair clippers and then branched out into other electrical appliances, including the Osterizer blender. The company was bought by Sunbeam in 1960.

"Martin had gone to work there," Mom explained, "and John Oster, Senior liked him and promoted him fast. Martin asked Herman to come work there too, but Herman kept turning him down, because the sauerkraut factory was so close in Franksville and he had friends there. Plus, it was easy work and they liked him. But Martin kept after him, and each time he'd offer Herman a little bit more money. Finally Herman did quit the sauerkraut factory and started working at Oster's."

"Then at some point, Oster's moved from Racine to Milwaukee and Dad had a longer commute."

"Oster's moved to Milwaukee years later, after Herman's dad retired and the family moved from the farm on K to that little house in Franksville."

"I remember the little gray house there." Though it was almost forty years ago, I clearly remembered the huge lilac bushes and the piles of leaves we'd rake on fall weekends.

"Before Oster's moved to Milwaukee, before we were married and you came along, well, the war in Europe came along and Herman got a draft notice. John Oster wrote to the draft board in Burlington to keep Herman out of it, because Oster's was making war material— everybody thought it was just a matter of time before the U.S. got pulled into it. But finally, Herman did have to go.

He was drafted on June 6, 1941—exactly three years before D-Day. He joined [Company I of the 32nd Armored Regiment] and began training at Camp Polk, Louisiana. The recruits drilled with rifles and marched for miles in the heat."

Recalling, she said, "Herman was always a good shot and got a medal for shooting at targets. But his feet kept swelling up so awful and he landed in the hospital. At first, the doctors thought surgery could solve his foot problems, but in the end, the Army gave him an honorable discharge. Herman came home and went back to Oster's in early September."

"I've seen Dad's honorable discharge papers." I rose to refill our coffee mugs, and then asked, "When did you and Dad marry?"

"We married in 1944 and it was hard to find places to rent. First we found this little place on Howe Street, way south in Racine. Herman could walk to work, but I had to take a bus, because it would take too long to walk to Western Printing. Finally, my sister Pat said that she and her husband were moving out of their apartment on Douglas Avenue, above the movie theater, and they subleased it to us. This apartment was only two rooms, but it was much nicer. We lived there for three years before we moved here to this house on Spring Street."

"You must have stopped working when you moved to Spring Street."

"Yeah, I worked at Western from 1931 to 1947, and I always liked working there."

"Did Elsie work there at the same time that you did?"

"No, she worked there later. Earlier, Elsie worked at a convenience store on the corner of the Four Mile Road and Charles Street." Mom added more milk to her coffee and stirred it. "Even if we had worked there at the same time, we wouldn't have seen each other. Elsie worked second shift, and Roy worked second shift at Massey-Harris, which was not far from Western Printing. Elsie's shift ended a little earlier, so when she finished work, Elsie would walk to the Hotel Thomas [at 1029 State Street] for a cup of coffee. Then, when Roy finished work, he would pick her up there."

[Later, I realized Elsie had not consistently worked during her marriage to Roy. In a 1941 note to Dad, she wrote: *"Roy is gone to work for he still works nights, so Pal my dog and I are alone."*]

"Moving to Spring Street must have been a big change for you and Dad," I said.

"When we moved from an apartment to one and a half acres, holy cow, there was so much space! And then, of course, Herman went overboard. Right away we had to buy a real big freezer and we had to get a little tractor, and build a chicken coop."

"I remember the chickens and the eggs—and Dad chopping their heads off in the backyard, you and Dad cleaning them in the basement, and the challenge of removing all the pin feathers."

"The amount of work involved was why we finally got rid of the chickens; plus, we always had to ask someone to feed them whenever we took a vacation."

I scratched a series of years on my notepad. "You must have stopped raising chickens about 1956," I said. "Was that also about the time that Grandma Green moved to the trailer on Pete's farm?"

Mom glanced through the window toward the chicken coop, which now held hoes, shovels, and gardening supplies. "She moved from that Franksville house a little sooner, I think. Let's see: Grandpa Green died in 1950 and for a few years, Grandma Green lived there on her own. Then, Pete's idea was that in the summer, she had a lot of grass to cut, and in the winter, she sometimes had problems with the furnace, so if she had a trailer in his backyard, he and Edna could check on her every day."

"And Grandma was living in the trailer when Elsie died?"

"She was living in the trailer then and when John died [two years later], too. When Elsie died, Pete and John went up there to Mattoon. They thought something was fishy, which I thought, too.

"Anyway, Clara was mad when her mother moved to the trailer, and ..."

"Clara didn't want Grandma to move to Pete's place?" I interrupted.

"No, not at all! And Clara would not go there. Absolutely, she would not go in that trailer. Then when

Elsie died—it was either Elsie or John, but I think it was when Elsie died—no one wanted to tell Grandma. See, Elsie was real good to her, so she was a favorite," Mom said with smile.

"Once, Elsie knitted Grandma a maroon sweater, and she would make her all kinds of things. Then, Pete called up here and said Herman should go and tell her. And then Herman said, 'Well, I'm not going by myself. Somebody's got to come with me.' So he called up Clara, and at first Clara didn't want to, but she did. When Grandma saw them two come together, she knew something had happened, because Clara had never been inside her trailer—not until then."

Later, I would learn Mom's memory was incorrect: Clara and Dad visited the trailer together in 1962 after John's death.

Mom talked a bit more about Elsie's death but offered no real revelations—at least, not then.

14

Not in a Vacuum: A Timeline

*T*he pages of my typed transcripts from Mom's and Pete's interviews lay scattered about me as I sat cross-legged on the loveseat in my tiny office, one of several compact rooms in my 900-square-foot house in Madison. Comparing their stories, I wondered where the truth lay. How could I begin to understand the complex relationships among all my Green relatives? How to keep track of what happened in correlation with other events?

These questions prompted the creation of a detailed timeline that would eventually stretch more than a century—from Roy's birth in 1901 to the present. It would record the births, deaths, marriages, and significant events relating to almost one hundred individuals in twenty-plus pages—information gathered from government vital statistics, newspaper files, family photos, land records, published histories, and more.

This timeline would reveal juxtapositions and context, as well as relationships. It would help attune me to the world of my elders and, of course, lead to ever more questions as I tried to puzzle out what happened to Elsie. Among the multitude of events noted, the following stand out:

- **1901**: Roy is born to Charlie and Nora (Ferguson) Woodson in Peoria, Illinois, on August 10.

- **1903**: Andrew Green (born December 26, 1876) and his wife Cecilia (born January 14, 1878) emigrate from Denmark to Wisconsin, arriving in October with their four sons–John (born June 17, 1897), Peter (born September 15, 1898), Carl (born September 25, 1900), and Martin (born March 16, 1903).

- **1905**: Cecilia gives birth to her first daughter, Laura, on July 7.

- **1908**: Charlie Woodson is listed for the first time in the Kenosha city directory.

- **1909**: Cecilia gives birth to a fifth son, Andrew, on May 4.

- **1912**: Elsie Christine Petersen Green, Andrew and Cecilia's second daughter and seventh child, is born on May 16.

- **1914**: Cecilia gives birth to her sixth son, my father Herman, on August 10.

- **1918**: Roy Woodson appears for the first time in the Kenosha city directory, living with his parents and an older sister, Velda.

- **1920**: Cecilia gives birth to her last child, Clara, on May 26.

- **1920**: The U.S. Census records the Woodson family (including Velda, age twenty-three, and Roy, age eighteen) living on Fremont Avenue, Kenosha. A niece, Helen B., age eight, lives with them. Charlie, Velda, and Roy all work in an "auto factory"—Charlie as a foreman, Velda as a stock clerk, and Roy as an apprentice machinist.

- **1922**: According to the 1930 Census, this is the approximate year of Roy's first marriage (specifically, between August 10, 1921 and August 9, 1922 if Roy's was age twenty-one at the time).

- **1923**: Although their parents are listed, neither Roy nor Velda appear in the Kenosha city directory. Maybe their names were inadvertently omitted. Or maybe Velda had married and Roy was working elsewhere.

- **1925**: Mrs. Beatrice Woodson is listed as a waitress at The Tea Shop on Church Street in the Kenosha city directory. She and Roy live at 819 Drew Street, and he is employed as an autoworker.

- **1927**: Roy and Beatrice now reside at 5819 21st Avenue, according to the Kenosha city directory. Roy is still an autoworker, but no employment is given for Beatrice.

- **1927**: Charlie and Nora Woodson are listed for the first time in the Racine city directory. Charlie is a repairman at the Nash Motors plant in Racine.

- **1929**: Roy Woodson appears in both the Kenosha and Racine city directories this year. The Kenosha city directory lists his job as "assembler." The Racine city directory lists his residence as the same address as that of his parents, 2614 Twentieth Street.

- **1930**: The U.S. Census records that Roy lives with his parents in Racine. Both father and son work as machinists at a tractor plant. Roy's marital status is "married" and his age at first marriage is twenty-one. But there is no mention of Beatrice.

- **1931:** According to Elsie and Roy's marriage certificate, Roy married Beatrice Stewart on April 21.

- **1931:** The Racine city directory lists Roy and his father, Charlie Woodson; both work at Massey-Harris—Charlie as a repairman and Roy as lathe hand. The family still all resides on Twentieth Street.

- **1933:** Roy is not listed in the Racine city directory. Charlie works at Nash Motors.

- **1935:** Roy reappears in the Racine city directory, working at Young Radiator Company and residing with his parents on Twentieth Street. Charlie again works at Massey-Harris.

- **1937:** Roy continues to live with his parents on 20th Street, according to the Racine city directory. No employment is listed for either Roy or Charlie.

- **1937:** For the first time, Elsie Green appears in the Racine city directory, living at 2110 Geneva Street. Ann Litzkow is not mentioned.

- **1938:** Elsie (almost age twenty-six), 811 Orchard Street, marries Roy Woodson (age thirty-five), 1116 Romayne Avenue, on April 23. Roy is a tool grinder, according to their marriage certificate.

- **1939:** The Racine city directory reports that Roy and Elsie Woodson live at 2036 Hickory Grove Avenue. Roy works as a toolmaker at Massey-Harris.

- **1943:** Roy still works as a toolmaker at Massey-Harris. He and Elsie now live at RD 1, Box 459, according to the Racine city directory.

- **1947:** The Racine city directory reports that Roy is now a foreman at Massey-Harris.

- **1950**: The Racine city directory states that Roy and Elsie live on Swamp Road. Roy is still a foreman at Massey-Harris. Elsie is a factory worker at Western Printing and Lithographing.

- **1952**: The Racine city directory again reports Elsie and Roy's address as RD 1, Box 459. No employment is given for Elsie.

- **1954**: The Racine city directory reports that Roy is still a foreman at Massey-Harris.

- **1955**: Roy and Elsie do not appear in the Racine city directory; maybe they were away from home when the canvasser was in their neighborhood.

- **1957**: The Racine city directory now states that Roy is a factory worker at Massey-Harris.

- **1959**: Roy is listed as a machinist at Massey-Harris in the Racine city directory.

- **1959**: Roy and Elsie buy a tavern and move to Mattoon, Wisconsin. They live in an apartment above the tavern.

- **1960**: Elsie Christina Petersen (Green) Woodson dies on July 31.

I tacked these pages to a bulletin board to better see the entirety of this flow. In my effort to focus on Elsie, I omitted all of the other marriages and births taking place in our family during the 1930s, '40s, and '50s. Everybody was having babies—by 1960, Grandma Green's eight other children had given her a total of twenty-six grand-children, with great-grandchildren arriving regularly.

Elsie alone remained childless. How had she felt about that? Had Elsie grieved for the loss of children unborn?

Also missing from this summarized timeline were world events and the context they provided. Elsie had married Roy, for instance, during Adolf Hitler's rise to power in Germany, just before the Nazis moved into Austria and before their 1939 invasion of Czechoslovakia. By the time the United States entered World War II, Roy was working long hours as factories built production in preparation for both battle- and home-front needs and most citizens were focused on winning the war.

Elsie's timeline showed the clear discrepancy in the reports of Roy's first marriage, recorded by the 1930 Census as about 1922, compared to 1931 as listed in his marriage certificate to Elsie. The timeline illumined the progression of Roy's career, from spotty employment during the Great Depression to moving up—and then down—the ladder at Massey-Harris. And it recorded Elsie and Roy's moves from a Racine apartment to their own home and finally to their Mattoon tavern.

Exploring a variety of research side roads was tempting since any tiny lead might reveal a crucial discovery. Roy, for example, seemingly followed a challenging career path. In his early thirties, he lived with his parents, and in 1931, worked with his father at Massey-Harris, which like J. I. Case and other farm implement manufacturers, was hit especially hard by the Great Depression. But in 1933, when his father returned to work at Nash Motors, Roy's name was absent from the

Racine city directory. Father and son might have been laid off from Massey-Harris. Could Roy have moved to another city seeking employment?

By 1935, Roy was again living with his parents and working at Young Radiator Company. Considering that Roy continued to live with his parents and that the directory interviewer presumably talked with his mother, it seems unlikely that his name was simply overlooked in the 1933 directory.

When Roy married Elsie in 1938, he worked as a tool grinder; in 1939, he was employed as a toolmaker at Massey-Harris. How long did he work at Young Radiator? Given the data available, he might have worked there only a few months or as long as three, or even four, years.

I reached to a shelf for a volume I'd often consulted, *Racine: Growth and Change in a Wisconsin County*, edited by Nicholas Burckel, and learned that Young Radiator, founded by Fred Young in 1927, was itself a young company in 1933. It was also a company in turmoil.

After Young Radiator fired eight men in August, allegedly for union activities, a major strike occurred with picket lines and daily rallies. A Racine County Workers Committee member even entered the plant to "chase out a strikebreaker," according to Burckel. "The police refused to arrest the offender, saying they had not seen him." Burckel also reported another incident in which "a taxi driver narrowly missed hitting two picketers while trying to drive two strikebreakers through the plant's rear entrance."

I wondered whether Roy might have been a strikebreaker; anything seemed possible. The strike ended in October with the company's recognition of the American Automobile and Accessory Workers Federal Union, affiliated with the American Federation of Labor (AFL).

By 1935, Young Radiator would have been a more or less peaceful union shop, although a strike again broke the peace in 1937 before it was settled in ten days by another Roy, Racine Mayor Roy Spencer.

Massey-Harris, a Canadian company that had bought the J. I. Case Plow Works in 1928, signed a contract with the United Automobile Workers (UAW) in 1937. "The president of Local 244, the UAW local at Massey-Harris, had his own telephone at his workbench in order to handle problems," Burckel wrote. The company met with union representatives weekly and "there was never any need at Massey-Harris for an arbitration clause, since the union 'assumed' that any grievance would be fairly settled."

The company boomed during World War II. Massey-Harris received in 1942 a large defense contract to build tanks at the former Nash plant. And by 1947, Roy had become a foreman at the plant.

Burckel reported that the firm greatly reduced its presence in Southeast Wisconsin, after Massey-Harris Company Ltd. and the Harry Ferguson Companies merged in 1953 to form Massey-Harris-Ferguson Limited (later as Massey-Ferguson, Ltd.), with headquarters in Toronto, Canada. Deciding to concentrate its tractor production in Detroit, the company closed the Racine plant, retaining only a parts warehouse. Massey-Harris, which had employed as many as 2,600 workers, employed only about 460 in 1960.

What did these facts mean for Roy—that he was lucky to have a job in 1959? I leaned back on the loveseat and thought about the implications. The plant where Roy had worked for almost twenty years was sold out from under him when he was in his fifties. Reason enough for a nervous breakdown.

I DREAMED ABOUT ELSIE AND ROY that night. I saw them standing in a Depression-era breadline and then taking flight together, like Peter Pan and Wendy, dipping and soaring above the Racine harbor and Lake Michigan, their coats furling out behind them.

The next morning, coffee mug in hand, I settled at my desk, beset by memories. Growing up, I believed Elsie had not worked outside of the home. If she had still been working at Western Printing in the late 1950s, her income certainly would have helped when Roy was demoted from his foreman position. Western Printing was expanding in those years, continuing to publish Whitman children's books and other titles in association with Walt Disney Productions.

Roy was about age fifty-five when he was demoted. Elsie turned forty in 1952. Childless, she witnessed the marriages of all her siblings and the births of more than twenty nieces and nephews. And, of course, by the late 1950s, Martin had moved to Mexico, Laura to Alaska, and Andrew to Marinette, Wisconsin. Did she feel stuck while everyone else had moved on?

I continued to build the family timeline, and years later, after the 1940 census was released to the public in 2012, I would learn that early in their marriage, Elsie and Roy had moved frequently—in quick succession from 2036 Hickory Grove Avenue to a home they rented for $33 monthly at 1007 Seymour Street (today, Lombard Avenue) as listed in the 1940 federal census to Charles Street (the former Swamp Road).

After Elsie and Roy married, Mom remembered, they first rented a house from Ann Litzkow's father. This may have been either the Hickory Grove Avenue or Seymour Street address. Elsie and Roy then built their house on a half-acre lot at 5138 Charles Street.

By 1947, according to the Racine directory, Elsie's sister Clara and her husband, Roy Miller, lived next door at 5128 Charles Street. For the Woodsons, having familiar faces as neighbors—family members who would always have their back—must have been a boon, occasional dust-ups between the two sisters notwithstanding.

As Clara and Roy and their growing family were settling into their new house, people were rebuilding a warred-out world. Japan had surrendered on my father's thirty-first birthday, an age he might not have seen had his feet been healthy. Had he fought and survived, Dad would still have been unmarried in 1945, though in that case, I believed Mom would have waited for him to come home, and I'd have come along on cue three years later.

What if this? What if that? My mind overflowed with too many options. On the plus side, all the possibilities pulled me forward in the search for answers about Elsie's life and death.

15

THE WAY CLARA REMEMBERED IT

Seven years after my interview with Pete, I braced myself and called my formidable Aunt Clara from Mom's home in Racine, asking for a family history interview. Mom wanted to come, too, and that was fine with me, given that Clara could be unpredictable.

Clara met us at her door and led us into the kitchen, where we each sat at a different side of the rectangular table. Hospitable as always, she asked if we wanted a drink. Mom and I declined, but Clara poured herself a tumbler of amber whiskey, which she would replenish repeatedly over the course of our conversation.

I placed my notepad on the table, along with Pete's transcribed interview and Gladys's family history. After setting up the cassette recorder, I began with the basics: "Please tell us when you were born and where."

Clara smiled at the easy question. "I was born on May 26, 1920 in Paris, Kenosha County."

"Do you remember Grandpa and Grandma talking about their life in Denmark?"

"They told me a few things. They did go to school together. You want the funny parts, too?"

"Especially the funny parts."

173

"When they were in school together, Grandpa said he thought she was a little butterball. You know, she was so short and she was chubby. And, then he left to work in a different part of the county for a while. When he came back, he said, 'Boy, she was good looking!'" Clara laughed, brought the glass to her lips and took a healthy swallow.

"Pete said Grandma worked as a milkmaid?"

Clara nodded. "They both worked on the same farm. And even then, she had trouble with her hands, with arthritis, so he'd sneak over and help her milk the cows because he knew that she was suffering."

"It sounds like it was a big farm." I envisioned the fields and pastures of southern Wisconsin.

"At the farms over there, the houses come in like a circle … and then each farm expands out beyond the circle of houses," Clara drew her hands together and then spread her arms wide.

"When the men worked on the farm, they were living under the barn—that's where my dad lived, in the barn. The women did the milking and inside, they did the cooking because there was always quite a few hired men. On the table they had little hooks for the forks and knives, and everyone had their own things at their place. After everyone ate, they hung them there and each of them had their own utensils hanging up."

"What kinds of food did they eat?"

"For one thing, the men would catch a chicken, kill it, and pack it in clay. They wouldn't pluck it or clean it.

They would bake it on a fire outside. That clay would bake onto the chicken. And when it was done, they would peel the clay off and that would take the feathers off."

I thought I must have misheard: "But they must have cleaned it first?"

"No!"

I shook my head and decided to move on. "How old were Grandma and Grandpa when they got married?"

Clara sipped her drink, considering. "They got married in 1896, and John was born in 1897."

"What year were Grandma and Grandpa born?"

"Grandpa was born in 1876 and she was born in 1878. But they were really only a year apart because his birthday was December 26 and her birthday was January 14."

"Did they talk at all about the kind of house they lived in, in Denmark?"

"The house they were renting was near the church where they went. That was right in Stenderup."

"What was the house built of?"

"I don't know."

"The reason I'm curious is that Pete said it had a thatched roof."

"Oh, I imagine that would be right, because most of the roofs were, over there."

"Why did Grandma and Grandpa decide to leave Stenderup, to leave Denmark?" I asked.

"Earlier, maybe before my folks were married, my dad had wanted to go into the Danish Army but they wouldn't take him because he had only one eye."

"He was totally blind in one eye?"

"Right, and then when they come [sic] over here, he could see a little bit—like colors a little bit in that bad eye."

"So his eyesight returned a bit in that bad eye?"

Clara nodded and passed a hand in front of her own eyes.

"Besides working on someone else's farm, there weren't many opportunities in Denmark, so Grandpa and Grandma decided to come to the United States?"

Clara shrugged her wide shoulders and explained that America offered both more opportunities for work and family connections. "His mother was already here. She was here with Uncle John, my dad's half-brother, and Aunt Mary, my dad's sister."

I looked down to consult the family tree. Gladys recorded that John had married Karoline Jorgensen in 1885 in Kolding, Denmark, before immigrating to Michigan in 1889. John's stepmother, Karen Bramsen Green, and her daughter Mary, then age nine, emigrated with the couple—even though Karen's husband and Mary's father, Peter Grøn, was still living in Denmark, where he would die five years later. I considered: Curious. Though only age fifty-one, had Peter believed he was too old or ill to make the grueling trip?

Across the table, Clara watched me, smiling.

"Gladys wrote that John came to Milwaukee in 1897, and then to Racine in the spring of 1903," I said. "When Grandpa came over, did his half-brother help him find a job?"

"No, Jess Winum, Mary's husband, was working at Case's and got him into the factory. And, then my folks bought a little farm on Randolph Street. It was off of Taylor Avenue near the Taylor orphanage at that time. They lived there long enough to get things organized, and then they got a chance to rent a farm in Kenosha County."

"Wasn't that where Herman was born, on that farm?" Mom interjected.

"Mmm...hmmm," Clara said. "And then I was born on Mike's farm on County E."

I wondered how best to move Clara's storytelling along, to reach the Great Depression, World War II, and the rest of the story.

But Mom was on a roll: "Wasn't something said one time when they lived downtown and they first came here, that someone got their foot caught in the railroad tracks? John? And, then there was a train coming, and he cut his shoe off?"

Clara frowned. "I think it must have been Pete that got his foot caught in the railroad track. And my mother almost got hit by the train, too. Their house and garden were on either side of the railroad track. Once she was going to the garden, and I don't know what she was thinking of, because she said that she just stepped off the track and the train went by. That's how close she was to getting hit."

I looked up from my note taking. "Sounds like something I would do!"

Clara raised her glass in a toast. "Herman was the one. Every other Sunday after church, my mother and dad would walk to visit Jess and Mary Winum, and the next Sunday, Jess and Mary would visit my folks. One Sunday, they went to Aunt Mary's house and they were in the house for quite a while before they noticed Herman wasn't there. All of sudden, everyone is looking for Herman. Finally, they found him outside—he was still walking up the street. He didn't know the rest of them went in the house; he just kept on going."

"How old was he?" Mom asked.

"He was real little. But Herman was like that, you know. If he was thinking, he didn't pay attention to other things going on."

Mom looked at me. *Suddenly, I remembered those times that she had tried in vain to get my attention when I was glued to a book.* In an effort to regain control of the interview, I asked, "What are some of your earliest memories?"

"When we rented Mike Stollen's farm on County E, we had half the house, and he lived in the other half."

Aha! Here was a clue to Mike's farm. It was Mike Stollen's—or was it Stolen's—farm, located in Kenosha County. This clue, however, never did help me to learn much more about the farm owner.

"On our side there was one bedroom downstairs, and there were three bedrooms upstairs," Clara continued. "My mother and dad had the room downstairs. At first, I must just have slept in a buggy in their room. Later, Elsie and I had a room, and Andrew and Herman had a room."

"Where were the older kids? Was Laura still at home at that time?"

"No, by the time I was in the room with Elsie, there was just Andrew and Herman and Elsie and me."

"Were all of the older kids married by that time, or just working?"

"Pete was the one that got married the youngest. He got married when I was a year old. John didn't get married until he was in his thirties, and I wasn't very old when Carl got married. Martin didn't get married right away; he was working other places. And then Laura got married young. She was seventeen maybe."

Once more, I referred to Gladys's history. Pete had married Edna in 1921, and John had married Inez in 1930. Carl had married Peg in 1923, when Clara was age two. Martin married his first wife, Frances, in 1927. And Laura married her first husband, Bert, early in 1923, ten months before Carl and Peg's wedding in November.

"So, a couple of the brothers were older when they married," Clara was saying. "Herman was ..." her voice trailed off.

"Thirty exactly," Mom supplied.

"Yeah," Clara agreed.

"There's a big span between the kids in your family," I said.

Clara took another swallow of whisky. "Yeah, John was twenty-four years older than me."

"When did you get married?"

"I started working out when I was fifteen."

"Where did you work?"

"First I took care of kids for a family that lived just up the road. Then I went to work for my former teacher for a while, and after that I worked in town at quite a few different places. I was working for a family with four kids when I got married myself."

"Had Elsie been married a long time at that point?"

"She got married, oh, I don't know, about four or five years before I got married."

"Can you talk a little bit about Elsie—about her later years and her death?" I turned to a flagged page in the transcript of Pete's interview. "Pete told me how he and John went up to Mattoon afterward and brought Elsie's body to Racine, but he didn't really have a lot of ideas about what had happened."

"I think something did happen, but there's no way to prove it." Clara emptied her glass, stood to refill it from the bottle on the counter, and resettled herself at the table.

"Woodson left in the morning, and the bartender and undertaker were in the bar—and Elsie was drinking with the undertaker. Then, she went upstairs, and all of a sudden, they heard a thump up there—and that's when she died. When Woodson got home, he went in the

The three Green sisters: Elsie, left, with her sisters
Laura and Clara at the Franksville farm about 1940

bathroom, brought out a bottle of sleeping pills, and said
that she must have taken them. Well, she wouldn't have
been taking sleeping pills in the morning. So there's
something wrong with the whole story."

Mom leaned forward. "Pete and John went up there,
because the undertaker wanted to have her buried up
there. The undertaker didn't have an autopsy done. The
undertaker was everything in town."

"I think he might have put something in her drink,"
Clara said.

"Why would he do that?" Mom asked.

"Because Woodson was going with that woman down here [in Racine]." Clara looked past us toward the doorway to the living room.

My eyebrows rose. Her words brought to mind overheard, half-remembered whispers about Roy having an affair with a woman in Racine, but this was the first time anyone had mentioned this in conversation with me.

"Elsie had left Pete's number by the telephone," Clara was saying, "and I'm not sure if that woman who worked there [the bartender] called him. Anyway, we had my mother over for dinner, so when Pete called me to tell my mother, I suppose I said enough that when I got off the phone, she said, 'Did Elsie die?'"

I glanced at Mom, remembering her interview. Was this really what had happened? Was our memory of Pete calling Dad, and then Dad calling Clara a complete fabrication? Or, were we conflating the event of Elsie's death with what happened two years later, when Dad and Clara together visited Grandma to tell her of John's death? Could I not trust my own memory as a twelve-year-old—never mind Mom's memory?

I struggled to put the pieces (both documented facts and distant memories) together. In any case, there had been two calls around the time of Elsie's death: first, Elsie's request to come get her, and then the announcement of her death.

Mom was following a different line of thought: "Pete and John wanted to bring her body to Racine for an autopsy, but then they never did an autopsy on her, did they?"

"The undertaker wouldn't let them."

"What did they put on the death certificate?"

I stared at Mom. I'd shown her a copy of Elsie's death certificate, so why ask Clara?

"I don't know." Clara went on, "Elsie and Roy didn't go to church up there, and they hadn't gone to church down here. John and Pete wanted to take her to a funeral home in Racine, on Washington Avenue, but that Mattoon undertaker said, 'No, she's not going into a funeral home.'

"They finally got her into that church where the funeral was, but then the undertaker didn't want anybody to look at her. The family all got to the church before the funeral service and we were all told to go down to the basement before the service. But I went back to the room with the casket by myself. The undertaker come chasing after me and says, 'What are you doing up here?'

"She's my sister. I want to take another look at her before they close the casket.'

"He says, 'That's what I'm doing. I'm going to close that casket. You weren't supposed to come back up here.'

"'Well, I'm still going to look at her,'" I says. "And I walked up and looked at her, but he slammed the casket shut."

"Nowadays, if there was a question, you could have the coffin opened after they're buried," Mom said.

"I know," Clara said, "but at the time, Pete didn't want to do an autopsy because of my mother. She was so upset. Elsie was really her favorite daughter."

"Elsie's death was a shame," Mom said. "I thought there was something crooked about it. She wasn't sickly or anything. We had visited Mattoon the week before, and she and Roy took us out to eat. Oh! She was like nothing wrong with her at all! And Carl and Glenys had been there, I guess the day before she died."

Clara regarded Mom. "Something like that," she agreed. "I think the undertaker and Woodson had a lot to do with it, and no one knows what happened to his first wife either."

I looked directly into Clara's shrewd eyes. "Elsie knew he'd been married before?"

"When he started going with Elsie, Woodson told her that he was divorced. For them to get married, Woodson needed proof of the divorce. He must have figured, 'I got to do something.' You had to put an announcement in some newspaper then; maybe you don't now, I don't know. He didn't have the announcement put in the Racine paper. He had it put in a Chicago paper and some other paper."

"Maybe he didn't want Elsie's relatives to know he was divorced." I pondered the puzzle. "Or, maybe Elsie didn't want all her relatives to know he was divorced."

"Ma wouldn't have liked it that Elsie was marrying a guy who'd been divorced. But Elsie was living on her own, and Ma and everyone else in the family would have supported the marriage because Elsie wanted it."

"Then why didn't Roy want the divorce announced in Racine?"

"I don't know exactly, but a funny thing happened after we were both married and living next door on Charles Street." Clara took a swallow of the whiskey, audible later every time the tape was replayed.

"When we'd drive to town for groceries, Elsie would sometimes go with us. One time, she had said that she was going to go with us. When the time came to leave, there was a car parked in their driveway, so we thought Elsie had company. I says, 'We'll just go by our car and see if she might come over.'

"By the time I come out of the door, Elsie comes flying across the lot and comes over, and then says those visitors are relatives of his first wife and they didn't know that anything had taken place. When Elsie heard a knock and come to her door, they asked for Mrs. Woodson, and she said, 'Well, I am Mrs. Woodson.' But they were looking for his first wife. They thought Woodson was still married to his first wife."

"Oh, that's odd," Mom said.

"I know it! Where is she?"

"I never heard that before," Mom said.

"And Woodson once claimed that he just told his first wife to get on a train and go, and I don't know where he sent her." Clara picked up her glass but set it down without taking a swallow.

I envisioned the scene. *Where might I have gone? Maybe California.*

Clara picked up her tumbler and finally drank. "He could be a nice guy, you know, but he did a lot of odd things."

"Once he painted each cement block in one of their basement walls a different color," Mom chimed in. "One block would be red, the next blue, green, purple, whatever. Elsie said, 'If you go down there, you'll think you're drunk.'"

Clara set down her glass. "Another time—long before they moved Up North—he hung a noose down in the basement and told Elsie she could go down and use it."

Mom looked like she wished she had accepted Clara's offer of whiskey. "He did?"

"Mmm...Hmmm."

"Oh, for crying out loud! Elsie should have left him before she went up to Mattoon with him."

"Yep," Clara agreed. "She should have left him a long time before that. He used to be pretty tough."

Clara paused, seemingly out of words, though I still hoped to confirm the motivation for the move to Mattoon. "Did Roy lose his job down here?"

"No," Mom answered. "He had a nervous breakdown. His job was too stressful, and he was in the hospital for a while. He was like a foreman and he was supposed to have a lot on his mind."

Clara swallowed another mouthful of whiskey. "I imagine he did have lots on his mind!" She thumped her empty glass on the tabletop.

I felt empty, too—empty of hope and empty of answers. But how much of Clara's testimony to believe?

16

BACK TO THE STACKS: ROY'S THREE WIVES

*B*ack home in Madison, I sat hunched over the cassette player, replaying the interview and stopping the tape every few phrases to accurately transcribe it. Clara had certainly built a case against Roy, who was possibly having an affair with another woman from Racine and supposedly hung a noose to suggest suicide to Elsie. But what did I know about suicide?

No matter how many times I heard the story of Elsie's death, one question lingered: *Had there been a suicide note?* One had never been mentioned. If there hadn't been a note, how could the cause of death have been rendered so quickly? When Roy brought that bottle of pills out of the bathroom, he must have been a very credible witness. And the person who might have best refuted him was dead.

Then, there was the thump heard from above when Elsie fell to the floor. That thump bothered me, too. It suggested either a very fast-acting drug or one administered earlier when she was downstairs drinking with the undertaker. I stretched out on the loveseat, head resting on one of its ample arms, legs propped up on the other. If I were going to commit suicide, I'd leave a note for Roy to find. I'd also comb my hair, lie down, and arrange my clothing—I certainly wouldn't want to drop like a load of bricks.

I also couldn't see what motivations Elsie might have had for taking her own life and tried to imagine what would it have been like to live with Roy, the glad-handing, social bartender. Elsie had one advantage I'd never had: a brother to ride to her rescue. Elsie had options other than staying with Roy. She knew that my dad (not to mention Pete or John) would come get her on the weekend, even if not in the middle of a work week.

A new thought struck me. What would it have been like to have Elsie live with us—at least until she found a job and a place of her own? With her cheeriness and skill at baking rich desserts, she'd have been a joy in our house. She could have taught me how to make a torte that I'd have entered as a 4-H project in the Racine County Fair. Blue ribbon guaranteed. If only.

My eyes flew open. While I couldn't know what was going on in Elsie's head that day, I could learn more about the drug that caused her death. The next Saturday, a breezy April day with the grass finally turning green, I walked from our little house along the railroad tracks across Monona Bay to the University of Wisconsin-Madison medical library to read about Nembutal.

Consulting several medical dictionaries and texts, I learned that Nembutal (pentobarbital) was one of hundreds of barbiturates available in the mid-twentieth century and widely accepted before their danger was truly understood.

The chemical formula for pentobarbital is Na (sodium) + ethyl + methyl + butyl + al, with the first letters of these words leading to Nembutal®, trademarked in 1930 by a Danish pharmaceutical company, Lundbeck. Used as a sedative and sleep aid, the drug is highly addictive and as tolerance to it develops, the margin between an intoxicating dosage and fatal dosage becomes smaller.

Accidental overdoses can happen easily, and the lethal dose is far less if alcohol is also ingested. Large doses can cause effects that mimicked drunkenness: staggering, blurred vision, and slurred speech. Symptoms of a Nembutal overdose include headache, confusion, sleepiness, low blood pressure, and weak pulse— followed by slowed or stopped breathing and heart failure. A victim will typically fall unconscious and lapse into a coma before finally succumbing. Sometimes a rash or blisters appear on the victim's skin.

Leaving the books I'd consulted to be re-shelved by student workers, I left the library for the glorious spring sunshine. Daffodils and hyacinths had begun to bloom in front yards as I walked from campus toward Monona Bay and the tracks. The rhythm of the questions running through my head matched my footsteps. Whose prescription did Elsie take? Did she have a prescription for Nembutal, or had the pills been prescribed for Roy's earlier breakdown?

I paused to watch a pick-up basketball game at a park on the bay. Though the temperature was still chilly, a couple of the players had doffed their sweatshirts to play in bright tees. The fast-paced game had drawn another observer, and the older man, bundled in a winter jacket, leaned on his cane to watch the action.

Elsie's death certificate stated that the "interval between onset and death" was a half hour, at least according to Roy, who did not always appear trustworthy. Yet that time frame probably rang true given witnesses who watched her go upstairs, heard a thump, and arrived in the apartment to find her barely alive—or already dead, according to Clara.

Again, the thump seemed to present a problem. If Elsie experienced symptoms and went upstairs because she wasn't feeling well, wouldn't she lie down? That thump suggested surprise—she wasn't expecting to fall. And if Elsie wasn't expecting to fall, maybe that was because she didn't realize that she had been drugged downstairs.

Later, I learned more about Nembutal from online research and found Richard Davenport-Hines's 2001 book, *The Pursuit of Oblivion: A Social History of Drugs.* Davenport-Hines wrote that according to F. Scott Fitzgerald, airline stewardesses in the 1930s would regularly offer barbiturates, asking, "Do you want an aspirin ... or Nembutal?"

Then, there was the sad saga of Marilyn Monroe's 1962 demise, although her death was unlike Elsie's since Marilyn had clearly been addicted to alcohol and multiple prescriptions. It wasn't as if Elsie was our family's

Marilyn, even if she was the most alluring among her farm family siblings.

Despite the development of newer barbiturates, Nembutal continued to be used by veterinarians, as well as for executions and assisted suicides, in which context it was sometimes called the "peaceful pill."

I could not help but wonder how peaceful Elsie's death had been. Had she been aware of the people around her and their efforts to revive her? The bartender and undertaker must have called her name and shaken her—never mind their reported efforts to force mustard down her throat and get her to throw up.

EVER SINCE CLARA'S INTERVIEW, I had wondered how to research Roy's first wife, the Beatrice Stewart listed on his marriage certificate to Elsie. I had a distant memory of meeting his third wife, Agnes, when they visited our home some years after Elsie's death and Dad had given them a cold shoulder.

Agnes had waited in the car while Roy went to the house, maybe to see if we were home. Mom answered the door and asked me to go the garden and fetch Dad, who was running a cultivator up and down the rows. When I stopped in front of him and after he turned down the roar of the cultivator, I repeated Mom's request. Dad shook his head and returned to his work.

There was nothing for me to do but go back to the house and deliver a whispered message to Mom. By then,

Roy and Agnes were sitting together on the couch, drinks in hand. They did not stay long, but their brief visit made me curious to know more about her, too. Yet Beatrice was the bigger mystery. Where had she disappeared to?

Kenosha city directories had placed Beatrice with Roy in that city in 1925 and 1927, but they had not married in Racine, Kenosha, or Milwaukee. Clara had said that Roy had placed a divorce announcement in a Chicago newspaper, so back I went to the microfilm room at the Wisconsin Historical Society Library in Madison. There, I squinted through rolls of fuzzy newspaper images, my eyes growing as blurry as the text of the classified pages. It was a fruitless search.

The library also provided access to federal census records, so I searched the 1930 census but found no listing for a Beatrice Woodson or, for that matter, a Beatrice Stewart, age twenty-seven, living anywhere in the United States. Beatrice had seemingly vanished in the late 1920s. Lacking facts, imagination took over. What if Beatrice had run away from Roy and changed her identity? What if she had moved to another country?

I walked to the row of windows in the library's expansive reading room, but the sun-filled sky didn't brighten my thoughts. What if Beatrice had been so unhappy in the marriage that she had run away and killed herself? Maybe Roy had hung a noose in their basement and she had used it. Maybe Beatrice's dead bones still rested somewhere, buried in the Kenosha countryside or under a building only God knew where.

The hard truth was that many murders went unsolved and some went unknown, cases in which the victims simply disappeared.

Like a soldier missing in action or an unidentified body following a plane crash or tsunami, Beatrice might never be found. Or properly grieved. Is that why her family came looking for her in Racine long after Roy had married Elsie? In any event, Beatrice would most likely be dead by now.

I again saw Clara's face when she stated that Roy had put his first wife on a train and just told her to go. Go where? Where would I have gone under those circumstances? Maybe the most likely scenario was the simple explanation that Beatrice, like Roy, had remarried, changed her name, and created a new identity elsewhere.

This was not an insurmountable mountain in my research journey, at least that's what I tried to assure myself. I vowed to find a way around or over this barrier, but for now, the quest for Beatrice moved to a side track. I couldn't think where else to look.

TRACKING ROY'S THIRD WIFE, Agnes, proved much easier, again with the proximity of State Historical Society and its library subscription to Ancestry.com, the for-profit genealogy database. It led me to Agnes's surname, Harris, and her marriage date to Roy, April 20, 1962—a respectable one year and eight months after Elsie's death.

Eventually, I would learn all three of Roy's marriages had taken place in April, this last one three days shy of what would have been his twenty-fourth anniversary with Elsie. Roy had married Elsie immediately after his divorce to Beatrice became final, explaining the April choice of his second marriage, but I wondered why he and Agnes picked almost the same marriage date.

No doubt, in my obsessive search, I was reading way too much into every detail; the date of Roy's third marriage probably meant nothing more than a repetition of the age-old pattern of romance in springtime.

Paging back and forth among Racine city directory name and street listings from the 1920s to the 1960s, I learned that Agnes and her first husband Frank had lived on Mead Street and operated Frank's Market at the same address. Frank last appeared in the 1957 directory and the next year, Agnes was listed as a widow, living at 2066 Superior Street, a property she owned. In 1961 and 1962, she worked as a clerk at the Red Cross Drug Store, within easy walking distance from her home.

I remembered that drugstore from childhood. The one-story, tan brick building stood a few blocks west of Lake Michigan's North Beach, where Mom occasionally took Diane and me swimming once the water had warmed to fifty degrees. We'd alternately shiver in the frigid water and broil on the hot July sand—a land-and-sea version of the Finnish sauna-and-snow custom. Afterward, we'd towel off and change our clothes behind the bushes north of the beach, between the Racine Zoo and the lake.

Footsteps echoed on the stairway and then sounded on this lowest level of the stacks open to the public. I heard a light switch click on and then two people whispering in an aisle to my left. The aisles between the towering shelves of volumes were usually so dark and silent that any other presence put me on alert. But as two older women carried books to a desk at the end of their aisle, I relaxed and nodded to the pair, who smiled in return.

Checking a Racine map, I noted the site of the drugstore in relation to Roy and Elsie's north-side home and considered the implications. The Red Cross Drug Store had been more than three miles from their rural home, but none was closer. Might Roy have first met Agnes at this drugstore? Given the fallibility of city directories, she might have begun working there before her employment actually appeared in the Racine directory.

For the umpteenth time, I recalled Roy crying when our family visited him and Elsie on a winter evening. When Roy had his nervous breakdown in the late 1950s, maybe he had filled a prescription for Nembutal at that Red Cross Drug Store location. Impossible to prove, it was nevertheless a tantalizing possibility.

On yet another visit to the Wisconsin Historical Society (Couldn't I just set up a cot in an out-of-the-way corner?) I accessed Ancestry.com and located two death records. Agnes's first husband, Frank Harris, died on July 29, 1957. Agnes died on June 24, 1988, in Carney, Michigan, where she had moved with Roy from Mattoon about 1969. She died less than a year after Roy passed—on August 25, 1988, two weeks after his eighty-seventh birthday (giving him thirty-nine more years of life than Elsie had enjoyed).

Through the Wisconsin Vital Records Office, I eventually obtained a copy of Frank Harris's death certificate, which reported that he died at St. Mary's Hospital in Racine, from a "central hemorrhage." Born in Poland on March 3, 1891, the World War I vet and butcher had suffered from hypertension. Fifteen years older than Agnes, Frank died at age sixty-six, about two years before Roy and Elsie moved to Mattoon.

A copy of Roy and Agnes's marriage certificate revealed they received their marriage license from the Shawano County Clerk and then married in Kenosha, with Roy's sister, Velda Nelson, and her husband Raymond signing as witnesses to the ceremony. The marriage certificate noted that Agnes, born in Pennsylvania, was age fifty-five and usually worked as a "clerk." Roy, age sixty, was listed as "tavern owner." No surprises or revelations there.

The more I learned, the more determined I was to tell Elsie's story. Yet any witnesses to her life and death were passing on, one by one, and there was little hard evidence to document a true crime—even if that was what Elsie's death had been—as Ann Rule, author of *The Stranger Beside Me* and other bestsellers, might have done.

Still, there was one other option: Could I tell Elsie's story as historical fiction?

I explored the possibility by writing a "practice" novel. *Dark Tunnels* was set on a dreamscape version of Mom's home farm. This mystery turned on a plot involving the illegal drug trade, contained a romantic subplot, and featured a tunnel leading from the sesquicentennial farm to the Root River. Drug dealers could float downriver to reach an underground outdoor club headquarters resembling a similar cellar hangout in a student union at the University of Wisconsin-Madison.

An Iowa college writers' workshop fueled my inspiration, though I was somewhat taken aback when another participant, a former Madison mayor, admitted he had an unfinished novel stashed away in a drawer. Nevertheless, I hired the workshop leader to review my romantic mystery manuscript. He—a prolific author of paperback tales of murder, torture, and the Old West— pronounced my draft "very well written." I was further buoyed when a publisher called to express serious interest.

But hold the applause. The caller turned out to represent a vanity publisher, and his confirmation letter asked me to pay $5,875 for book design, printing of 10,000 (!) copies, and distribution. No one else called and I was ill- prepared to self-publish. In those days, self-publishing meant buying cartons of books, storing them, and selling them one by one, before the pages foxed and curled. Still, the experience met the goal of writing practice.

The publisher's phone call came in the midst of packing for a move. The phone was one of the last items still in place inside a largely empty living room cluttered with moving boxes. Five years after Clara's interview, Michael and I moved from Madison to a log house on a wooded hillside overlooking the Wisconsin River south of Spring Green. It lacked many amenities—dishwasher and cable, to name two—but more than made up for these omissions with a woodstove, plentiful woodlot, and abundance of wildlife. For a year, I commuted to my job with a Madison newsletter publisher, but then resigned to have more time for writing, as well as researching Elsie's story.

During that first transitional year, the country proved exciting in unwanted ways: lightning struck the antenna, igniting the between-log insulation, which cascaded downward in tufts like Molotov cocktails into the wet woods; and, a giant tree limb punched a gaping hole in the roof. Woodpeckers occasionally hammered away on the house and later, flying squirrels took up residence in the roof, reluctant to leave despite efforts by a variety of wildlife exterminators and building contractors.

The flying squirrels now and again appeared in the house proper and provided much entertainment, as when one landed briefly atop Michael's head to re-launch itself upward to a spot high on the log wall. But such challenges worked like barbells to strengthen resolve for the Elsie project—at least, that's what I kept telling myself.

Research forays from rural Spring Green to Madison became easier after a freelance assignment turned into a part-time job with the University of Wisconsin-Madison. Surrounded by campus buildings, the Wisconsin Historical Society's world-class library was not far from my new office—either a short stroll along the Lake Mendota Lakeshore Path in fair weather, or a quick march up and over Bascom Hill when icy winds blew. At least the Bascom Hill walkways were salted and sanded. (Harking back to my high school Latin verb conjugations, I created a new one while stepping gingerly along the steep grade: *Slippo, slidere, falli, bumpus.*)

In the early 2000s, I also juggled a handful of writing assignments—from freelance articles to contracted training guides for the Credit Union National Association. When a Michigan publisher ceased producing a Wisconsin banking magazine, I launched a bimonthly magazine for the Community Bankers of Wisconsin, writing and arranging for the design, printing, and distribution of each issue. This assignment would last, amazingly, to 2015. There was little time to think about Elsie's story.

Have I mentioned that I have a tendency "to spread myself too thin," as my father once commented? Yet I did not forget entirely forget about Elsie and her curious death. Haunted by that Cave of the Mounds family trip decades earlier, I submitted a proposal to a Wisconsin publisher, Trails Books. This time my query was accepted, and in 2000, *Wisconsin Underground: A Guide to Caves,*

Mines, and Tunnels in and Around the Badger State appeared on bookshelves.

Accompanied by Michael and friends, I traipsed around Wisconsin, Upper Michigan, northeastern Iowa, and northern Illinois to explore underground spaces. Damp or dry, all maintained a constant temperature in the upper forties Fahrenheit, and all had something to teach about geology and chemistry, not to mention physical flexibility. Two more Trails Books—*Minnesota Underground* (2003) and *Explore Wisconsin Rivers* (2008)— gave Michael and me more excuses to tramp about wild places.

Like the early novel, the guidebooks paved a circuitous route to the creative work of Elsie's story. Riverine outings offered recreation, as well as discoveries to share. Michael and I explored the headwaters of the Wisconsin River with our black Labrador Retriever Rumpus and hiked the historic portage route between the Bois Brule and St. Croix rivers. Such boots-on-the-ground research inspired renewed investigations into the physical world of Elsie and her generation. All roads, apparently, led to Elsie.

17

OUT ON A LIMB

*E*very question about Elsie's death had so far led to a rock-face dead end. Feeling blindly for handholds on this mountain of a mystery, I turned in 2004 to a strategy once tried in a different family puzzler: hypnosis.

After a cousin was seriously injured in a car accident that had resulted in the death of the other driver, investigators used sodium pentothal ("truth serum") combined with hypnosis to jog his lost memory of the event—albeit with limited success. Still, maybe hypnosis might reveal subconscious impressions locked away in my childhood that would throw light on the circumstances of Elsie's death. What did I have to lose?

Agitated and hyper-alert on the day of my scheduled appointment, I was not the world's best hypnotic subject. The hypnotist invited me to take a seat on a sofa in a darkened room at the front of her suburban home, while she sat in a chair placed at a right angle to the couch. She began by leading me through multiple relaxation exercises to induce me—finally—into a very light sleeplike state. At any moment, I could choose to throw my eyes open, but, of course, that wasn't why I had come to her home office.

One by one, beginning with my toes, I relaxed all muscles. One by one, we moved through the series of exercises. I envisioned a blackboard with a circle drawn on it. I imagined writing with my right hand and erasing with my left, I wrote each letter of the alphabet. When I had completed the task, I raised my right index finger. I counted backward from one hundred to one.

Judging that I might be relaxed enough to proceed, the hypnotist instructed me to walk into a gated garden and sit on a bench in the midst of its green and light beauty. From there, I walked down a flight of steps and finally met my guide.

My guide, who reminded me of my seventh-grade teacher, turned out to be surprisingly jovial. I asked him to protect me and if it was okay to continue to move forward and remember new information.

Permission received, I tried to view my own past as on a movie screen. Suddenly, I could see Elsie moving about the kitchen and dining room of their home in Racine. She was comfortable and conversational. Then I could see Roy. His movements were easy, smooth, and relaxed. He appeared like a storyteller, an entertainer— maybe an actor? Compared to Elsie, he seemed to be covering up more facts.

"Do you have a sense that it's acceptable or not acceptable to go back?" the hypnotist asked.

"There's a sense of fear," I decided.

"Ask the guide to set the fear aside."

Instead, I wanted to put my finger on the hesitancy. "It's fear of knowing what really happened and fear of knowing what other people thought at the time."

She again suggested putting it up on a movie screen. I envisioned myself in two places at the same time. Part of me was sitting in the theater watching the screen, while another part of me was standing in the projection room where I could turn off the projector at any time.

"Put on the screen anything in your memory bank that will help to understand Elsie," the hypnotist advised.

All at once, I could see Elsie as a girl, helping my grandmother in the kitchen. I could see her as a teenager asking my grandfather to send Dad—then a twelve-year-old boy—to high school. The movie wound forward and suddenly Elsie and Roy were traveling with Dad and Mom, a young Diane, and me to the Cave of the Mounds. I could see our group following the tour guide into the cave and sense that Elsie was speaking to me, but I couldn't quite make out her words, which sounded like water bubbling from a spring.

"I want to remember what I've forgotten." I must have spoken aloud, because the hypnotist suggested I ask my guide if it would be okay to bring forward Elsie's essence. I knew that would be fine as I had nothing to fear from Elsie. Soon, I felt my aunt's familiar warm presence and again saw her moving about the house she shared with Roy in Racine. I saw her set the table in the dining room and return to the stove in the kitchen.

Later, when I listened to the audiotape of this session, I'd be struck by the long silences. When the hypnotist prompted me by asking what was happening, I'd replied:

> I feel that sometimes I know her and yet there are things I don't know. I'm trying to sense more aspects of Elsie's personality than I sometimes saw. I want to know more about how she interacted with other people, especially Roy—and anything dark. I want to understand the difficulties and the challenges she faced. I see her almost mothering Roy, caring for him .... Elsie felt so torn because she did not want to go to Mattoon and saw no other choice but to go with him. Maybe one advantage was that ... if she knew he was having an affair in Racine, they would leave that behind. He must always have been the dark part of her life.
>
> And I wonder when Elsie first realized that the problems she maybe thought were minor weren't minor. Clara told a couple of intriguing stories— I'm sure the one [about the visit from relatives of Roy's first wife] was true. Why would she make it up? And I'm sure the second was true. If I can relax enough, can I figure out what Elsie did when my uncle suggested that she just go hang herself in the basement in Racine? Why would he do that? I need to understand him more.

The hypnotist responded, "Are there other things about Elsie that you need to understand?"

> Her relationship with my grandfather—He was a rough-and-tumble kind of guy [leading a] hardscrabble immigrant family lifestyle. They had to be very tough to survive, so it would have been traditional roles for the girls growing up. Yet Elsie's two sisters were very outspoken. Her older sister would have had a divorce long before Elsie and Roy moved to Mattoon, so divorce was not unheard of. Elsie would have been the most moderate of the sisters.

Out of the blue, I suddenly felt Elsie's death had been an accident—she had simply wanted to forget. Her sisters were independent and outgoing. Elsie was more disciplined and outwardly sophisticated, but did she hide more of her emotions? Elsie must have been holding things in and not expressing herself as freely as her sisters. She certainly appeared more poised, but that composure may have covered up raging emotions. While Elsie was not out of control that I ever knew, she must have been very disciplined. "I think I understand her well enough."

With the hypnotist's nudging, I brought forward Roy's essence:

> I can see him. He laughs and leads the conversation like a story teller—not like a conversationalist. He's more of an entertainer type. I guess we all are actors and he surely had to be acting if he had a relationship on the side.

Now I see him as very determined, a very determined person, more so than I'd have thought about before—determined to get his own way. I need to intuitively feel him more than I've done before—because if he was responsible for my aunt's death, I was sort of backing away from him.

Again, a well-timed nudge: "Ask your guide to bring the soul essence of Roy to be in front of you. If Roy is there, ask to communicate with him without judgment, just to know and understand."

In my mind, Roy turned to face me squarely and I focused on his emanations:

Roy is smiling. He thinks it is a joke that I want to find out about Elsie.... There must have been something not working in the relationship with Elsie and he clearly had needs that were not being met. He felt that he needed to move on. Elsie and her family must have seemed like a drag to him and on him. He wanted to be free and couldn't cope with her. I think he views her death almost as a good thing and that he bought the pills. But she took them and they carried her away.

Afterwards, when he visited our family with his third wife, he was just testing how we'd react and [learned] my father did not want to see him. I think the third wife was a disappointment and his life after Elsie's death was a disappointment. It was still better [than his marriage to Elsie] but it wasn't as freeing as he thought it would be.

As if through a veil, I vaguely sensed my father's scorn. "It's hard for me not to judge him."

"The judgment can come later," the hypnotist said. "Right now, we're just looking for information and data. It flows much more freely without judgment."

"I'm realizing that Elsie's death was an accident and that she took the pills, but I was trying to ask Roy about the role of the undertaker and why people saw him as suspicious and what he may have known. I guess he must have been Roy's friend and so protected Roy."

"Ask the essence of Elsie to come forward and ask her what you need to ask her."

> I see her as a light and Roy as a different type of light. Roy's light is more yellow, denser. Elsie is a lighter light—and I know that she took the pills. But I'm so overwhelmed by her light that I can't quite see for certain if it was an accident. If she was drinking, it would have increased the effect of the pills and so I don't really know if—I'm just so overcome by the taking of the pills that I can't see if it's really intentional or just wanting to forget for the moment.

"Can you just ask her that?"

"'Yes', she says 'yes'. Maybe she wasn't really thinking about it. Maybe it was just to forget—without really thinking about it too deeply."

The hypnotist's soft voice asked, "Is there more that you need to communicate with either Elsie's or Roy's soul essence?"

"I don't think so—I guess not right now. Maybe for Elsie now, death wasn't such a big thing."

"Thank them for sharing with you and tell them they can go from whence they came. And now I'd like to ask if you'd like to communicate with the soul essence of the undertaker?"

"Sure." I spoke without any other movement, as if I were lightly constrained on the couch.

"Ask your guide if that's acceptable and he can bring forward the soul essence of the undertaker."

> He is already here in the background and I've been sensing that he was Roy's friend. He really did run upstairs and try to bring Elsie around. He really did try to rescue her. This is an interesting perspective, different from Clara's. After Elsie died the undertaker and employee ... waited for Roy to come home and figured it was his place to call Elsie's family.

Finally, there was nothing else to ask. For now, I was devoid of questions, though of course, more would arise. But I needed a break.

With the hypnotist by my side, I bid farewell to my guide and slowly retraced my steps up to the garden, through its delightful paths, and out its wrought iron gates. When I opened my eyes, she reassured me: "Anytime you'd like to communicate with your guide and you find yourself in a relaxed position, take three deep breaths, and say to yourself, 'relax, relax, relax,' and you'll be able to come into the very relaxed state you're in right now. And you can call your guide forward to communicate with you at any time in the future."

The hypnotist suggested looking at Elsie's death from different perspectives. When family members visited her not long before her death, they observed her to be fine. But from Elsie's perspective, it may have seemed like everybody else was fine except her. Then when Roy left that Sunday, Elsie may have thought the problem she had left in Racine had followed her north.

"At the time Elsie took the pills, she wasn't thinking about your grandmother or anyone else. We are egocentric when we are stressed," the hypnotist said. "Ego operates as a protection for us—as does skepticism, when we're not ready or able to deal with something."

Dad, Clara, and Pete had all been skeptical of Roy's innocence in Elsie's death. Were they simply not ready to deal with the verdict of suicide?

When I drove away after the session, Bob Dylan's song, *Who Killed Davey Moore?*, played again in my mind as I'd long ago re-titled it, *Who Killed Aunt Elsie?*. Even if I was ready to believe my own revelation under hypnosis—and Elsie had swallowed the deadly pills on her own—I wanted to blame others for setting her up. The refrain that resounded in my brain pointed to the Mattoon tavern bartender, the undertaker, and above all, Roy. Yet the song's answer was always the same: "*It was someone else who let her die.*"

Years later, another music culture comparison would come to mind as I followed the news about Dr. Conrad Murray, convicted in 2011 of involuntary manslaughter following Michael Jackson's drug overdose and death. Even if Elsie's death had been an accident or suicide, didn't Roy bear some measure of guilt?

We all make mistakes and must wrestle with the consequences. I can't count the times I've asked, "How could I have done that?!" about a forgotten work assignment, a foot-in-mouth comment, or an overindulgence. But we don't all play a starring role in another person's death.

Like Dad, Clara, and Pete, I was not ready to let Roy go blame-free. I was not ready to let go, period. Perhaps I was as stubborn as Elsie.

While the hypnosis session stuck like a thorn in the back of my mind, I still hoped to find proof: solid evidence of one kind of crime or another. So I continued to probe genealogical byways, new historical databases, and whatever other trails might illuminate the truth about Elsie's death—and the facts needed to accurately depict her story.

At first, I had envisioned Elsie's story as a true crime drama, but as solid leads withered and dried up (a twenty-first century video cam in that mid-twentieth-century tavern would have helped), the nature of the search slowly changed. No longer was I focused only on what happened. Without at first realizing the fact, I increasingly concentrated on how to convey what most likely happened.

18

A Bad Novel

*P*erhaps I should have spent less time chasing freelance work and more time researching Elsie. This point was driven home (literally) on a drive back from my campus job in the spring of 2005. Near the junction of our county road and the state highway, I pulled over to watch a funnel cloud that was moving fast toward the edge of Spring Green.

Michael, meanwhile, was in the village of Spring Green when he heard radio reports of a tornado that touched down near Muscoda, Wisconsin, and was heading east, so he decided this would be a good time to go home. Though the sky looked nasty on the county road, the sun was shining when he reached the house.

But then he heard an odd noise and went out to the porch. There was a funny yellow color in the air and an odd rumbling sound. Near the house nary a leaf moved, but the trees to the west began shaking violently. Michael finally recognized the rumbling as the proverbial freight train.

He ran inside and rounded up Houdini the cat and Rumpus. As Michael headed down the basement stairs with an unhappy cat in his arms, the power went out. But that—thankfully—was it, at least at our property. We later found a corn leaf near the western edge of our land—there are no cornfields in our immediate, wooded vicinity.

In the aftermath, Michael was green with envy that I got to see a tornado; I was envious that he got to hear one. That's the kind of adventures to have—near misses that make for good storytelling. Still this near miss reminded me: Life had an endpoint, time was passing, and I was making little progress on telling Elsie's story.

The problem with my decision to continue searching for hard evidence, of course, was that there wasn't any. I considered this challenge while walking through our woods one day—pausing to locate the pileated wood-pecker that was the source of the jack-hammering above me—and decided to tell Elsie's story as an historical novel. After all, with the experience gained from my practice novel, how could the new attempt go wrong?

Using fiction, I could fashion links and proof while creating a memorial to a life that mattered. I could freely embellish and embroider to regale readers with more interesting people and events. In short, I could tell a "better" story. While professional historians will disagree, it might even turn out to be a more accurate story, in the way that *The Red Badge of Courage* by Stephen Crane successfully described the trauma and terror of the Civil War despite the author never having been to war.

In the prologue to the 2005 historical fiction account, I wrote: "Memory creates. The future hinges on how we frame the past … Elsie's story is mainly the truth—the truth framed through memory and dreams."

Parts of the fictional version tracked close to my memory of events. For instance, here's an excerpt from the embellished account of our family's visit to Elsie and Roy' tavern in Mattoon.

> Customers drizzled in, two older men in overalls hunched over a table in a corner, and three others lined up along the bar next to Dad.
>
> Elsie poured kernels into the bin at the top of a large popcorn maker and turned it on. While the last few kernels were still popping, she scooped a generous measure into a basket and carried to the table near the end of the bar where Mom, Diane, and I sipped our sodas….
>
> "Bill," Roy said, "you know better than to tell tales about me. I'm just an innocent bartender, trying to make a go of this place."
>
> "Yeah, right."
>
> "He always gets the last word," Elsie told Dad. "Bill's the undertaker."
>
> "He always gets you in the end," Roy agreed.
>
> Bill looked at Roy. "You're the guy in charge here. People know you mean business and not to cross you."
>
> "Mattoon isn't dangerous "at least not compared to Racine. And, I mean to keep it that way." Keeping his eyes on Bill, Roy reached under the bar and pulled out a revolver, brandishing it toward the entrance. "Maybe you noticed the sign on the door? 'No Indians' means 'No Indians.'

They can't handle their liquor and they get crazy after a drink or two. When they drink, they fight, so I don't let 'em in here.

"They go to Tom's Tavern down the street. It's a rowdier spot and sometimes a guy will take a poke at someone. Next thing you know, there's a regular riot." Roy glared around the room.

The men at the bar looked down at their drinks. Fascinated, I kept my eyes on Roy.

"I run a safe place here. We have a good time and maybe we get a little loud sometimes, but there's no fighting. Besides, I'm ready if anybody wants trouble." Roy rapped the gun against the bar.

Elsie moved next to him, reaching across him to pick up Bill's empty glass. "Have another?" When Bill nodded, she refilled the glass and set it back in front of him. "This will keep you cool. This heat gets to you after a while."

Roy took a deep breath and replaced the weapon behind the bar. He weaved his head back and forth, a bear scenting the wind.

You get the idea. Parts of the historical fiction version are only a little exaggerated. Other parts swung more widely from the truth. In the fictional version of Elsie's story, a mythical cousin snooped in Elsie and Roy's Racine bedroom and discovered they slept in separate twin beds (a fact, though what did it really mean—maybe Roy or Elsie was an insomniac).

The imaginary cousin found a suicide-special revolver in the drawer of Elsie's bedside table and accidentally discharged it out the window. In another chapter, Elsie discovered a Red Cross Drug Store receipt embellished with a hand-drawn heart and the words "I love you." When she confronted Roy (the bear in his basement lair), their argument turned ugly and he threatened her with a rifle from his gun rack. This was all complete fiction. City-boy Roy was never a hunter and did not have a gun rack.

With fiction, I could put words in their mouths and create what happened behind closed doors. In reality, of course, the truth of a couple's married life could only be discerned through their words and behaviors that were written down, filmed, or otherwise witnessed. Although fiction offered freedom to dramatize scenes that no one had actually seen, I felt immobilized by a desire to get it right. This desire for truth trumped the fun castle of fiction told for entertainment alone—and ruined my novel version of Elsie's death.

Maybe it was my Lutheran upbringing. I didn't know how to end Elsie's fictional story: suicide, accident, or murder? If I listed all the damning factors against Roy, the reader might believe him unarguably guilty, but I'd know the case wasn't so cut-and-dried. While I might be ready to portray him as a hunting bear and Elsie (forgetting for the moment Beatrice) as his victim, I was uncomfortable convicting him without more proof.

If I unjustifiably charged Roy with the crime, he might forgive me in the next life, but what if he had descendants? It seemed unlikely, but how would his descendants feel if, without sufficient evidence, I accused their ancestor of murder—even in a fictional account?

Maybe my conscience was overly active. Probably I worried too much. But the problem remained. In my experience whenever I've jumped to judge people, I've later often been proven wrong. Even in fiction, I could not bring myself to judge Roy, for fear the judgment would one day be proven unfair.

Caught between the desire for a good story and a need for proof, I waffled on the ending. First, I created a character whose existence at the time seemed incredibly unlikely. This character, "Will Mayhew," disclosed he was Roy and Beatrice's son. The plot grew wilder when Mayhew explained to my lead investigating character (me, in minimum disguise), "Roy was horrified when the undertaker admitted he had 'solved Roy's problem of Elsie.' But Roy lacked any solid evidence against his friend."

Thus, I pushed the blame onto the undertaker, whom I didn't know as well as I knew Roy, and concluded by placing Roy with me in the lack-of-evidence boat, an uncomfortable spot to sit. But the effort to twist away and escape the problem of blaming Roy by instead blaming a possibly innocent bystander did not ease my conscience. Clearly, this ending left much to be desired. I wanted both a credible plot and great climax, yet I still yearned for the truth—whatever it was.

Additionally, I wanted the truth for all of Roy's wives. I wanted to understand the truth behind his marriages to Beatrice, Elsie, and Agnes, because they were all connected as different chapters of his life. Each reflected and shaped his identity as a strong and sociable husband who, like all of us, had serious shortcomings and changed in response to experience. Maybe by the time Roy married Agnes, he had become a better husband.

Beatrice especially haunted me. I pictured her as a young, fair-skinned beauty, strolling down Kenosha's Fremont Avenue. I imagined Roy calling out to her when she passed his house and the two of them talking in his front yard. Maybe he invited her to go out for ice cream or to a movie downtown.

It was hard to envision Roy at eighteen. I'd never seen photos of him as a young man and only remembered the fifty-year-old. By the time he and Elsie had moved up north, he'd been almost sixty.

When had he gotten glasses? At eighteen, he was likely slender, with a full head of dark hair, but with the same wolf-like grin. And the same sociability.

Bea (*could I be so familiar?*) might have been flattered by his attentions and eager to know him better. He must have seemed supremely eligible, with a good job and steady family life.

Lacking facts, imagination took over. What if, after their marriage, Bea had run away from Roy and changed her identity? Worse, what if she hadn't run away at all? I kept returning to the unwanted image. Maybe Bea's murdered bones still rested, neglected, buried in a Kenosha backyard.

For a newsletter article, I had interviewed Dr. Pauline Boss, the former University of Minnesota professor who developed the idea of ambiguous loss to explain the kinds of unclear disappearances that defy closure and magnify the challenge of grieving for those left behind.

When the departed individual was a victim of a war or natural disaster that left no body or precise cause of death, the survivors were left to mourn the circumstance, as well as their loved one. No doubt Dr. Boss's theory at least partly explained my obsession with Elsie's death and those nagging questions about Beatrice's fate, though it did little to help my plotline.

Beatrice, Elsie, Agnes. Of these three, only Agnes's story had a clear-cut, well-documented ending.

19

FARTHER OUT ON A TWIG

*I*n the world of historical research, astrology is at best a sable sheep, a non-contender even in the broader documentary of human strife. Nevertheless, lacking facts, in an effort to leave no stone unturned, I found myself inching farther out along the branch of "alternative" research in 2007. If hypnosis seemed an unlikely stretch for truth, astrology begged all credulity for serious historians. Yet I was seeking personal and family truth, not global history.

Lacking physical and recorded facts about Elsie's death, I turned to intuition and the stars. Though some people dismissed astrology as "a load of bunk," I sometimes found it a reasonable weather forecast for my own life, particularly when I read the daily forecast at the end of the day and observed that, yes, I had felt anxious or confident, blessed or not in the previous twenty-four hours. Of course, like the weather forecast, many predictions struck far off the mark.

I'd always thought that Dad was in the "load of bunk" company and so had been surprised to find an astrological "reading" for Leo (copyright 1934) among his mementos. Born on August 10 like Roy—only in 1914 instead of 1901—Dad's reading claimed that Leo's "most outstanding characteristics are warm-heartedness, courage, pride and uprightness." I wondered how Dad, a farmer and factory worker, felt when he read that ...

> Leo men are especially fitted for bankers, financiers, brokers, promoters, architects, and lines pertaining to art and music. They usually attain success on the stage and in the motion picture field, as they possess all the characteristics so essential to acting.

While this profile did not fit my father, it did remind me of Roy.

Despite Dad and Elsie's intense loyalty toward one another, their astrological signs, Leo and Taurus, were not known for compatibility. As one popular astrologist put it: "Leos and Taureans are strong personalities known for their stubborn and ambitious nature. The similarities end right there." While Leos wished for fame and fortune, Taureans desired security and stability.

Other astrologers insisted that no sun signs were ever completely incompatible, especially considering all of the other planetary placements in every birth chart. Still, from first grade onward, we all knew individuals who would never be our close friends; they walked a different path.

Maybe a life reading based on Elsie's birth date of May 16, 1912, would shed light on her decisions and relationship with Roy. Or, even better, suggest new avenues of research to explore. I selected a recognized astrologist from a book about Wisconsin psychics and ordered readings for both Elsie and Roy. In addition, I asked for a reading detailing their relationship and another focusing on the last few weeks of Elsie's life.

Born with the sun in Taurus, Elsie was generally affectionate, quiet, and pleasant, according to the astrological report. Emotionally stable, she seldom got depressed and only rarely displayed aggressiveness or impulsiveness—all traits that, on the surface at least, seemed at odds with suicide. At the same time, she could be very stubborn. Elsie's fixed mind could hold onto thoughts for a long time, and if negative, they could alter her health. Letting go did not come easy.

Elsie would need "to learn to moderate her tendency to over-indulge in life's pleasures," according to the astrological report. "She should not drink alcohol or smoke." While a tavern may have been the perfect place for Roy, it did not sound like the best environment for Elsie.

Colors and sounds affected Elsie's emotions. Vivid colors like red and orange disturbed her, while soft colors like light rose and blue made her feel better. I envisioned the gray old lumber town of Mattoon and the tavern's dark interior. Had these shades made Elsie feel as bad as they made me feel? The report noted she found loud noises disruptive, whereas softer sounds soothed her.

Elsie had an instinctive affinity for music and the arts and was quite creative. At the same time, Elsie tended to be obedient and did not forget what she had been taught. She could be a bit fearful and did "not like darkness or ghost stories," according to the astrological report, which also stated that Elsie had "a romantic imagination." If these statements were true, I wondered how Elsie had felt that day in the Cave of the Mounds. Had she shared my unease?

Born beneath the light of the new moon, Elsie was spontaneous and energetic. She made a good impression on people and was not soon forgotten. Elsie usually acted with authority and sensitivity, and was occasionally guided by impulse and intuition rather than by reason. She could be restless and always ready to start new adventures. Yet Elsie could also be "shy, reserved, and insecure about her feelings [and] experience difficulty in expressing herself." Mattoon had certainly been a new adventure, but had Elsie's natural reserve held her back from expressing any doubts or anxieties about the remote location?

The sun's position in relation to Mars suggested that Elsie's great energy would allow her to take initiatives and achieve her goals "because of her great decisiveness and courage to live the everyday adventure," stated her astrology report.

She would also have a strong feeling of honor and personal integrity and would be protective of family and friends. When Elsie was born, Venus like the sun was in Taurus, suggesting she would be very attached to the people she loved. Elsie would "take care of her friends and family and show great loyalty in her affections."

The presence of Mars in Cancer indicated Elsie's actions would always spring from her moods. Whenever she felt positive and happy, as she usually did, Elsie would act with confidence. But when depressed, she would become irritable and impatient. Elsie would seldom "show anger or hurt ... she could keep it to herself and then become spiteful."

Mars' conjunction with Neptune pointed to a big imagination and intense emotional world. Elsie would "need ways to release the resulting inner pressure," her chart suggested. She would be idealistic and "become enthusiastic about people so quickly that she [might] make herself vulnerable to disappointment."

Like my own, Elsie's rising sign (ascending on the eastern horizon at the time of her birth) was Virgo, indicating an appreciation for details. Her big disadvantage was shyness and a tendency to hide her real potential because she felt inferior or insecure. Elsie usually did not assert her needs easily.

Despite a leaning toward decisiveness and courage, the astrology report noted that her great sensitivity sometimes made her close up and retreat into herself when a problem came up. Elsie could "live an intense inner life" and she tended to be "very sensitive, fragile and easily suggestible ... her fears [were] the fears of the adults around her."

I highlighted one other section in her astrological report: "Elsie [would] be very generous, although indiscriminate, with her friends and will give all of herself to them ... [She would not] see her friends the way they are, but the way she would like them to be; as a consequence, she may suffer a rude awakening or two, possibly being disappointed or disillusioned." That had certainly been true in Roy's case.

Next I turned to the comparison of Elsie and Roy's charts.

Born August 10, 1901, with his sun in Leo, Roy was just as strong-willed as Elsie. "Both [could] be infuriatingly obstinate and inflexible," and their styles and tastes were often in conflict. For instance, Roy was more social and would want to go out more often than would Elsie, the home-centered soul.

At the same time, once they dedicated themselves to each other, they were unlikely to part. Both took seriously their relationship, which was marked by "longevity, stability and loyalty." Each knew they could depend on the other. Both were "so resistant to change that even if [they] hated each other, it would be hard to disengage ... and move on."

Roy was more emotional, sensitive, and moody, while Elsie tended to be more steady, practical, and even-tempered, the astrologist reported. Elsie gave Roy a sense of security and was like "the Rock of Gibraltar during times of emotional stress and turmoil."

What Roy needed to be happy was rather complex, while Elsie's needs were more straightforward. She was less prone to send mixed messages. Roy felt pulled in contradictory directions, and this could lead to indecisiveness. Elsie would need to develop patience while Roy sorted out various issues.

Both could be impulsive and impatient with each other, and misunderstandings could easily spill into arguments. (I had a testament to their impulsiveness—a postcard mailed to our family in October 1958: "Made up our minds at noon today to leave, we are in Prairie du Chien [Wisconsin] tonite.")

"There [was] a tendency to rush or go at a frantic pace" when they were together, according to the astrology report. It was difficult for them to settle down and jointly accomplish practical, mundane tasks. They drew out the silly, childish, imaginative side of each other, and often would be unable to clearly focus on practical tasks. They would likely disagree on how to handle finances and budgeting.

I highlighted another sentence: "If either [had] a drinking, drug, or psychological problem, [the] relationship [would] highlight this problem; [there was] the tendency of both ... to over-indulge in these kinds of bad habits."

The comparison of Elsie and Roy's birth charts suggested their relationship might have "struck like lightning out of the blue" and would always contain an element of surprise and uncertainty. "It also might contain a sudden break from a previous ... way of life, which shocks everyone around you." I highlighted the sentence, which certainly fit Elsie and Roy's move to Mattoon.

A strong potential existed for Elsie and Roy to idealize and romanticize one another. Because of the stars in their eyes they could not always see one another clearly and disappointment would occur. Human imperfections and inadequacies that each might take in stride with other people might seem like a betrayal.

This idealization led to another—each might feel the need to sacrifice themselves for the other. I thought about their move to Mattoon. Had Elsie felt that she had sacrificed herself for Roy's career?

"Another potential pitfall," according to the comparison chart, was for Elsie and Roy "to encourage in each other excessive idealism, false hope, unrealistic fantasies, and an urge to escape into paradise." Not for the first time, I wondered how realistic their Mattoon business plan had been.

Elsie and Roy's relationship would never be lukewarm. Each evoked intense, complex emotion from the other and they got under each other's skin. They could inspire one another to be spontaneous and break out of restraints or inhibitions, which could be joyfully liberating—"or lead to foolish excesses and imprudent risk-taking." Elsie and Roy's adventurous and freedom-loving sides led to unpredictability, which made their relationship feel alive.

The chart comparison noted the difference in their ages and that the disparities in the trends and impulses of their generations could cause friction. In particular, Elsie's generation sometimes uncovered the illusions or deceptions of Roy's age group. I stuck a sticky note on the paragraph. Roy had possibly lied about the dates of his first marriage. What truths might Elsie have discovered about Roy's early life? Had any deceptions played a role in her death?

Finally, I turned to the report of the final weeks of Elsie's life.

Her chart for mid-July 1960 stated, "Friendships and cooperative endeavors flourish now. You achieve a harmonious balance of giving and receiving and of talking and listening, and any social or joint activity will benefit." The report was intriguing, as this was close to the period when Elsie had several visits from her family.

Her astrological report for late July went way beyond intriguing:

- **July 17 – 19 (position of Venus)**: You are prone to act erratically in your relationships. A sudden infatuation or an impulse to break free or make radical changes in a current relationship is likely.

- **July 17 – 20 (position of Mercury)**: You are likely to come to a very clear, definite decision at this time…. You are not in a very conciliatory mood…. You may speak or act in haste now, which can be a cause of regret later on…. You may hear from someone from the past or reach out to someone you have a long history with or who was once very important in your life.

- **July 19 – 24 (position of Mercury):** Your thoughts are dreamy, fantastic, and faraway right now. Your imagination and intuition is heightened, which benefits any creative or artistic work you may do. However, your practical reasoning ability and your ability to focus on the here and now are diminished. Your judgment regarding concrete matters is a bit fuzzy ... so you may wish to delay making important decisions.

Among her eight siblings, Dad was closest to Elsie in age and certainly had once been very important in her life. Might Elsie have planned to share with Dad her decision to finally break free from Roy and leave him? Her chart suggested she was up to the fight:

- **July 21 – 24 (position of Mars and the moon):** At this time you are more temperamental, impassioned, and inclined to act on the dictates of emotion and desire rather than reason. Minor annoyances and others' idiosyncrasies aggravate you more than usual. You are in a fighting mood.

- **July 22 – 25 (position of Mars):** You are prone to feel frustrated and to resent the limitations or drudgery of this time period. Perseverance and patient effort are required of you now. Try to avoid becoming discouraged or lashing out at the ones you are responsible for.

- **July 28 – Sept. 28 (position of Mars):** Ego conflicts ... may arise. Try to control or temper your ambition with consideration for others. Your urge to act and to do is so strong that you are prone to rush and to try to force your will in situations where waiting may be more appropriate.

If Elsie's chart had any truth in it, she was ready to stand up to Roy in late July—finally prepared to tell him that she felt imprisoned by their life in Mattoon—even if she had not yet worked out all the details about exactly where to go from there. Though it mentioned discouragement, Elsie's forecast did not portray a woman on the brink of suicide. If anything, it presented an image of a woman about to rush to war.

One friend, on listening to a bare outline of Elsie's story, suggested the sometime craziness of menopause might have added to Elsie's stress. True, given that Elsie was age forty-eight, pre-menopausal or menopausal symptoms could have intensified any tension she was feeling that summer.

PART THREE

Caught off guard—Elsie and Roy, about 1940

20

SOULS SHINING THROUGH: CARDS, LETTERS, CLIPPINGS

*T*he astrologist's report of Elsie's last days got me thinking about the whereabouts of the people in her life during the weeks leading up to her death in 1960.

Grandma Green, age eighty-two, was living in a mobile home in Pete's Racine County farmyard. Pete was operating a large farm with help from two of his children. Elsie's oldest brother, John, was a salesman for Murphy Products Company, an agribusiness firm in Burlington, Wisconsin, while Carl was working at the Barber-Greene Company, an equipment manufacturer in Aurora, Illinois.

Martin was heading up a John Oster Company plant in Mexico, and Laura was still working a variety of jobs in Alaska. Andrew was farming in Marinette and Dad was living in Racine and commuting to the John Oster Manufacturing Company in Milwaukee. Clara was living with Roy Miller and their children next door to Elsie and Roy Woodson's former home in Racine.

Not long before Elsie's death, Carl and Peg had visited Mattoon, reporting later that Elsie had seemed just fine. They had spent a good deal of the month on the road, vacationing in Florida from about July 4 to July 12 (according to a postcard our family received) and then staying at home only a week or two before driving north to Mattoon. Our family had visited Elsie and Roy a little earlier in the month, also finding her warm and welcoming.

Five weeks before Elsie's death, many Green relatives (not including Elsie and Roy, who were busy at the tavern) gathered in Racine to attend the wedding of Andrew and Adeline's oldest son. While they were in town, the Marinette clan—minus Andrew himself, who stayed on the farm to milk the cows and care for all the livestock—stayed at our house, since Dad and Mom had recently converted our attic into two large bedrooms.

On the drive to the church Adeline, wearing a new hat, sat in a car's front seat. One of the kids in the backseat pointed to a price tag swinging from the hat in Minnie Pearl style and Adeline laughingly removed the tag.

The wedding came only about a week after Adeline left the Marinette hospital following surgery. She must have really wanted to attend that wedding. On July 20 in a letter to Dad and Mom, Adeline complained of lingering pain and reported she planned to take it easy for a time.

Her next note, contained in an August 10, birthday card to Dad that I found years later, held a surprise:

*Just got your letter and sure are sorry to hear about
Elsie, that is quite a shock. It's funny that no one let us
know sooner. But I spose everyone was so shocked that
they didn't think of letting us know. Andrew said they
could have called us on the phone. But who can think
that fast? Did Carl come to the funeral? We hope that
everyone is well at your place....*

*With best wishes,
Adeline and family*

I read the note twice. Considering Adeline's health and
the fact that her family had made the trek to Racine so
recently, I had not been surprised when they didn't
attend Elsie's funeral. But I'd had no clue that they had
not known of her death until Mom or Dad wrote to them
afterwards. Of course, Adeline was right: Everyone was
in shock.

ELSIE'S DEATH MIGRATED TO A mental back burner as I dealt
with increasing, present-day work and personal de-
mands: the University of Wisconsin-Madison School of
Human Ecology planned a new campus building; the
community banking magazine grew and required more
time, and Mom faced growing health issues—leading in
2009 to a move from her home of sixty-two years into an
assisted living facility.

Besides commuting the fifty miles to Madison three or four days each week, I soon found myself driving the one hundred fifty miles to visit Mom and check on her former house in Racine every other weekend, more often when she was occasionally hospitalized with varied health problems—from appendicitis to pneumonia.

While I wouldn't want to repeat those crazed years on the road, blessings abounded. I found opportunities to recharge by walking on campus and around our wooded hillside south of Spring Green. In contrast to June 2008, when record rains had bestowed on our property a temporary, rushing stream and totally destroyed one Spring Green neighborhood, the summer of 2009 brought a return to normalcy and the usual return of wildlife.

We counted sandhill cranes on every drive along our county road and noted the migrating indigo buntings at our feeders, along with the usual grosbeaks and orioles. Driving on a town road, we watched a fawn sail gracefully through the middle bars of a pasture gate; soon it would be sailing over the top of that gate. At Blackhawk Lake, we spied a small mink on a platform along the marshy shore.

On the more frequent trips to Racine, I reconnected with Racine friends and cousins who kept a close eye on Mom, and with her former neighbors who kept a close eye on the house. When a van with out-of-state license plates turned into the driveway and backed up against the garage one day, alert neighbors called the police.

The house held its own lucky talismans. Ever so slowly, I began to sort through its contents—tossing, giving away, setting aside for resale, or keeping any items that I or a family member might want. I unearthed a treasure trove of memories, childhood toys, souvenirs, clippings, and family photos and letters. From obituaries of people who had died before I was born, to Dad's schoolbooks and the cache of letters from Laura in Alaska, many boxes of paper "followed" me home.

Old toys such as a tin barn, boy doll, and View-Master® slides (including three reels of magnificent Alaskan scenes) sent me back to the late 1950s. My own school papers—all the way through graduate school— reminded me of lessons learned, the primacy of writing, and dreams fulfilled, unfilled, and yet to be realized.

All this time travel led me to a life review of sorts. Early writing critiques of research papers rang true today (I still needed to keep the primary premise in mind!), and photos of old boyfriends had me asking: How could I have been so dumb? Far past the moment, I was free to see my younger self more clearly and to be less protective and more honest about her shortcomings. Then, every situation was dead serious; now, I could sometimes laugh at my younger self: What had she been thinking!

Mom's longevity proved a similar blessing. Her fading memory of recent events led to conversations about better-remembered, long-ago events. She regaled my Makovsky cousins and me with humorous tales of her own childish behaviors and pranks played on older siblings. At first it was hard to envision my respectable Mom lying in wait with her brother in a ditch along the road to softly call out, "Ooohhh, ooohhh" when their older sisters hastened home one night. The two elder sisters, already hurrying, went into top speed when they heard the ghostly emanations, while Mom and her brother doubled over in silent laughter.

Once our roles had firmly reversed and Mom had settled into her new living environment, our relationship relaxed. Only a few years earlier, when she had been in her early nineties and I'd suggested a move to an assisted living facility, Mom had fought back. After visiting one site, Mom dreamt about moving to—and running away from—the proposed facility.

When a hospitalization finally forced a move and Mom found herself the center of attention among the wonderfully caring staff of Elizabeth Residence, our relationship turned a corner. Less burdened by day-to-day concerns about medication schedules and eating routines, we went for drives, played gin rummy, and talked both about the long-ago past and current happenings—"What a lovely shade of nail polish!" "Here's a card from your niece." and even "What a beautiful day!" More and more, they were all beautiful days.

The focus on the past engendered by Mom's memories and the rediscovered treasures in the house rekindled my quest to learn more about Elsie. A casual comment from Mom or a photo or card pulled from yet another box brimming with papers never let me forget the search still simmering on that back burner.

A benefit of the campus job and the freelance work was that I grew accustomed to spending countless hours at a computer. Over time, I took advantage of the growing number of genealogical documents available online. Ancestry.com was increasingly trendy, and television series like *Who Do You Think You Are?* showcased the adventure and possibilities of family history research. Developments in DNA testing and the aging Boomer generation's interest in leaving a legacy further fueled popular interest in genealogy along with my own quest.

While searching public records, directories, and newspapers had once required hours of eye-blurring scouring of faded print or microfilm, more and more records could now be found faster and easier online. Publishers, libraries, universities, and historical societies were scanning and making available digital documents at an astounding rate. Online newspaper archives proved a most helpful resource, sometimes providing the human connection and fleshing out the simple facts of vital records.

That's where I found Elsie's recipe for Toasted Potatoes in the July 21, 1940, *Journal Times* column, "Racine's Favorite Recipes."

Elsie's instructions ran as follows:

> *Four white potatoes*
> *Two eggs*
> *Three-fourths teaspoon salt*

Four tablespoons butter
One cup cracker crumbs

Pare the potatoes and cut them into slices about one-third inch thick. Dry the slices well. Beat the eggs and roll the potatoes in seasoned crumbs, then in egg and again into the cracker crumbs. Place the slices into a well buttered casserole and cover. Bake for about 1 hour in a 375-degree oven.
—Mrs. Roy Woodson, 1007 Seymour Avenue.

I couldn't wait to try the recipe and added potatoes to our grocery list as soon as I'd read it. The result was less than spectacular. The potatoes I used were large, so I needed almost twice as many crumbs to cover them. And Elsie's published recipe was unclear about how to add the butter (beyond greasing the casserole dish). I decided the butter had to be added to the crumb-and-salt mixture so that it would adhere to the dry potato slices when they were first dipped into it.

More seasonings would help, too—next time, I'd add pepper, garlic, onions, and maybe rosemary or oregano. Crumbled bacon or ham would make this recipe a good supper casserole. As it was, I topped my first try with grated cheese for the last ten minutes in the oven—just long enough to melt the cheese. By then, I'd tweaked Elsie's post-Great Depression recipe into practically a different dish. *Face it*, I finally admitted. *I'd rather have found one of Elsie's cake recipes.*

BadgerLink, the Wisconsin public library system's statewide newspaper database, also offered several *Journal-Times* social-notebook reports of Green family parties in the early 1940s. This is where I learned that Martin's first wife, Frances, held a bridal shower for her daughter on March 21, 1940. "Cards and bunco were played, with prizes going to Mrs. Roy Woodson, Clara Green, Margaret Baumstark [the bride-to-be] and Charlotte Tennessen of Kenosha." Among the guests were several men, including Roy Woodson and Bert Olsen, Laura's husband.

Later the same month, Roy's parents, Charlie and Nora Woodson, celebrated their fiftieth wedding anniversary with an open house on Saturday and Sunday, March 30 and 31. The article confirmed: "To them were born three daughters and one son. One daughter died in infancy; their other children include Mrs. Leona Steinway of Peoria, Ill.; Mrs. Velda Nelson of Kenosha; Roy Woodson of this city." The report noted the couple had three grandchildren and I wondered which of their children had children of their own. Might Roy and Beatrice have had children?

When Racine was a younger, smaller city, every event within miles—no matter how small—appeared as a news story. As the thirteen-year-old reporter of the Hoods Creek 4-H Club, I had written short reports of each monthly meeting in long hand. Mom drove me to the *Journal-Times* office, where I'd bravely marched into the newsroom and presented my article to the man behind the editor's desk. He'd looked up from the copy he was reading, perused my short article, and—always to my great surprise and relief—thanked me for it.

Racine County had a population of over 94,000 in 1940, spread across about 800 total square miles and comprising thirty incorporated and unincorporated communities. The city had a population of approximately 67,000 in 1940 and 89,000 in 1960, when Mom believed it was "getting too big" to feel comfortable. To me, it seemed just right.

Like many small-city newspapers in the forties and fifties, the *Journal-Times* covered confirmations and birthday parties, as well as visits from faraway relatives and lakeside bonfires. In September of 1940, the paper reported Pete's surprise birthday party, held in Kellogg's Corners, the tiny community located just over the Kenosha County line where he then lived and farmed:

> Peter Green was surprised by a party of relatives, the occasion being his birthday anniversary. Dinner and supper were served to [his parents] Mr. and Mrs. Andrew Green [Sr.] and [his brother], Herman, and Roy Miller of Franksville, Messrs. and Mmes. Andrew Green [Jr.] … Roy Woodson, Bert Olson [sic], Misses Clara Green and Marjorie Makovsky, … [and his brother] John Green ….

This short announcement taught me much. It confirmed that Mom (then Margie Makovsky) and Dad (Herman) had known each other well before their 1944 marriage. Surprisingly, Roy Miller, who had reportedly wed Clara in June 1940, also appeared separately from "Miss" Clara. From the names of individuals not listed, I inferred they were the party's hostesses—namely, Pete's wife Edna, John's wife Inez, and sisters Laura Olsen and Elsie Woodson.

Later articles explained why Roy Miller and Clara appeared to be unmarried in the 1940 story—it was because they *were* unmarried. Although Gladys's original family history had placed their wedding in 1940, it actually took place in 1941. Eventually, I would review several "Additions and Corrections" sheets that Gladys had circulated to family members from 1985 – 1995 and would notice the corrected year of Clara's marriage.

Gladys also corrected the date of Elsie's marriage and added many names to the ever branching family tree. Her labor both clarified my timelines and proved a valuable truth: The work of a genealogist is never really done. No matter how we shape the stories as they come to us—through either the rose- or dark-colored lenses of our relatives—they remain open to revision and up to interpretation and reinterpretation by the reader.

Clara's May 6, 1941, engagement party made *Journal-Times* headlines, as did a June 26 wedding shower hosted by her sisters Elsie and Laura at Laura and Bert Olsen's home on Kearney Avenue, Racine. Again, the extended family attended, including Mom (Margie Makovsky) and John, Pete, Carl, and Martin Green, along with their growing families and assorted friends. "Decorations were in pink and blue with gifts and streamers hung by clothespins to a line strung through the rooms." Prizes were awarded in games of *Schafskopf*, Five Hundred, and Bunco.

The *Journal-Times* report described the May 6 gathering as a "special occasion party" that also observed "the birthday anniversaries of Andrew Green Jr., Miss Clara Green, Mrs. Roy Woodson and Mrs. Carl Green." There was always a birthday to celebrate in any gathering of a family this large! In addition, the party "feted … Herman, who will leave for military training this month." Dad received a wristwatch as a going-away present, though he never got rid of his old pocket watch, which I would find years later in his top dresser drawer.

Decades before the Internet, Facebook friends, and matches made online, the news reports bore witness to a more primary network: During the early and mid-twentieth century, everyone's chief set of contacts was found within their families. Besides the news reports, I had a few letters and cards that sealed the deal. Social life revolved around family. In a January 1941 note to Dad, bedridden with mumps at the home farm near Franksville, Clara wrote:

> *Saturday night we went to a show, after the show we went out to Stoll's [Bar in Franksville]. Elsie and Roy were out there. We had to take them home because their car wouldn't start. [Then] we took them out there*

*Sunday to get it. We could have started it Saturday
night, I suppose, but it was pretty late. [Roy Woodson]
just had too heavy oil in it [for the cold weather]. Roy
[Miller] pushed him with his car and it started. Maybe
you heard us go past home Sunday. I blew the horn all
the way.*

A different kind of newspaper announcement in the
spring of the following year caught my eye. Roy Woodson had placed a classified advertisement offering a
reward for a lost dog—Teddy, a "large reddish brown
collie." The ad listed no phone number, only an address:
"Route 1, Box 507A, Swamp Road, Racine". I tried to
picture the big dog. Had Teddy ever been found? I
recalled my cousin's story about how Roy had replaced
their family's dog after accidentally backing over it. Roy
seemed to genuinely care for dogs, regardless of any
issues he may have had with people.

That same spring of 1942, another *Journal-Times*
classified ad seemed to leap off the page. The notice
corroborated the sale of "lot 1, block 2, Oaklawn" by
"Joseph Mrkvicka, et al. to Roy and Elsie Woodson."

By the time I read these news stories, I had come
across the names of Joseph Mrkvicka and Charles and
Elizabeth Mrkvicka during an earlier search for land
records. A warranty deed notarized November 5, 1941,
and not recorded until March 9, 1942, after the United
States had entered World War II, transferred the house
and corner lot at 5138 Charles Street to Elsie and Roy

Woodson. A second sale, recorded in 1945, transferred the house and lot next door at 5128 from the Mrkvickas to Clara and Roy Miller.

This sequence at first confused me, since I thought that one of Clara's children had told me that their family was the first to move to Charles Street, and that Elsie and Roy Woodson then purchased their house from Clara and Roy Miller. But by now I was becoming accustomed to stumbling across inconsistencies, so the ambiguity didn't bother me—too much.

The Mrkvickas sold one other property to the Woodsons. On January 30, 1948, the Mrkvickas transferred to them the title of a parcel at 1501 Oak Lawn Drive outside the city limits in the township (now village) of Caledonia. Elsie and Roy immediately sold this parcel on February 7 to Clark H. and Ida M. Nichols. Both sales were recorded February 9.

No doubt both the Mrkvichas and Woodsons profited from these sales in the post-war housing boom. Already in 1948, it seemed that Roy was seeking alternative ways to earn money, aside from working in a factory.

I thought again about the Swamp Road/Charles Street transactions and pictured the Woodson and Miller houses side by side. Despite their differences, the two sisters shared more than family background and had more in common than was at first obvious.

Like Elsie, Clara married a man named Roy (Roy Miller, in this case) who was more than a decade older than his bride. I wondered whether Grandpa, their Pa, had presented such a strong male figure that both sisters looked for—and found—an equally strong husband in an older man, toughened by experience.

Their elder sister Laura had also married older men, though her first husband, Bert Olsen, was only five years his wife's senior and her second husband, Reuben Larsen was only four years her senior. Not for the first time, I speculated on the relevance of age in the success of any marriage.

Along with their adjacent addresses, the Woodson and Miller properties shared a drain tile system and well. The well was dug in 1941, according to a note Elsie wrote to Dad that August: "Roy is getting pretty tired of hauling water, especially now during the hot weather, because we use so much more."

The deeds to both properties contained a curious stipulation against using these lots for a tavern:

> The … premises shall not, nor shall any part
> thereof, or any building or buildings thereon
> erected or to be erected, be at any time hereafter
> used or occupied as a tavern or other public house
> of any kind. Nor shall intoxicating liquors be
> produced or sold upon said premises or in or
> from the buildings erected or maintained thereon,
> for a period ending January 1, 1960.

My mind rapidly went down a number of alternate roads. Perhaps the Mrkvickas were ardent teetotalers even nine years after Prohibition had come to an end. Had the

Mrkvickas known even then that Roy Woodson wanted to run a tavern someday and attempted to block his efforts—at least on their former property? I had failed to uncover any evidence that Roy had ever worked as a bartender, but this lack of documentation did not constitute proof. Or, had the Mrkvickas simply been aiming to maintain the respectability of the neighborhood?

Years later, searching online from the loft office of our hillside log house, I stumbled across a description of Wisconsin Historic Marker 354, which lent credence to the respectability theory. The marker, in Milwaukee's Merrill Park, noted that Sherburn Merrill, general manager of the Chicago, Milwaukee and St. Paul Railroad, created a housing development in 1883, near the railroad shop complex, which employed 2,500 workers. "Desiring a 'respectable' neighborhood, Merrill placed deed restrictions on his prop-erty, prohibiting 'intoxicating liquors' and 'livery stables.'" I understood how taverns might impact the reputation of an area but had no idea how livery stables might render a neighborhood less than respectable—maybe by increasing horse-and-buggy traffic or contributing to the presence of horse poop?

Aaargh—stop! I closed my eyes, pushed back in my chair, and mentally regrouped. There were entirely too many family and local history roads to travel. Get back to the main quest.

21

BLACK, WHITE, AND READ
FROM RACINE TO CARNEY

*F*or all the social notices carried by the Racine *Journal-Times* that made Green family history come alive through the war years, the newspaper nevertheless failed to contain all the news I sought. Not for the first time, I wondered who had submitted our family stories to the newspaper; Elsie (the family glue) or Laura (the Alaskan scribe) seemed the most likely candidates.

The family background these stories provided sparked many reveries of the years before my own birth. In May of 1943, for instance, Laura's oldest daughter celebrated her confirmation with a big party. Again, the attendees included Elsie and Roy, Clara and Roy, and my dad and mom—Herman Green and Margie Makovsky—who did not marry until the following year.

Yet when I searched genealogybank.com and other websites for articles about Roy's family, few social announcements came to light. There was, however, an obituary for Roy's father, Charlie, on October 28, 1943:

CHARLES J. WOODSON, 75, retired Massey-Harris employe [sic], died early today at the home of a daughter in Kenosha. Mr. Woodson was employed by the Racine concern as a machinist from 1928 to 1940. Making his home in Racine until April, 1943, when he moved to Kenosha to live with his daughter, Mrs. Raymond L. Nelson. He was born in Bloomington, Ill., March 4, 1868, and lived in Peoria until 1903 when he and his wife moved to Kenosha prior to coming to Racine....

Survivors are his wife, a son, Roy Woodson of Racine; two daughters, Mrs. Nelson of Kenosha and Mrs. Theodore Steinway of Peoria, Ill.; two grandchildren, a great grandchild, his mother, Mrs. John Woodson, and a brother, Harry Hazelwood.

The cryptic words proved both helpful in reporting some information and frustrating in what they left out. At least the obituary told me that Roy had moved to Kenosha with his parents at age two, the same year my grandparents had emigrated from Denmark. But his parents' move back to Kenosha from Racine was less clear—might Roy's mother, as well as his father, have gone to live with his sister in Kenosha that spring?

I wished the obituary had included the names of the grandchildren and great-grandchild, all the while realizing that listing the names of estranged or disappeared children would be unlikely. There were also questions about Harry Hazelwood: Why did he have a different last name? Where did live? And, was there any chance Beatrice might have fled to his family after leaving Roy? Alas, a later search would turn up a Harry Hazelwood in northern Illinois, but no evidence that Beatrice ever lived with this family.

Similarly, when my Grandpa Green died in 1950, his obituary failed to list all of his grandchildren by name, though to be fair, in addition to his nine children plus siblings, there were way too many of us grandkids to list individually—twenty-two, along with nine great-grandchildren. Again, when Roy's mother Eleanor (Nora) died in April 1959, her obituary omitted the names of her three grandchildren and eight great-grandchildren. Might one or two of the grandchildren have been Roy and Bea's kids?

Regardless of what Nora Woodson's obituary left out, I was grateful for the documented basics. The obituary recorded: "Passed away April 18, 1959, at Brookside, after a long illness." Brookside Care Center still provides skilled nursing care in Kenosha today. Nora may have entered the facility as early as 1943 when Charles went to live with their daughter in Kenosha.

When I added Nora's death to the timeline, it clearly revealed that the spring of 1959 had been especially demanding for Roy. After deciding to finally leave a stressful job and move north, his mother died only a month before Roy and Elsie finalized their tavern purchase and relocated to Mattoon.

On a roll, I looked for other obituaries. Of course, I already had Elsie's obituary, carefully clipped from the

August 2, 1960, *Journal-Times* and saved by Mom in a cigar box of death announcements and funeral cards:

> WOODSON, MRS. ROY (ELSIE), Mattoon, Wis. Age 48. Passed away July 3I, 1960. Mrs. Woodson was born in Racine County on May 12, 1916, daughter of Mr. and Mrs. Andrew Green. On April 22, 1938, she was married to Roy Woodson, and had lived in Racine County until 1959 when they moved to Mattoon, Wis. She was a member of the Immanuel Lutheran Church, Racine. Surviving are her husband Roy; mother, Mrs. Andrew Green; two sisters, Mrs. Roy (Clara) Miller of Racine and Mrs. Reuben Larson [sic] of Alaska; six brothers, John Green of Burlington, Peter of Sturtevant, Andrew of Marinette, Carl of Aurora, Ill., Herman of Racine, and Martin of Mexico City, Mexico; nieces and nephews. Funeral services will be held Thursday, 10 a.m. in the Immanuel Lutheran Church, Rev. Cornelius Hansen officiating. Internment will be in West Lawn Memorial Park.

The short announcement offered no new information, and I again noted the errors in Elsie's birth date. Maybe the family member who supplied the information (Pete?) had been too upset to get the details right, or maybe the linotype operator had been in a hurry and inadvertently exchanged the numerals of the day and year.

I sighed and returned to searching for additional obituaries online. Even though I had his death certificate, I could not find an obituary for Frank Harris, who died of a central hemorrhage—two years before Roy and Elsie moved to Mattoon and five years before Frank's widow, Agnes, would become Roy's third wife. I wondered whether Agnes had simply been too upset to publish a notice of her husband's passing. Reflecting on her full name, it seemed ironic that Roy would eventually marry a woman with a similar last name as the company (Massey-Harris) that had provided him employment, but then sabotaged that job through downsizing and demotion.

The lack of an obituary for Frank seems particularly odd in light of an earlier newspaper story that document-ed Agnes Harris' interest in genealogy and the preserving of family history. The *Journal-Times* Social Notebook of August 23, 1941, recorded her "extended trip" to the Southwest and Pacific coast. "As national chairman of junior membership in the Daughters of the American Revolution, Mrs. Harris will visit many DAR chapters during her western trip." Genealogy had been important to Roy's third wife and I wondered whether she had ever researched Roy's family history or what she had known about his previous wives.

Later news stories confirmed that Agnes had a son with Frank, as the *Journal-Times* Cradle Roll announced the christening on August 2, 1963, of David Harris, "fourth child of Mr. and Mrs. Robert A. Harris (Rose Marie Eppler) of 3600 20th St.... Grandparents ... are Mr. and Mrs. Roy Woodson of Mattoon, Wis."

Even before Agnes and Roy Woodson moved from Mattoon to Upper Michigan, social notes about them began to appear in the Escanaba *Daily Press*. For instance, on November 7, 1968, the paper reported three married couples from Escanaba had traveled to visit a patient at St. Joseph Hospital in Marshfield, Wisconsin, and en route "also visited with Mr. and Mrs. Roy Woodson in Mattoon, Wis."

Four years later, after Roy and Agnes had relocated to Upper Michigan, the *Daily Press* noted that a group including Mrs. Frank Pokladowski, Bark River; Mrs. Willard Ledger, Spalding; Mrs. Anna Deptula, Escanaba, and "Mr. and Mrs. Roy Woodson of Carney attended the wedding of the latter's grandson, Robert Harris to Marie Dacquisto, in Racine's St. Edward's Catholic Church at noon Saturday, June 17."

Not two months later, the Escanaba newspaper reported a success for another son of Agnes, this one named after his father: "T.Sgt. Frank J. Harris, son of Mrs. Roy Woodson of Carney, is a member of the team which has earned the Communications Electronics Maintenance Award for the Aerospace Defense Command's 25th Air Division." This son was a communications equipment maintenance technician at McChord Air Force Base in Washington.

The Racine *Journal-Times* published a sad follow-up, announcing the death of Frank Harris, age fifty, in 1977:

> HARRIS, F R A N K JOSEPH ... passed away
> unexpectedly at his residence on Tuesday,
> November 8, 1977. Mr. Harris was born in Racine
> on May 13, 1927. He was retired after 28 years in

the Air Force. Surviving are his wife, Elizabeth, sons, Frank, Jr. and Michael; daughter, Donna; mother and stepfather Agnes and Roy Woodson of Carney, Mich.; brothers, Robert and Richard of Racine and John of Hawaii; cousin, John Harris, of Racine; aunts, uncles, nieces and nephews. He was preceded in death by his father, Frank, on July 29, 1957. Funeral services will be held on Friday, November 11, ... in Tacoma, Washington.

So, Agnes and Frank Harris had had four sons. I wondered whether Agnes and Roy had traveled to Washington for the funeral of Frank, Jr.

Agnes and Roy lived in Mattoon eight years before moving to Upper Michigan in 1970, according to land transfer records—suggesting the tavern business succeeded in providing them with a living. One other newspaper story shed a little light on their life in Mattoon, like a kerosene lamp throwing flickering shadows into a dark corner.

The Appleton *Post-Crescent* published a feature, "Shawano County Village Looks Back on Prosperity" on December 9, 1962. As the subhead ("Mattoon Was Creature of Sheboygan Manufacturer Until Lumbering Fell") suggested, the town seemed almost imprisoned by its past. Yet, modern-day boosters—including tavern-keeper Roy—touted its new attributes as a vacation destination. The story began:

> This tiny community, set in the rills and rocks of the northern reaches of Shawano County shows a laconic face to the world. Its Main Street is quiet

and bears the scars of a shifting economy. The tell-tale sign of reverses can be read in the empty stores which punctuate the broad order of its principal avenue.

The fact is that Mattoon was once a lumbering town with a bustling population of 2,000; and the fact is that the 1960 census gave it a minimum total of 435. The distance between those two populations is 64 years.

The writer continued in the same vein, recalling the lumber-era boom and bust, the closing of storefronts and local schools, and, finally the evolution of the cut-over land into a sportsman's paradise. "Today, Mattoon is still a pretty place tucked in amidst the hills and the woods, and blessed with the presence of two fine trout streams—the Red River and a fruitful creek which feeds it—which run directly through the village."

Noting that deer were plentiful and hunting good, the reporter quoted Mattoon Postmaster Ernest Thorpe: "'Mattoon isn't as busy as it used to be and there are some empty stores, but I like to hunt and fish and I have my good share of it here. That's the reason I stay.'" The writer also interviewed Roy along with the village president and other prominent residents:

Roy Woodson, proprietor of the uniquely original Flamingo Tavern, one of four here, came from Racine to settle here four years ago.
Said Woodson: "Sure, this is a nice town. We like it here and we hope to stay here. Just about everybody has a job—some of them at the mill

Coin purse notes "Roy Woodson, Prop."

and others—maybe about 50 per cent of the working population here—is employed outside, at places like Antigo and Manawa. And besides, people like it here because there's good hunting and fishing. Most of the men are sportsmen."

A Chicagoan, Raymond Burris, moved to Mattoon for reasons of health and retirement. "'Take it from me,'" he told the reporter, "'Living in Mattoon—this is the only way to live. It's a good life.'"

The reporter concluded: "And prowl the streets and the woods of this rather attractive little community as you will, nobody has a bad word for Mattoon—and neither do I."

ABOUT THE THIRD TIME I READ this story, a new realization finally registered. All those years ago, when I had found that red plastic coin purse in Mom's house and puzzled over its words, "Flamingo Inn," I had mistakenly

257

believed it was Roy's first name for his tavern, subsequently discarded. Now, I understood that it was the last name he'd given his tavern—renamed after Elsie's death. And I'd been wrong about how it came to rest in a dusty box: It must have been a gift from Roy after Elsie had died, not a gift from Elsie at all. What other errors had I made? None crucial, I could only hope.

Other news stories fired my imagination and occasionally led far afield from my Elsie search. I read about the missing wife of a Racine dentist. He had been convicted in 1932 of wounding a dental assistant "after spending the night with her in a Root River cottage" and was subsequently sentenced to the state prison at Waupun. Given circumstantial evidence and the forensic science of the time, the missing wife might—or might not—have been an unidentified dead woman found near Mattoon. How many other deaths might connect Racine and Mattoon?

Around the same time, an Oconto County jury, overriding the objections of the parents, ruled that the hanging death of a fifteen-year-old boy was suicide. Later fingerprints proved the presence of a stranger at the scene and that the parents had been right to suspect foul play. How many other Wisconsin suicides were in fact mislabeled murders?

I closed the web browser, looked at my notes, and tried to refocus on the essentials while chipping away all the extraneous facts to leave only the truth. Was there evidence anywhere of either murder or suicide?

22

DOUBLING BACK:
MORE LAND AND LIFE RECORDS

S hawano County officials assured me there was no probate record relating to Elsie's death, so that any life insurance or other property passed seamlessly to Roy. But I could follow the history of the tavern property through recorded land transactions, which also added context to Elsie and Roy's sojourn in Mattoon.

Four days before Elsie's forty-seventh birthday, she and Roy sold their cozy home in Racine to Victor and Edna Smith and closed on the tavern in Mattoon. They took on an $8,000 mortgage at 4.5 percent interest, with the entire sum due in ten years.

I pictured Elsie and Roy sitting side by side at the closing in a Langlade County bank office. Did Elsie perceive the tavern as an early birthday present and a grand adventure? In hindsight, it may have seemed more like an albatross, and the experience of running it like signing on to a voyage to Antarctica.

Elsie and Roy bought the tavern from Rudie and Barbara Mondl, who had purchased it for $8,500 just ten months earlier. I wondered why they held the property so briefly. Had one or the other fallen ill? Findagrave.com noted that Rudie did not die until 1973; Barbara died in 1979. The couple had bought the property from John and Mildred Willut of Milwaukee County, who had paid $7,000 and owned it since 1950. Besides the land and building, the purchase agreement enumerated a lengthy list of furnishings and equipment:

- Liquor cabinet
- Candy showcase
- Bar and back bar
- Walk-in cooler refrigerator
- Tap box—refrigerated
- Seven-Up Cooler—refrigerated
- Coca-Cola Coolers—refrigerated
- Three-hole rinse tank
- Cash registers
- Clock
- Deer mountings
- Estate Heatrola
- Tables
- Chairs
- Bar stools
- Kerosene lamps
- Suction fan
- American flag

- Jet water system—electric
- Hot water system—electric
- Water Softener
- Refrigeration unit
- Assortment of mirrors
- Steel Venetian blinds at all windows
- 33 eight-ounce glasses
- 15 six-ounce glasses
- 21 one-and-one-half-ounce glasses
- 19 five-ounce glasses
- 8 two-ounce glasses

I could picture the candy showcase, soda coolers, deer heads, and other fixtures and supplies, but what was an Estate Heatrola? A quick Google search supplied the answer: a coal stove. Now I could see it in my mind's eye, too, situated in a corner near the stairs. When I visited the tavern as a child, it had also contained a popcorn maker, dollar bills tacked to the back wall, a television, and mounted fish. I speculated on whether Roy had added these items or they had also been included in the sale.

The next land transaction was recorded seven months after Elsie's death, when Shawano County documented the official termination of Elsie and Roy's joint tenancy, leaving Roy as sole owner of the tavern property. Four months later, Roy purchased an adjacent parcel for $1,200. Was it possible that Elsie had had a life insurance policy and Roy bought this parcel with its proceeds? Sure, it was possible, I decided, but so what? If family suspicions had any basis and Elsie's death involved foul play, love—not money—remained the most likely motive.

Roy married Agnes in April of 1962 and in March of the following year, he filed property ownership changes, establishing "a deed of joint tenancy" for Roy and Agnes Woodson in Shawano County. They held the property and operated the tavern until selling both parcels on May 27, 1970, when they moved closer to Agnes' family in Carney, Michigan. Roy turned sixty-nine that year and Agnes turned sixty-three—time to retire.

Roy lived another eighteen years, dying on August 25, 1988, in Menominee County, Michigan. Agnes followed him less than a year later, passing away on June 24, 1989. Roy had been married to Agnes for twenty-six years, compared to his twenty-two–year marriage to Elsie and his five-plus years spent living together with Beatrice (estimating they had married in 1922 and that Beatrice had left Kenosha between 1927 and 1929, as recorded by city directories).

I didn't begrudge Agnes her happiness with Roy if, indeed, they had been happy. And I had no problem glossing over her possible affair with Roy while he was still married to Elsie. But could I ever forgive Roy, who lived almost four decades longer than Elsie had—years he spent in the natural beauty of the Wisconsin and Michigan northland?

Of Roy's three wives, Agnes was the only one whose death was definitively documented. Again, I lamented the lack of proof of Roy and Beatrice's divorce. Their divorce certificate might have provided clues as to what happened to Beatrice. Roy's first wife had seemingly vanished after appearing in the 1927 Kenosha directory. I complained about the destruction of divorce records to a genealogist Makovsky cousin. She offered to double check for me in Racine and Kenosha, and (to my astonishment!) subsequently discovered the elusive divorce certificate, as well as a summary of the divorce court proceedings.

By the spring of 2014, I had retired from my campus job, so on one rainy weekday my cousin and I drove to the Wisconsin Historical Society's Area Research Center at the University of Wisconsin-Parkside in Kenosha to view court files of Roy and Beatrice's divorce case. The Wisconsin Historical Society and University of Wisconsin System support a network of thirteen area research centers; each focuses on documenting the stories of its local region.

Thanks to the Parkside center, on a summer day in 2014, I saw with my own eyes the Judgment and Order Book of the Racine County Municipal Court, which recorded the divorce, and the Racine County Municipal Court Minute Book, which recorded the dates the case was filed and heard, as well as the names of all involved.

Every element of the case seemed straightforward: No Perry Mason twists and turns complicated this divorce. Roy's attorney, Gerald T. Flynn, filed the summons and complaint against Beatrice Woodson on March 4, 1937, and the "Proof of Publication of Summons" on March 25, a full decade after Beatrice last appeared in the Kenosha directory and a year before Roy married Elsie. The case was called on April 21 and resumed the next day. Beatrice never appeared in court and following testimony from Roy and his mother, Eleanor Woodson, Judge E. Roy Burgess granted the divorce.

The Minute Book noted that the testimony given by Roy and his mother was "reduced to writing and filed." Oh, how I wished for a transcript of their testimony! But, these records were not retained. I later learned that Wisconsin courts are not obligated to keep complete family court case files longer than thirty years if no support payments are ongoing. Retention of court records is governed by Supreme Court Rule 72, which mandates that family case files need be retained for:

> Thirty years after entry of judgment of divorce, legal separation, annulment, or paternity, or entry of a final order, except that after 30 years, for any case file for which related support or maintenance payments are continuing to be made, 7 years after final payment or after an order terminating maintenance is filed.

Even without the testimony and complete details, the basics of the case recorded in the Judgment and Order Book and Minute Book stunned me on several counts.

In my 1984 interview with Pete, I learned that Judge Roy Burgess had once rented a farm to my grandfather. In fact, Judge Burgess owned the Kenosha County farm where Dad was born in 1914. Twenty-three years later, the judge granted Roy the divorce that left him free to marry Elsie. Additional research revealed that Judge Burgess served the municipal court from 1919 until 1941 and as an attorney continued to represent clients until his retirement in 1960. What a small world my family lived in during the early and mid-twentieth century!

The Judgment and Order Book both corroborated a statement by Clara and answered a question that had come up during her interview:

> *When he started going with Elsie, Woodson told her that he was divorced. In order for them to get married, Woodson needed proof of the divorce. You had to put an announcement in some newspaper then…. He didn't have the announcement put in the Racine paper. He had it put in a Chicago paper and some other paper.*

While the Judgment and Order Book did not name a Chicago newspaper, it did identify the "other paper" as the *Waterford Post*, noting that the defendant had "been duly served with the Summons and Complaint by publication in the *Waterford Post*, a paper of general circulation in Racine County." The choice of newspaper seemed odd, given that Waterford was a relatively small community (the entire township had a population of 12,396 in 1940) in northwest Racine County and I had found no evidence that Beatrice ever lived there. Why not place the ad in the *Kenosha News* or Racine *Journal-Times*?

Waterford seemed like the last place that Beatrice might go and the *Post* the least likely newspaper she might read. Maybe that had been the point. Might Roy have feared that Beatrice would show up in court? Had Roy neglected to sue for divorce all those years before Elsie came into his life because he was afraid of Beatrice's justified accusations—accusations she might have been happy to proclaim in court? Of course, there was still a simpler, more straightforward possibility: Maybe Roy had reason to believe Beatrice had some connection to Waterford. Despite the mounting questions, I was elated to find the added documentation.

I later located the summons published in the *Waterford Post* on microfilm at the Wisconsin Historical Society Library in Madison. The summons appeared in the classified advertising section for three consecutive weeks in March 1937. It identified Roy Woodson as plaintiff and Beatrice Woodson as defendant, summoning her to appear in court. "In case of your failure to do so, judgment will be rendered against you," the summons read, and continued: "The object of the entitled action is to obtain a divorce from the bonds of matrimony." The notice also contained the name and address of Roy's attorney and the fact that a "verified complaint herein is on file with the Clerk of the Municipal Court for Racine County, Wisconsin."

The discovery of the Waterford newspaper announcement substantiated Clara's claim and moved my research a small step forward, but the real bombshell buried in Judge Burgess's ruling came farther down in the document. After dissolving the bonds of matrimony between Roy and Beatrice and allowing each to "keep such properties as they are now possessed of," the judge ruled "that the defendant shall have the care, custody, and control of all her children."

I stared at the words, needing time for them to completely register. All her children! Did Roy and Beatrice have children together? Or had Beatrice already been a mother when she married Roy?

Grateful for the bureaucracies that had archived even these incomplete records, I noted the court prohibited Roy and Beatrice from remarrying for a period of one year and that the Judgment and Order Book provided the date of the divorce certificate. A month later, I located the certificate at the Wisconsin Office of Vital Statistics in Downtown Madison. The certificate added important details about Roy's first marriage:

- Roy and Beatrice had married on May 8, 1924, in Pekin, Illinois, while they both resided in Peoria.

- They had been separated since March 19, 1927.

- Beatrice's occupation was listed as "waitress" and Roy's as "machinist."

- He was age thirty-five in the spring of 1937. Beatrice was reportedly thirty-one—born in 1905 or 1906—and so would have been age eighteen or nineteen when she married Roy.

- Following the words, "Nature of decree," the certificate read: "Absolute Divorce granted; defendant to have care, custody and control of children."

- Roy and Beatrice had one child together. In response to the line on the certificate, "No. of children by marriage", "None" at first had been entered, then the "N" later crossed out, leaving the response "one."

No one in our family had ever said anything about Roy having a child. Likely no one knew, though I wondered whether Roy had ever told Elsie that he was a father. Considering that Beatrice was given custody of "children," I also wondered whether—and when—she might have given birth to additional children fathered by someone other than Roy. Might Beatrice have given birth to a child by another father before she married Roy, during their life together, or after they separated? This last possibility seemed the least likely, unless Roy had had some communication with or about Beatrice after her 1927 departure.

WITH A WRITTEN APPLICATION AND small fee, the Wisconsin Office of Vital Statistics will perform searches for individual records and mail them to you, but I opted instead to apply for a two-hour, in-person appointment to perform several searches. Besides the divorce certificate, I retrieved Elsie's birth certificate, documenting her arrival at the farm in Paris Township, Kenosha County, on the afternoon of May 16, 1912.

Her father, my Grandpa Andrew Green, Sr., was age thirty-six; Grandma Cecelia was thirty-five. This certificate, at least, contained no surprises and raised no new questions. Chasing Elsie's path did not always feel like walking on shifting sands.

Next a clerk led me to a chest-high counter, hefted up a heavy, old ledger-style book, and opened it. The volume contained an index of Wisconsin births, beginning in 1924, the year of Roy and Beatrice's marriage. She paged through the volume to 1927, the year that Beatrice had reportedly left Kenosha. "Nope, nothing here," she said.

Unbelieving, I moved closer and looked at the pages for myself. Had Beatrice and Roy had a child or had they not? Or, had they perhaps had a child before they married when Beatrice would have been a teenager? I skimmed the list of hand-scrawled names and pointed to one: "Isn't that 'Woodson'?"

The clerk peered at the list over her glasses. You're right. I'm sorry, I missed that."

She pointed out the shelves where I'd find the birth certificate, filed by date and county. Another genealogy lesson learned: double-check everything. It's not only long-ago census takers who made mistakes. Mistakes in reading and recording still happened every day.

I gaped at the clerk and couldn't believe my genealogical good fortune. There was a child and a birth certificate to prove it!

The certificate turned out to be easy to locate. Elated by the find, I read it carefully. Though the certificate contained little information, all of it was important. Joan Ruth Woodson was born on July 30, 1926, in Kenosha. Her parents, Roy M. Woodson, age twenty-six, and Beatrice Stewart, age twenty-one, were both born in Peoria, Illinois, and now resided at 322 Wescott Street, Kenosha. Roy worked as a mechanic and Beatrice was a housewife. Beatrice had no other children

Eager to absorb every fact contained in the brief record, I examined the paper closely and turned it over. At the top of the reverse was a penciled note: "verif. 7/21/41 Juvenile Cook County Illinois Courthouse."

I carried the certificate to a clerk at the front desk and asked, "What does this mean?"

She studied the faint notation. "It means that the Juvenile Court in Chicago called to verify the birth in 1941."

Joan would then have been almost fifteen and on summer break. I wondered how she had come to the notice of the Chicago Juvenile Court. Had she run away from home? Had she been arrested for shoplifting or another crime? Might she have been pregnant?

While I hoped the faded note would one day lead to more information, I never did find additional Juvenile Court documentation. Most of Chicago's early juvenile files were destroyed. Still, something out of the normal had happened to Joan that summer.

The visit to the Office of Vital Statistics affirmed a truth that most family historians discover one way or another. Occasionally, a researcher must personally visit a particular library, cemetery, courthouse, or other site to get all the facts. If I had not visited the state Vital Statistics office, I might not have found Joan's birth certificate, and I certainly would not have seen the penciled note on the reverse, which placed Joan in Chicago during the summer of 1941. Contrary to common expectations about Ancestry, genealogy research is not always as easy as clicking on a leaf!

Driving west into the setting sun toward Spring Green and home, I pondered the implications of Joan's birth and Beatrice's disappearance eight months later. I recalled Clara's memory of Roy telling her that he "told his first wife to get on a train and go." A new image sprang to mind of Roy putting Beatrice on a train to who knew where—while she carried an infant in one arm and a battered suitcase in the other. For all I knew of this event, Beatrice might even have been pregnant again— with or without Roy's knowledge.

Regardless of Clara's version of the story, the divorce ruling ten years later placed blame for the separation on Beatrice. Nor did the court order Roy to pay child support, though to be fair, he may not have known Beatrice's whereabouts.

The innumerable possibilities and unanswered questions made my head spin. If Clara's version was correct, why had Roy told Beatrice to leave? Was there a chance that Beatrice had been having an affair with another man and Joan was not Roy's biological daughter? Or, maybe Joan was Roy's daughter but Beatrice subsequently became pregnant with another man's child? Was that why there was no alimony? Might Joan still be living? Surely Beatrice was dead by now, but Joan and her descendants (if she had any) could easily be alive—somewhere. Could I find them?

Questions were still roiling through my brain an hour later when I drove up the long drive to our hillside log home. The trip had been supremely worthwhile, yielding several leads to follow.

In addition to Joan's birth certificate, Roy and Beatrice's divorce certificate offered leads to the record of both their marriage and Beatrice's birth. Searching online, I ordered an uncertified copy of Beatrice's birth certificate from Peoria County, as well as a copy of the marriage certificate from the county clerk in Pekin, administrative seat of Tazewell County, Illinois.

Not expecting a swift reply, I was surprised to find a letter in our mailbox from the Tazewell County Clerk less than a week later, on Saturday, November 1, 2014. Once more, public agency workers had done a great job in quickly replying to my request.

I breathlessly hiked up the drive, climbed the stairs to the house, and dumped the mail on the kitchen table before grabbing the envelope and tearing it open. Folded inside was the marriage certificate, confirming the date of the wedding in May of 1924. Roy's age was correctly listed as twenty-two; Beatrice was only seventeen. Roy's occupation was chauffeur. Beatrice had been born in Peoria to Louis Stewart and Carrie Oltman Stewart. Witnesses were Elmore Prince and Carrie Bragg, and H. C. Witte had performed the ceremony.

Paper in hand I practically danced up the stairs to my loft office. Talk about leads! Now I could search census records, as well as Pekin and Peoria city directories for more information.

Through www.familysearch.org, a website sponsored by The Church of Jesus Christ of Latter-day Saints, I quickly located Beatrice in the 1920 census—listed as "M. Beatrice C. Stewart," age thirteen. Her mother E. Carrie Stewart, age thirty-six, was a widow who was born in Illinois and owned her home. Six other people lived with them:

- Louis R. Stewart, Beatrice's brother, age ten

- George E. Stewart, another brother, age four

- Frieda M. Stewart, Beatrice's sister, age one

- Enoch J. Stewart, Beatrice's paternal uncle, age forty-nine

- Charles F. Oltman, Beatrice's maternal uncle, age thirty-nine

- Ray Simpson, a roomer, age thirty-six

Considering her mother's name the "C" in "M. Beatrice C. Stewart" might stand for "Carrie," but "M" could be one of a thousand different names. If Beatrice Stewart/Woodson in later years used her first name, how could she ever be traced?

The census corroborated Beatrice's birth year of 1907, which synchronized with her certificate of marriage to Roy. But neither matched their divorce certificate, which had given Beatrice's age in 1937 as thirty-one, thus pointing to a birth date in 1905 or 1906 and a marriage age of eighteen or nineteen. Was this discrepancy simply an honest mistake on Roy's part? Or had he intended to report in the divorce filing that Beatrice was at least age eighteen at the time of their marriage? Was this another example of Roy's dissembling?

I recalled that Eleanor had offered testimony during the divorce proceedings; perhaps he did not want his mother to know that Beatrice was only seventeen when he married her. The discrepancy added another question to my list and another niggling doubt about Roy's motivations.

Since Carrie was a widow in 1920 with a one-year-old daughter, I searched for information about her husband, Louis, and found he had died at age forty-one on May 27, 1919—maybe in the global flu pandemic that killed millions from 1918 through 1920. His death took place in Pekin, Illinois, where he worked as a machinist. I marveled at the parallel in the lives of Carrie and Beatrice: both had "lost" husbands soon after they bore a daughter. Like mother, like daughter, sort of.

Carrie Stewart did not appear in the 1930 census, but I found Beatrice's brothers, "Luis" and George, as well as her sister, Frieda Stewart, age twelve, living with Carrie and Elmer F. Prince in Peoria. Three other children were also listed—Velva Stewart, age eleven; Burl Stewart, age nine, and Elizabeth Prince, age two. Might Velva and Burl have been Carrie's niece and nephew? Maybe Carrie gave birth to two children before remarrying Elmer Prince, with whom she then had a daughter.

In addition to being listed as living with the Prince family in 1930, Beatrice's brother Louis, then age twenty, was listed as a prisoner in Peoria, presumably in the county jail where he lived with thirty-three unrelated individuals, age eighteen to seventy-three. Maybe being the eldest stepson in his mother's new household had been a strain that pushed young Louis toward crime. The thought sparked another. What if the senior Louis had died so young as the result of criminal activity? Like father, like son?

I pulled back from the brink: Such speculations were certainly unwarranted. Yet any imaginative flight might point to a signpost on Beatrice's trail. And every possibility examined—even those that led nowhere—pushed forward the search for Beatrice.

The name "Prince" rang a bell and I remembered the names of the witnesses to Roy and Beatrice's Pekin marriage: Elmore Prince and Carrie Bragg. Surely "Elmore" could have been "Elmer" and maybe the father of Carrie Stewart Prince's middle children had been named "Bragg"? Since Beatrice had only been age seventeen at her marriage, she would have needed parental consent. I considered another possibility: Carrie could have born two children (Velva and Burl Stewart) with a man named Bragg before eventually marrying Elmer Prince. In any case, Beatrice's mother and step-father had certainly witnessed her marriage to Roy.

By the 1940 census, Carrie (now listed as "Elizabeth Caroline") and Elmer Prince had moved to Pekin. The only child still at home was Elizabeth. Neither the 1930 nor 1940 censuses listed a Beatrice Woodson or a Beatrice Stewart who could be definitively linked to the Beatrice born in Peoria about 1907, so Beatrice had not moved back home after she left Roy. Had I reached another dead end? Too soon to tell.

Carrie Stewart Prince died at age eighty-four in 1967, according to FindAGrave.com, which reported her burial in Peoria's Lutheran Cemetery. Elizabeth Caroline Prince was the eighth of eleven children born to George and Jane Edwards Oltman, who had emigrated from Germany and Wales, respectively. If only I could so easily find documentation of Beatrice's death! But all my early searches yielded no results.

Three days after receiving the copy of Roy and Beatrice's 1924 marriage certificate, an employee of the Peoria County Clerk's office called to say he had so far not located Beatrice's birth certificate and to ask whether I might know her parents' names. Births were not required to be recorded in the early 1900s, although many were, he explained, sometimes listed only by the father's name followed by "F" or "M" to denote gender. Since I now had the name of Beatrice's father, I provided it—to no avail, as it later turned out.

Disappointed by the lack of birth and death data for Beatrice, I was nevertheless heartened by the new discoveries. I'd have been even more buoyed if all the facts had lined up neatly, but discrepancies abounded:

- Presumably "Elmore" was "Elmer" Prince.

- Also presumably, Carrie "Bragg" was both Carrie "Stewart" and Carrie "Prince". (If not, the coincidence was so large as to seem unbelievable.) I reflected on Carrie's relationships and final marriage to Elmer Prince. How comfortable had Beatrice felt in the home of her mother and stepfather? Had Beatrice viewed marriage to Roy as an escape? If marriage to Roy had turned out to be less than idyllic, had Beatrice then run away from him, as well? She would have been only twenty years old, even too young to vote at that time.

- The date (1931) for Roy's first marriage, listed on the certificate of his marriage to Elsie, was clearly incorrect—either due to a clerical error or to Roy's lying about the timing. Now I wondered: Might he have lied in an attempt to cover up the fact of Joan's birth in 1926?

- The lack of details about Beatrice leaving Kenosha left several questions unanswered: specifically, who had left whom? What were the circumstances of Roy and Beatrice's parting? And, especially, where did Beatrice go?

These questions added to the mystery surrounding Elsie's death. But what did I expect? Whose life was ever straightforward, rational, and well-documented? If, fifty years from now, a researcher looked back at my life, what would she find? Even with the resources of the Internet and ever expanding public agencies, who would know my motivations or decision-making processes? If I wanted to leave a record, I should have kept a journal.

In Beatrice's case, the dead end appeared particularly final—a pinched-down funnel at the end of a narrow Cave of the Mounds passage, with no hint of a breeze going anywhere. If, like her mother after her father's death, Beatrice had remarried and changed her name following her divorce from Roy, finding her could be an insurmountable challenge without her birth record, particularly if she began using her real first name. "M" could stand for hundreds of names—from the ubiquitous Mary to Mabel, Meg, Millie, Mona, and Molly, among many other possibilities. To further complicate tracking Beatrice, Stewart was a fairly common surname, so every online search turned up numerous possibilities.

23

TRACKING BEATRICE AND JOAN

R oy and Beatrice's May 1924 marriage certificate recorded Roy's occupation as "chauffeur", so at the first opportunity I returned to Madison and the Wisconsin Historical Society Library to look in the stacks for the Peoria city directories of the early 1920s. As usual, the lowest level of stacks where the directories were shelved was empty of people.

I found the Peoria volumes and lugged an armful to one of the small tables provided. I opened each volume and paged to the W's. Sure enough, Roy's name appeared, showing him as living at the YMCA in 1922 and again in 1924, when he was working as a "yard man" for Red Fox Petroleum Company, possibly a satellite office of a company of the same name headquartered in Fort Wayne, Indiana.

While the listings answered the question of Roy's whereabouts—and his absence from Kenosha directories during this period—they gave rise to additional questions—for instance, what was the attraction in Peoria? The U.S. manufacturing economy was booming everywhere, so he probably didn't move in search of a job.

Family had been important to Roy, and his parents may have preserved ties with family and friends in Peoria. Yet Roy himself was only two when they moved to Kenosha. So why move back to Peoria at age twenty-one? Might he have known the Stewart family? After all, there had been that 1920 census listing of a Stewart family living next door to the Woodsons in Kenosha.

Later, I would find a letter Elsie sent to my dad when he was at the U.S. Army's Camp Polk, Louisiana, in 1941:

> *We had company from Peoria most of last week. Some old friends of Roy's. We took them to the zoo and the beach. It was kind of hard to find much to do. They happened to pick ... some real hot and sticky days. They were so disappointed because they [had] come up to Wisconsin to cool off.*

These "old friends of Roy's" must have been very good friends to remain with Roy and Elsie for most of a hot and sticky week. Yet these friends were unlikely to have been Beatrice's relatives—at least not the relatives that Clara reported had visited Racine, believing that Beatrice was still married to Roy.

In the library stacks, I leaned forward in the straight-backed wooden chair and propped my elbows on the study table. Roy had two occupations in 1924: chauffeur according to his May marriage certificate and petroleum company yard man according to the city directory. Which had come first or had he done them simultaneously?

Unbidden, my imagination leaped to answer, providing all sorts of fantastical solutions. Remember, I told myself, Beatrice's younger brother was a jail inmate by 1930, according to the federal census. And she married during the 1920s, when Prohibition made bootlegging a viable career option. Peoria had reputedly been a gangster hangout. Maybe Roy had gone to work as a chauffeur for an old family connection affiliated with the mob. I pictured Roy as a dark-suited driver for a kingpin.

My mind spun along a new, bizarre pathway. Like Peoria, life in Wisconsin's North Woods had sometimes been a wild ride during the 1920s, when Chicago gangsters hung out in spots like Al Capone's summer home near Hayward and John Dillinger's resort, Little Bohemia, at Manitowish Waters. Perhaps Roy's interest in tavernkeeping dated from his years as a young man in Peoria. And maybe (okay, this was a stretch), the mob later helped him purchase the Mattoon tavern, only a few miles from the dry Menominee Indian Reservation. As Elsie learned more and more details about Roy's mob connections, she became a threat and was killed for what she knew. I took a deep breath. Not likely.

Chin in hand, I stared at the rows of shelves in this cemetery of information. Despite the mounds of data available here and online, bits of crucial information had either disappeared or never been recorded.

Perhaps I'd have better luck with Beatrice. The Peoria city directories listed three Beatrice Stewarts, but thankfully, identifying "my" Beatrice was easy. My Beatrice lived at her parents' address, 221 Easton Avenue, in 1923 and 1924. She worked as a waitress, which agreed with her occupation listed on her divorce certificate—not to mention her experience at The Tea Shop in Kenosha city directories.

I returned to the library's expansive reading room, claimed an open computer, and searched online databases for Illinois newspaper stories from this period. Several intriguing hits mentioned a Roy Woodson in the Springfield *Daily Illinois Journal*. In a series of classified announcements in May and June of 1925, for example, a Roy Woodson advertised wall papering and general house cleaning services. But Springfield Roy was not my uncle, who by 1925 had reappeared in the Kenosha city directories, along with Beatrice.

Returning to the quest for Beatrice, I scoured Ancestry.com and FamilySearch.org, clicking for details on any document that might conceivably have recorded an event in her life. I searched for "Beatrice Stewart," "Beatrice Woodson," and other permutations that seemed at all conceivable—including the first names "M. Beatrice C." and "Beatrice Caroline," but came up with nothing certain.

Finally, I gave up for the day and, bleary-eyed, left the Wisconsin Historical Society Library to find my car in the Lake Street ramp. Walking across the University of Wisconsin-Madison Library Mall, a breeze from nearby Lake Mendota chilled me. The cold wind felt foreboding: what had happened to Beatrice—not to mention Elsie?

As usual, I drove home on the familiar roads on auto-pilot. When I descended into the Wisconsin River valley, its broad agricultural fields bordered by steep wooded hillsides, I wondered whether any other person would ever care about Elsie's story. Would anyone be drawn to the murder-suicide-accident dilemma? Or to the decades-long search for an ending to her story?

Just then, a bald eagle swooped across the road, heading toward the river. I pulled onto the shoulder and stopped, watching the magnificent symbol soar above the trees on the shoreline—and took its presence at that moment as a good sign. Suddenly recharged, I felt ready to continue the quest.

For several days each week, I continued to chase down leads from my home computer, trying to find a cross-reference that would definitively identify a particular Beatrice as Roy's first wife. If only Beatrice's mother, Carrie, had been the subject of my search—her life had been so much easier to document, from birth to the grave!

Initially, I was excited to find two "Beatrice Stewart" death records in Chicago, but both women would later turn out to be African American, one the stillborn daughter of the other, according to their death certificates, which I ordered online from Cook County.

My Internet search of census records also produced an African American Beatrice Stewart who had been born in Alabama. Another Beatrice "hit" that initially seemed promising—a Michigan death certificate of a Beatrice born in 1905—had, additional research revealed, a different middle initial (F.). Still, given the frequency of clerical errors, this Beatrice, who died in 1983, might be a possibility, as might a Beatrice Stewart who worked in California as a waitress, although both seemed long shots whose lives did not well match what I knew to be true about the life of Roy's first wife.

After countless hours of computer time, I could find no connection between Roy and the various Beatrice Stewarts living in the United States in the 1930s and 1940s. Following another long morning at my desk, I pushed back my chair. After a trip to the kitchen to warm up my cold coffee, I refreshed the screen and considered Beatrice's mother—Carrie Stewart, Carrie Bragg, and Carrie Prince.

Might Beatrice have used any of those names, as well as Beatrice Woodson? Face it, I finally lectured my dogged researcher self, there isn't enough information here to know what name Roy's first wife used after leaving Kenosha.

THE NEXT DAY—A WARM, SUN-FILLED wonder of orange-flashing orioles and iridescent butterflies—I carried quart-sized fruit boxes to the garden and picked the sugar snap peas. Then, I attacked the weedy strawberry patch, growing hot and sweaty while yanking out misplaced grasses and dandelions. The effort loosened Beatrice's grip on my mind.

I returned to the computer and tackled a different quest: examining every fact available about Joan Ruth

Woodson. At least I had her birth certificate, with its penciled notation about the Cook County Juvenile Court query.

Joan had a potential Michigan connection in the form of yearbook photos that showed up in an Ancestry.com search. Born "about 1927" according to Ancestry, a Joan Woodson had attended Ottawa Hills High School in Grand Rapids in the early 1940s.

I studied the photos of the dark-haired teen. Was it only my imagination or did she indeed resemble Roy? Could Beatrice have given up Joan for adoption and might she have been raised by a distant relative of Roy's? Cross-checking census and other records, however, revealed this Joan had been born in Ohio to parents not named Roy and Beatrice. Clearly, this was not the Joan Woodson I sought.

Of more interest were three marriage records noted in Ancestry.com—two from Chicago and one from Minneapolis. Of the two Chicago records, I dismissed one immediately, as the age of the much, much older groom made the match seem unlikely. But the other was intriguing: A Joan Woodson had married a John Bigham in 1947. The Ancestry document was intriguing enough that I ordered a copy of the marriage certificate online from the Cook County Clerk's Office.

Even though I'd paid for it ($15.00 plus a $12.45 processing fee), the resulting email link seemed like a birthday gift to me in mid-June 2015, and I quickly downloaded and printed the certificate. It reported the bride's age as eighteen ("my" Joan would have been nineteen) and the groom's age as twenty. It did not list the bride or groom's parents, though the groom's unnamed father had given his consent for the marriage. I drummed my fingers lightly across the computer keys. If this was the Joan I was seeking, had Beatrice also approved of the match? Was she even in the vicinity? Maybe Beatrice had by now married someone else and was living elsewhere.

I started when the ringing telephone interrupted my thoughts. The American Red Cross Blood Services wanted to know whether I'd come to the Madison center to donate platelets. "Yes, of course."

As soon as I had refocused on the marriage certificate, the phone jangled again—with a reminder of Michael's upcoming optometrist appointment. Then, a window on the computer popped up: several new emails had arrived, so I responded to them. As I hit "send" for my final reply, a knock sounded at the front door. Why were there so many interruptions today?

I climbed down from the loft to find Shane and Logan, two young, clean-cut Mormon missionaries. After I (politely, I hope) got rid of them, our cats—Pookie and his trusty sidekick, Watson—set to caterwauling, so I paused on my way back upstairs to give them a snack.

Back at the computer, I wondered at all of the distractions and delays that had gotten in the way of Elsie's book. I could only hope each byway had a purpose—even if that purpose served only to force a period of reflection or a shift in perspective that resulted in a new angle on an old question. Thinking about all the interruptions over the past ninety minutes, I wondered whether I had somehow attracted them. Had I needed a mental break?

While not as common a name as Beatrice Stewart, there were, of course, multiple John Bighams in and around Chicago. Three were not nearly the right age (the oldest was born in 1886) to have been Joan Woodson's likely groom. But one, born in Cook County, Illinois, on April 13, 1926, was exactly the right age to have been Joan's 1947 husband.

However, subsequent searches of death certificates and other records failed to turn up any possible connections to Joan Woodson Bigham or that 1947 marriage. The 1950 federal census has not yet been publicly released, and Chicago published no city directories after 1929, although there are a few Chicago suburban directories. I scribbled a note to check suburban city directories and Chicago telephone directories.

At first glance, a 2006 newspaper account of John Bigham's death caught my attention. Born in 1957, this John Bigham had applied for a Social Security number in Illinois. Might he have been the son of John and Joan Bigham? The answer was apparently "no," as additional records revealed his father's name to be Richard.

Another death certificate proved more tantalizing: a John Bigham, born in 1946, had died in an Indiana car accident in 1960. Was there a way to efficiently search

Illinois vital records for any children born to John and Joan Bigham—say, between 1940 and 1960? Was there a way to narrow the search? I also wanted to know whether they remained in Illinois after their 1947 marriage, and, of course whether Joan Bigham might have once been Joan Woodson.

There were a half dozen Joan Woodson leads equally intriguing. I pursued, examined, and eventually discounted each, usually because the Joan in question was the wrong age, or in the wrong place at the wrong time. Each such trail taught me something—about my Joan's most likely whereabouts, search methods, or even patience, though most advanced Elsie's story only by its elimination as a potential route forward.

Yet one Minneapolis marriage needs mentioning. *The Minnesota Marriage Collection, 1958 – 2001*, recorded the marriage of Joan Woodson and Joseph Kelly in 1962, when my Joan would have been almost age thirty-six. The online record noted the age of the bride as thirty-three and listed the groom's age as thirty-four. Was it even possible? Could this be my Joan Ruth Woodson?

I ordered a copy of the actual marriage certificate from Hennepin County, Minnesota, and in early July found a business-sized envelope in our mailbox containing a copy of the one-third page certificate. Big disappointment. Except for the groom's full name, the copied certificate contained less information than the online record, omitting the ages of the bride and groom. There was nothing about their parents, birth places, occupations, or any other useful facts—well, harrumph!

Obsessive, perhaps—nevertheless I kept pulling at the slender threads of Elsie's story, including the whereabouts of Beatrice and Joan. Whenever leads disappeared, I continued to take heart from various wildlife sightings on my walks and drives around Iowa County.

In March, a large fisher ran in front of my car as I was driving east on busy U.S. Highway 14. In all the years we have lived in Iowa County, I had never had such a good look at a fisher, never mind one braving heavy commuter traffic. A later Internet search led me to the Wisconsin Department of Natural Resources' website, which confirmed that what I had seen was a male fisher, which averages fifteen pounds, compared to the average-sized eight-pound females.

Encouraged by the sighting, I kept fishing in the Wisconsin Historical Society Library. Returning once more to the city directories housed on the lowest publicly accessible level in the stacks, I searched Minneapolis and St. Paul directories for a Joseph and Joan Kelly throughout the 1960s without luck. I headed back to the library's reading room and also came up dry in an Ancestry search online. A vital record, public notice, or any connection would have been a most welcome gift.

I deserted the dim corridors of the stacks for the bright sunshine of the Lower State Street Mall, where, city and campus meet in a celebration of colorful food carts, occasional performers, and panhandlers. From pita pizza to multi-ethnic cuisine and southern barbeque, the enticing aromas made me hungry and I bought an empanada to eat at one of the concrete tables scattered across the renovated landscape. I ate absent-mindedly, watching the crowds and thinking about Joan.

All in all, Joan Bigham was more likely to be my Joan than was Joan Kelly. Joan Bigham was closer to being the right age at the time of her 1947 marriage and she lived in Chicago, precisely where that note on her birth certificate had placed her in 1941. It was time to put the Joan who had married in chilly Minnesota into cold storage.

24

FINDING JOAN

*E*nsconced once more beneath the skylight above the computer in my loft office, I flashed on a years-ago event, when Dad took me fishing on the Root River and I hooked an ugly crawfish. Dad laughed and released it, but the unwanted catch stuck in my mind. With few leads to follow, I would need to cast into less promising waters.

I decided to visit the Newberry Library in Chicago to search for the names Stewart and Woodson in any area phone and suburban city directories. The trip would entail a drive into Chicago's snarling downtown traffic and held little promise of finding useful clues, but what else to do?

But before scheduling the Chicago trip, I returned in the summer of 2015 to the University of Wisconsin-Parkside Area Research Center to ask one last question about Roy and Beatrice's divorce records, which included copies of Minute Book and Judgment and Order Book pages. The minutes stated, "Testimony reduced to writing and filed." My question: Was there any chance of locating this testimony, which included comments from both Roy and his mother and might provide a clue to Beatrice's whereabouts?

The Parkside reference librarian had no answer and referred me to the State Historical Society Library Archives, so on my next trip to Madison, I returned to the society headquarters on the University of Wisconsin-Madison campus and went through the now familiar routine of placing my purse in a locker and registering at the fourth-floor archives.

A senior archivist suggested I re-contact the Racine Clerk of Courts—even though I'd been told decades ago that all early Racine divorce records had been destroyed. Occasionally, she explained, records can be difficult to find, or are misfiled or lost for a time.

The archivist restored my optimism. I vowed to contact the clerk directly and report my results to the archivist. On the drive home, I envisioned a Godzilla-sized version of myself grabbing the Racine County Courthouse in one fist, turning it upside down, and shaking it until the testimony miraculously dropped out.

At her suggestion, I went to the top and emailed Roseanne Lee, clerk of the circuit court for Racine County. Lee, a sixty-four-year-old woman who had graduated from my alma mater, Horlick High School, replied, "Wow, long time ago! I don't think we have anything that far back. We only have to retain records on family cases for thirty years, so we would not have that information. So sorry!"

In a quirk of fate that left me wondering whether my Elsie quest was doomed, Lee died of a sudden stroke a couple weeks after our email exchange. And when I reported back to Fritzsch, she unearthed the state statute mentioned above confirming that family case records need not be kept longer than thirty years. So, no divorce testimony.

The archivist referred me to another Historical Society reference librarian, a reputed expert at finding people, and I made an appointment to meet her in the library's vast reading room, But, she, too, was unable to suggest research avenues I had not already explored. If nothing else, these exchanges left me confident that I hadn't inadvertently missed critical sources.

THEN ONE EVENING, WHILE mindlessly trying FamilySearch.org for the umpteenth time, I typed Joan's name into the search boxes. To my astonishment, a marriage record popped up at the top of the hit list. This was not simply another false lead—the bride's parents were Roy Woodson and Beatrice Stewart!

Finding Joan's marriage record rekindled my research and emphasized the value of revisiting sources. In this case, FamilySearch.org had by now posted eighty percent of Iowa's marriage records. Given this new marriage document, there was no need to visit Chicago and the Newberry, and I triumphantly crossed the item off my search list.

So, what did the marriage record reveal? Near the end of World War II, in 1945, at age eighteen, Joan married a young man who was only sixteen years old.

Despite the disappointment of the Woodson-Kelly, Minnesota marriage certificate, I wanted to see this Joan Woodson marriage certificate and hold it in my own hands, but when I called the state's vital statistics office, I was told that only certified copies were available and only to close relatives.

Next, I contacted a state genealogical society, but its spokesperson said she could provide marriage records only into the 1930s. She referred me to the county web page for more recent records; however, the website offered marriage certificate copies beginning after World War II. How to find a marriage certificate from the war years?

The county web page did list an email address for the local genealogical society. Its secretary, who replied to my query within hours, was planning a library visit in a few days and vowed to find the certificate—for a fee of all of $3!

When the envelope arrived, I ripped it open at the kitchen table. The certificate revealed that both bride and groom resided in Crown Point, Indiana, where the groom, Karl Cochran, worked as a pipe-fitter helper. The big news, however, was that Joan had been married previously.

I sat down and stared at the paper in my hand. Our cat Pookie leaped to the table and sniffed at the page. If only I could sniff out the details of the past as easily as Pookie nailed a flying squirrel. By age eighteen, Joan had already married twice.

While waiting for the copy of this marriage certificate, I had revisited other online sources and found one more tantalizing clue to Joan's life path. When I checked Google.com for Joan using her married last name, Cochran, an intriguing Social Security Administration-related record appeared.

Ancestry's database had combined information from the Social Security Death Index with data from the Administration's application and claims processes. The resulting Ancestry record noted that Joan had died in the central United States about a month before her sixty-fourth birthday in 1989. She had applied for a Social Security number in June 1943, using a surname I'd not seen before, "Joan Ruth Gerts." Then in March 1945, she had changed her name to "Joan Ruth Kelly" (there was that Minnesota surname again) before changing her name once more in January 1959 — to finally match the surname of her 1945 marriage, Cochran.

I stared at the screen. Did this make any sense at all? I wrote to the Social Security Administration for a copy of Joan's application in hopes that it might clarify the confusion of her multiple names.

Might Joan have first married a man named Gerts in the early 1940s? A FamilySearch.org search for Gerts marriage records yielded several possibilities (of course!), including a Jack C. Gerts, who married a Joan Adler in Lake County, Indiana, (Gary is the county seat) on the eve of the United States' entry into World War II. The marriage took place on August 14, 1941, when Joan

Woodson would have been barely age fifteen. And what about the name "Adler"? Might Beatrice have remarried a man named "Adler" who then adopted Joan?

Eventually, I received a reply to my Social Security Administration request from its acting Freedom of Information Officer with a copy of Joan's application for an account number. It recorded her address as RR1, Box 71, Crown Point, Indiana, her age and birth date, and the fact that she was unemployed.

Her signature seemed curious: She had at first signed "Mrs. Joan Gerts," then crossed out "Mrs." Was Joan already separated—or divorced or widowed—from Jack Gerts by 1943? What if he had been drafted and lost or killed in World War II?

A quick online search led to an obituary and 2002 Social Security Death Index listing for a Jack C. Gerts of Illinois, who had indeed served in—and survived—that war. Yet maybe the war and its separation of the young couple had contributed to the end of their marriage, possibly leaving Joan to raise a child alone as her mother Beatrice had raised her—and as Carrie had at least for a time raised Beatrice.

But there was a problem with Joan's Social Security account number application: the acting Freedom of Information Officer had whited out the names of Joan's parents—when I'd been hoping the document might clarify Beatrice's surname in 1943. The officer wrote: "We have deleted the names of the parents, however, as they may still be living ... If you can provide proof of death for the parents, and if there is enough information available to us to determine that the proof of death refers to the same individuals shown on this document, we can disclose this information."

"Flabbergasted" almost captures my reaction. Roy was born in 1901, so he'd be age 114 in 2015, certainly one of the oldest men alive—never mind the fact that I had his Social Security number and death record. Beatrice, born in 1907, would be age 108. While I had no proof of Beatrice's death—nor proof of her exact birth date for that matter—I did have both for Roy, along with that 1920 census notation and other documents that gave an approximate age for Beatrice. I wrote back to the Social Security Administration, appealing the deletion:

When the phone rang six weeks later on December 7, 2015, and the caller identified herself as an employee of the Social Security Administration in Baltimore, I at first wondered whether there was an issue with my retirement benefits checks, which I'd begun receiving some months back. Then, the light slowly dawned, and I asked, "This is about a genealogy question?"

"Yes." The caller explained that since what I wanted was simply the name of Joan's mother as listed on her application, the Social Security Administration could provide it. The mother's name appeared as "Beatrice Stewart." Confounded at receiving the call (from a real person!), I thanked her and hung up.

Since Joan had listed her mother's name as Stewart, at least this, combined with the Stewart name on Joan's marriage certificate, suggested that Beatrice might still have been Beatrice "Stewart" in the 1940s—or simply that Joan still thought of her mother as "Beatrice Stewart" even if she by then had changed her name. On a whim, I rechecked the 1940 census, but, once again, none of the Beatrice Stewarts listed appeared to be "my" Beatrice Stewart.

Periodically, I revisited various web resources both from home and at the Wisconsin Historical Society Library and learned that Joan's second marriage had lasted. If I was correctly interpreting various documents and news articles, she had had six children—four were still living—and many grandchildren.

Joan's eldest had been named after his paternal grandfather, and her second eldest, another boy, had been christened "Roy," presumably after his maternal grandfather. Joan probably never knew Roy Woodson, yet she named her son after him. Had she hero worshipped the father she never knew? Perhaps equally significant, none of her daughters was named "Beatrice."

After much consideration, I crafted a short list of questions and one quiet morning, called Joan's second son, Roy. His sister-in-law picked up the phone. She said this Roy never talked about his family, but agreed to give him my message. I could only hope—and wait.

Four days later, the living Roy returned my call. He verified that he was Joan's son and confirmed his grandfather's name. The living Roy and I exchanged email addresses and I sent a brief timeline of Roy Woodson's life. His reply:

> *WOW!!! I have a grandfather on my mom's side I never knew of … Roy is definitely my Grandfather. So that is where the name Woodson came from for her maiden name. I was told over the years that Woodson was a fabricated name because she never really knew her real last name.*

Now I knew for certain that Joan's descendants existed. Hard to believe that I actually spoke with her son, a possible, tangible living link to my Uncle Roy.

While I'd like to know more about Joan and discover what happened to Beatrice—how she lived and where and when she died after leaving Kenosha in 1927—I no longer needed to learn her fate to illuminate Elsie's story.

Joan's birth and the fact that she lived into adulthood, combined with the summary of Roy and Beatrice's divorce ruling, proved without a doubt that Beatrice had survived her years with Roy and went on to live out her life somewhere after her disappearance from Wisconsin public records. There had been no foul play, no fatal accident.

Yet a hint of a possible reason for marital discord would come to light in 2017.

25

BONES, DIGGER, AND THE
EVOLVING FUNERAL INDUSTRY

The whereabouts of Beatrice Stewart had become unimportant by late 2015, as the search for answers about Elsie's death led elsewhere. The behavior of Bill "Bones" Johnson, for instance, still raised questions. First, why not call a doctor or ambulance? After the undertaker and the bartender heard that thump on the floor above them and rushed upstairs, why not call for help?

A discussion with a present-day Racine funeral home director helped resolve these questions. He reminded me that few rural communities had ambulance services in 1960 and said, "Not calling an ambulance was not that unusual." In addition, Mattoon lacked a local physician who might have rushed to the tavern on a Sunday morning or any other time.

I tried to set aside judgment and re-imagine the scene in the apartment that day from the perspective of the undertaker and bartender. They did not know how much time they had before Elsie might die. If they had taken the time to carry her down the stairs, place her in a car, and drive to the nearest hospital in Antigo—perhaps a twenty-minute drive—it might be too late to save her. Bill

Johnson and the bartender did the best thing they could think to do: surmising that Elsie had swallowed pills (was there an empty glass nearby?), they forced mustard down her throat in an attempt to encourage vomiting. This was a big risk, as Elsie could easily have choked on the mustard. Maybe they believed she was near death and there was nothing to lose.

Had Elsie ingested a fatal dose of barbiturates today, many circumstances would be different. The undertaker and bartender would have called 911 right away and first responders or emergency medical technicians would have quickly arrived. Elsie might have survived.

Even if the failure to call for help could be reasonably explained, other questions about Elsie's death remained.

When Roy returned to the tavern and found his wife dead, why did he not immediately contact Elsie's family in Racine?

Why make arrangements to bury her in Mattoon? Roy and Elsie had been married twenty-two years; during that time he had attended innumerable Green gatherings—including funerals—and would have known how important they were to the family. Yet, had not the bartender called Pete, Elsie would have been officially declared dead and buried before any of her brothers or sisters or even Grandma Green had a hint of her demise. No wonder family members were suspicious of Roy!

I ran the scenario past the Racine funeral director and, again, he did not find the facts unusual. The circumstances simply revealed family dynamics. "I see this all the time. If a spouse is not getting along with the rest of the family, they won't tell the family until after the burial. [Roy's failure to communicate] doesn't surprise me."

Another idea hit me. Maybe Roy's failure to communicate was simply another example of his penchant for secrecy. Maybe being secretive was a defense mechanism against a family that stood together with Elsie. The bartender had sided with Elsie, too, when she called Pete to tell him of his sister's death.

When Pete and John entered the tavern in Mattoon to lay claim to Elsie's body, Roy at first objected, as did Bill Johnson. Was the undertaker simply supporting his friend Roy? Or were there other reasons for his resolve against transporting the body to Racine? When the decision had finally been made to return Elsie's body to her family, why did the undertaker insist on accompanying it and remain adamant that it not be taken to another funeral home?

Again, I put these questions to the twenty-first century funeral director, and his answer came as a revelation. Transporting the body "may have been more expensive [for Roy]. Roy may have been demanding the quick burial. Or, [the undertaker] did not want to deal with a funeral director [in Racine] who had a close bond with the other part of the family. Or, he had a desire to be paid—pay me, not them."

Yes, economics could be a factor, the funeral director explained. Or, Bill Johnson could just have been an inexperienced funeral director. "The industry has a high turnover in the first five years."

If Bill Johnson was relatively inexperienced and did not orchestrate a large number of funerals in the village of Mattoon, might he also be inexperienced in the legalities of filing a death certificate? After all, there had been no inquest, no examination of fingerprints on the bottle of pills, no questioning of witnesses.

I shuffled through my files and pulled out Elsie's death certificate, again noting that two-thirds of the document had been completed by one hand and signed in that hand, "William W. Johnson, Mattoon." L. E. Hoeff (whom I had learned was Louis Hoeff, deputy coroner) and the registrar had also signed the document, certifying information provided by Roy.

Only a year older than Roy, Bill Johnson had clearly assisted his friend during those dark days following Elsie's passing. While he would certainly have known the general legal requirements for pronouncing and recording Elsie's death, might he have helped Roy hide any of the facts or circumstances surrounding her demise?

Had Elsie's death occurred today, "… there would have been more investigation, with a qualified medical examiner who would have looked at the person's medical history," said the present-day funeral director. In the past, a coroner didn't routinely investigate every death, especially if he thought he had no reason to be suspicious.

I had one more question: But why shut the casket in Clara's face? Was the undertaker seeking to hide evidence of murder or his own inadequate embalming techniques? Since the original plan had been for a quick burial, perhaps Elsie's body had not been treated to ensure good preservation for the time needed to transport it to Racine and hold a proper funeral.

Once more, the funeral director's answer came as a possibility I had never considered: "That seemed to be the way things were [back then. The undertaker] thought, 'Okay, it's time to start the service.' Everything was more structured. The attitude was we know best. [The undertaker] was in charge."

This attitude of old-time undertakers reflected the attitudes of society as a whole, in which the public generally showed more respect for law enforcement, elected officials, and other leaders. The old-time undertakers "assumed a protective attitude around their [clients]," according to the Racine funeral director. Their attitude was, "Everyone knows best except for the people who are grieving. [In contrast,] today funeral directors try to work with [family members and accommodate] what they want. It's a more open society, less structured."

Of course, I realized, remembering a comment Mom had made during Clara's interview: "The undertaker was everything in town."

Like law enforcement, government, and other entities, the funeral industry changed immeasurably before and since 1960.

A century ago, many deaths and funerals took place in the home; but by the mid-twentieth century, more deaths occurred outside of the home in hospitals or nursing homes, embalming became the norm, and more death-related services moved to funeral "homes."

When care for the body of the deceased moved out of the caring hands of family members into the hands of professionals, suspicions arose about these professionals and the mysterious services they performed away from family scrutiny. A decline in mortality rates further fueled distrust as death became a less frequent, more mystifying visitor in many family circles.

By the 1960s a growing number of Americans had mixed feelings about funeral directors and the funeral home industry. When Jessica Mitford published her industry critique, *The American Way of Death* in 1963, she gained an avid readership, especially following President John F. Kennedy's televised funeral in November that year.

Gary Laderman, author of *Rest in Peace: A Cultural History of Death and the Funeral Home in Twentieth-Century America* (2003), noted that as death and funerals became more removed from everyday life, television scriptwriters introduced undertakers "to promote either laughs or gasps." The best example was the character who first appeared on radio, then television in the pioneer family sitcom, *The Life of Riley*, as a friend of factory worker Chester Riley.

Digby "Digger" O'Dell often delivered an episode's most memorable lines: "You're looking fine, very natural," and "In my profession, we have a saying: Never give up, though things look black, 'till a case is closed a man can bounce back."

Digger provoked fear as well as laughter. In one 1949 television episode, Riley "has to have a tonsillectomy and enters the hospital trembling with fear," Lademan reported. Digger visited Riley in the hospital, giving him a bouquet of lilies and the book, *The Good Earth* by Pearl S. Buck, saying, "You haven't lived until you've buried yourself in a good book."

The friendly undertaker then added, "When you're ready to leave this place, I'll be waiting for you." Though played for laughs, these lines, Lademan stated, "betray serious public suspicions about the motives of men in the business of death and a strong discomfort with their presence in life."

The funeral director, Lademan wrote, was "sometimes portrayed as laughable and buffoon-like, sometimes as malevolent and crafty as the devil." These stereotypical roles also reflected "the ambivalence and fear associated with the corpse itself, and the conflicted desire to see a pleasing image of the deceased before burial."

Maybe that was why Clara's description of Bill Johnson's slamming Elsie's casket shut stuck in my mind. Though Elsie's body no longer held her spirit, her visage remained to imprint a memory for those left behind.

Bill Johnson, I later learned from a local Mattoon historian, had a funeral home on County Highway Z. His nickname (I shouldn't have been surprised) was "Digger" — not "Bones" after all. Though not too far off the mark, here was yet one more proof of my fallible memory.

The local historian also supplied the identity of the bartender — Barbara Mondl, who, with her second husband Rudie — had sold the tavern to Elsie and Roy. Mondl must have agreed to stay on and help Elsie and Roy learn the ropes of tavern-keeping following the sale of the business.

FROM THE OUTSIDE, ROY AND Elsie's former tavern has changed little in the past half century. While Racine and its outlying townships of Mount Pleasant and Caledonia have undergone tremendous development with many new residential and retail areas, Mattoon continues as a quiet village with a population of about four hundred. The village lies a few miles west of U.S. Highway 45 and fewer miles east of Menominee County/Indian Reservation.

I drove north on an overcast February Wednesday, the clouds giving a quiet tone to the day, which was enlivened by the presence of multiple flocks of wild turkeys along the Shawano County roads leading to the village. When turkeys moved close to the road, I slowed, knowing from shattering experience the damage they could do to a windshield when accidentally struck.

The exterior of Driftwood Inn as it appeared in the winter of 2016, similar to Elsie and Roy's tavern of 1960, although new siding had replaced the old, gray asphalt shingles.

Then I noticed a big beast loping west through a leafless, open woodlot. I braked to a stop on the empty road. It couldn't be, could it? I'd never seen a wolf in the wild, but this was what I'd always imagined one might look like—larger than a coyote or German shepherd with its tail flat out and parallel to the ground. Still, it was a ways off the road, so maybe a coyote after all?

Later, I read about wolves on the Wisconsin Department of Natural Resources website and learned that, indeed, there were several packs in Shawano County, including one just west of Mattoon and two to the east in Menominee County. Though extirpated from the state when Roy and Elsie had lived in the village, wolves had slowly returned and now numbered perhaps eight hundred animals across northern Wisconsin. Maybe this region was in some ways wilder now than it had been fifty years earlier, when the vestiges of lumbering still held sway.

Driving into town via County Highway D was like arriving on the set of a Western ghost town, minus the boardwalks: Except for the occasional vehicle passing through, the gray street lay broad as an empty interstate—with all the width needed to accommodate snow piles and snow removal. It rested open and devoid of people, pets, and activity, ready and waiting for a person (or a ghost) to make a move.

Two blocks off the main street, the mood inside the Mattoon Community Library offered a welcome contrast to the gray outdoors. Recent releases lined the bright shelves, a checkers game lay set for players on one table, and ice skates lined up beneath a shelf, ready for children to use. Three young girls followed me inside; one moved to restock a candy bowl on the librarian's desk.

I'd come to see what Mattoon historical materials the library held, though there turned out to be little of relevance to Elsie's story. Still, the scrapbooks filled with newspaper clippings that overflowed three shelves of the back room were mesmerizing.

A collection of scrapbooks contained themed clippings—for example, about the Dionne quintuplets and U.S. presidents from Ronald Reagan to Bill Clinton. Others contained a hodgepodge of national and local news including obituaries, so I focused on these volumes for the years 1958 through 1960, but found nothing relating to Elsie, Roy, or anyone else connected with their story.

The library also held a couple of manila folders containing local history materials, and Bill Johnson's name did appear there, in a typescript history of Mattoon and Hutchins Township.

Beneath the section heading "Business Past and Present" and following a paragraph about William Blum, Mattoon's first undertaker, who had also operated a furniture store in the early twentieth century, two short sentences mentioned Johnson: "In later years, the William Johnson Funeral home was established in Mattoon. Mr. Johnson remained only a year or two." If true, Bill Johnson and Roy shared another common tie in addition to their similar ages: both were new in town and likely open to new friendships.

My own adult interactions with funeral directors were entirely positive, as when Mom died in September 2015, two months shy of her 101st birthday. She had suffered from some dementia due to a narrowing and hardening of her arteries and had moved to a residential facility in 2009. During those six years, we had a number of intriguing conversations, like the one that occurred the month before she died. The brief exchange left me wondering about the malleability of identity and the extent of our human potential.

Mom said, "You can choose any name. You can have a different name." So I asked what name she would like. Mom's answer: "Lydia"—the name of her oldest sister who had died many years before.

I picked up a photo album and asked Mom whether she could identify any of the people clustered in a group for the camera. She took a quick look at the black-and-white image before turning away. "Cousins," she replied, as if she did not want to bother with the work of identifying each face—or, more likely, as if she knew she would not be able to name them all. When I tried to explain that they weren't really cousins, Mom said: "All cousins. You are a cousin."

To this, I said, "I'm your daughter."

She replied, "You could be a cousin."

My takeaway from her words: We are all cousins. Indeed, the first definition of "cousin" in our worn *Webster*'s dictionary is "originally ... descended from a common ancestor." And if we are all cousins, then surely we are all our cousins' keepers, responsible not only for their welfare, but also for the stories they leave behind.

26

ELSIE

More than five decades after the fact, I understood more about Elsie's death, had a better grasp of Roy's motivations, and had gained a deeper appreciation for the culture, lifestyles, and norms of the post-World War II era. Yet stubborn questions remained.

On the day she died, both Elsie and Roy's behavior still seemed curious. Why on that summer Sunday morning was Elsie drinking in the tavern with their friend, the undertaker? Where had Roy gone? He certainly hadn't stepped out to get a Sunday newspaper or a cup of coffee. Or had he? Maybe Roy had simply driven into Antigo for a break: to have breakfast and read the newspapers.

I imagined Elsie's death examined on a modern TV mystery series and pictured a hard-driving investigative reporter interviewing Roy. How might he have defended himself?

Despite my suspicions, I had to admit that yes, Roy's responses might reasonably be those of an innocent man. Maybe there had been a suicide note, which Roy had destroyed because in it Elsie blamed him for her decision to take her own life. Even if Roy's Sunday morning foray

Elsie Christina Petersen Green Woodson

away from the tavern had involved an affair with Agnes, that fact wouldn't make him a murderer. On the other hand, Roy might lie about his involvement in Elsie's death: His life seemed to reflect a pattern of untruths. In my mind, the arguments flew back and forth.

Roy could be secretive and unstable. Captured by the bright lights of a television production set and held in the steely gaze of a hard-nosed reporter, would Roy have broken down under a barrage of tough questions? Would he have confessed? And if he had confessed, how had he committed the crime—considering his absence from the tavern that Sunday morning?

Circumstantial evidence abounded, like the lack of a suicide note and Elsie's own behavior that day. Did Elsie go upstairs because she was feeling ill after the undertaker had put Nembutal in her drink?

If she had willingly taken the Nembutal, she would have had time to write a farewell note and lie down on her bed, not fall to the floor with a thump that could be heard in the tavern below. If she consciously committed suicide, why not leave a note naming her reasons?

And why commit suicide at all, when at least one other escape was available to her? Dad (never mind other siblings) was only a few hours' drive away. Of course, if Elsie did commit suicide, she might not have been thinking so clearly.

The key to Elsie's death resided in her relationship with Roy. While many of my Green relatives held Roy responsible for Elsie's death, not all were convinced that he was a murderer. In fact, Clara's daughter, who lived next door to Elsie and Roy in Racine as a girl, never saw Roy as a murderer.

My cousin Karen lived with Elsie and Roy for a couple of months after running away from home the afternoon of Halloween, 1957, two months before her sixteenth birthday—picking the holiday so that she could go trick-or-treating and would have food to eat.

After hiding in the rear of the family's property until dusk, my cousin collected her stash of treats and ran to hide in Elsie and Roy's car, which would have offered some shelter during a chilly, late-fall night. There was even a blanket in the back seat. But, as she recalled in 2015, "I must not have closed the door all the way." Elsie and Roy noticed the light on in their car and went outside to close the door.

Surprised by the stowaway, Elsie and Roy faced a quandary: What to do with the teen? In addition to my dad and mom, Elsie and Roy sought advice from Grandma Green, who also told them to go to the authorities—and so they did.

A social worker visited Clara and Roy Miller, interviewing them separately, as well as talking with Karen. The result was that Karen went to live with Elsie and Roy; however, she stayed only nine weeks, returning to her own home for her father's birthday on January 5.

Two years after Elsie's death—when my cousin was married and living in Racine's near-west-side neighborhood—Roy Woodson visited her. Clara's daughter was surprised to see him. "I didn't think he knew where to find me."

By then, suspicions about Roy's possible role in Elsie's death had spread throughout the Green clan. Somehow, the tainted thoughts had reached Roy. If my cousin was surprised to see Roy at her door, she was even more astonished by his words: "There are rumors, but they are just rumors."

In an effort to dispel the rumors, Roy may have hoped that Clara's daughter, who had once run away to take refuge with him and Elsie, would lend him a sympathetic ear. If so, he was right. In answer to my question, "What do you think happened to Elsie?" my cousin replied, "Maybe she was sick and no one knew it."

More likely not, considering the reports of relatives who had visited Mattoon soon before Elsie's death. All had reported that she was welcoming, happy to see them, and appeared healthy. Yet even if my cousin was wrong about the state of Elsie's physical health in the summer of 1960, she nevertheless did not believe Roy had killed our aunt.

Karen's answer reminded me of a comment Mom made shortly before she entered the assisted living residence. As if realizing her mind was failing and knowing of my interest in Elsie's fate, Mom made a point of telling me during a lucid moment what she deemed to be the truth: "Elsie believed that Roy was going with another woman, but he wasn't." We stood in the sunny kitchen, but like a call past midnight, I knew this was important.

Her comment sounded like something Roy might have said. After learning about his visit to my cousin and his attempt to deny family rumors, I wondered, *Had Roy made a similar statement to Mom in an effort to clear his name? Maybe Roy thought that Mom, who was a generous soul and not Elsie's blood relative, might be open to his words. If Roy had been trying to clear his name, was his the voice of a man wrongly accused — or one who doth protest too much?*

In any case, Roy was right to expect a sympathetic hearing from Mom, who apparently forgave him far more readily than did Dad. Aside from Dad, no one had heard the strain in Elsie's voice during that first, fateful telephone call in July 1960. No one else had heard her plea for help.

After Elsie's death, Mom and Dad had naturally reacted differently. While Mom had opened the door to Roy when he visited with his third wife, Agnes, and invited them in for drinks, Dad had refused to see him.

Mom's comment took me back to my aunt's and uncle's horoscopes. The astrologer had observed that once Elsie and Roy dedicated themselves to each other, they were unlikely to part. Both took their marriage seriously and it was marked by "longevity, stability, and loyalty." Each knew they could depend on the other. Both were "so resistant to change that even if [they] hated each other, it would be hard to disengage ... and move on." Roy had deep attachments to family and to the familiar, and Elsie was resistant to changes in her domestic or personal life. Whether or not Roy was having an affair, his friendship with Agnes must have left him conflicted.

Even if Mom believed Roy was no murderer, she hardly believed him an innocent man. I reread Clara's interview, during which Mom had stated: "Oh, for crying out loud! Elsie should have left him before she went up to Mattoon with him."

Many members of the Green family believed Roy guilty—or at least wondered about his possible complicity. Laura's eldest daughter, Audrey, stated, "I think he killed her." She added, "Grandma Green was also suspicious; you could see that when the subject came up at a family reunion."

Audrey recalled visiting Mattoon after Roy had remarried. Roy was behind the bar when his new wife, Agnes, had irritably yelled down from the second-floor apartment that dinner was ready, and he immediately headed upstairs, deserting Elsie's relatives. My cousin concluded, "And he could have had Elsie!"

Early in the spring of 2016, I contemplated Roy and Elsie's behavior from my loft office while gazing at the Wisconsin River visible through the still-leafless trees. When I drove the local back roads, I could see houses tucked away in the woods, as well as the skeletons and foundations of homes that had once stood strong and sheltering. Hidden during leaf-on and snow-filled seasons, these remnants of past lives could be seen clearly.

My mind turned back to November and I remembered the feel of the approaching winter snows. Now I felt the clarity of winter draw near that unyielding question: Murder, suicide, or accident? The answer felt at hand.

SINCE 1960, I HAD PERSONALLY encountered only a few suicides, in contrast to one friend's family who had experienced several suicides, most related to physical and mental illness. My friend's father committed suicide about the time she became engaged to her first husband, who later also committed suicide. Her second husband, two children, and one grandson also took their own lives. Yet suicide did not so routinely run in the Green family, though it could be as dysfunctional as any—my obsessive self included.

Family suspicions bloomed like mold on wet wood due largely to the unanswered questions revolving around Elsie's death. Regardless of the reason—a terminal or painful illness, for example—any suicide might seem senseless to the survivors left behind. Unless the circumstances were incontrovertible, family members don't always accept a verdict of suicide easily. In Elsie's case, the circumstances left plenty of room for doubt.

All these years, I had not wanted to accept a verdict of suicide. Yet if Elsie had been murdered, this had not been a crime of rising passions, committed in the heat of argument or delusion.

At the same time, I could not quite accept—or face the prospect of—Roy being a cold-blooded killer. The Roy I had known never struck me as a psychotic killer, but, of course, as current headlines sometimes attest, that's often what the neighbors say after the fellow next door has been arrested for murder. Even serial killers often appear normal to their neighbors, according to one *Psychology Today* article, "Serial Killer Myth #2: They're Dysfunctional Loners" (posted on July 28, 2014).

In *AMERICAN GHOST: A FAMILY's Haunted Past in the Desert Southwest,* Hannah Nordhaus wrote of her quest to uncover the truth about her great-great-grandmother, who reportedly haunted the hotel that once served as her ancestors' home. Part memoir, part historical research, the book haunted me, too. Soon after reading it, at 4:30 a.m. on what would have been Dad's 101st birthday, August 10, 2015, I woke from a dream:

> *Michael and I, along with two or three other people, were exploring the upper floor of a big, old house, trying to see where renovations had been made, where walls had been removed, and where a bedroom and bed had once been positioned. The floor was now wide open, with no individual rooms or partitions. Clutter filled the vast space—old furniture, boxes, and shadowy forms. As we investigated the enormous hall, one of the other people announced that he saw a half ghost—the*

upper half of a woman's body—floating toward him, just above his head.

AFTER I AWOKE AND JOTTED A note about this dream, I thought about what I'd learned about Elsie's life and her generation. Although I'd found only half a ghost and would likely never find the whole truth, that half truth now seemed to be enough. I'd done what could be done. I'd done what I had come to do. Time to move forward.

If Elsie's death had occurred in 2017, as an adult, I'd have immediately understood she was no paragon. Though I'd loved her, I would have wondered what dark thoughts boiled beneath her calm and friendly exterior. I would not have wanted to think her capable of suicide.

But when she called Dad in mid-week and asked him to come get her, what had she been thinking? When he had reasonably pleaded that he needed to go to work the next morning, why did she neither press her point nor get an immediate commitment from him to come on Saturday? Moreover, why did she not then follow up with him on Friday?

Decades after the fact, Elsie's call seems to point toward ambivalence and uncertainty, and to reveal a woman in considerable distress. Picking up the phone to call Dad—and admit problems in her marriage—was both a desperate and a courageous act.

Elsie's astrological report had addressed her possible mental state during the two weeks before her death:

- **July 19 – 24**: [Y]our practical reasoning ability and your ability to focus on the here and now are diminished. Your judgment regarding concrete matters is a bit fuzzy ….

- **July 21 – 24**: [Y]ou are more temperamental, impassioned, and inclined to act on the dictates of emotion and desire rather than reason. Minor annoyances and others' idiosyncrasies aggravate you more than usual. You are in a fighting mood.

- **July 28 – Sept. 28**: Ego conflicts … may arise … Your urge to act and to do is so strong that you are prone to rush and to try to force your will in situations where waiting may be more appropriate.

Not for the first time, I wondered what Elsie had been thinking and feeling during the days leading up to her death. *Had Elsie asked Roy to take her away from Mattoon and the tavern?* The recent visits from her vacationing brothers (Carl and Dad) had showcased their more settled lives and perhaps reminded her of the family reunions and fun she was missing. While Elsie worked in the small-town tavern, her relocated siblings (Laura, Andrew, and Martin) thrived in their far-flung new homes.

I recalled one of Laura's 1956 letters to Mom and Dad. Four years before her death in 1960, Elsie angrily ordered Laura to pick up the spinning wheel, sewing cabinet, and Nesco that had been stored at Elsie and Roy's home ever since Laura's move to Alaska three years earlier. Laura's handwritten words slid before my mind's eye: *"Elsie's gone off on one of her wing-dings and there is no use asking her. When Elsie wants to get mad—she gets mad—she doesn't have to have a reason."* Maybe Elsie resented Laura for her Alaskan adventure. Maybe Elsie went on another "wing-ding" near the close of July 1960.

After a full year in Mattoon, Elsie might have berated Roy for the move that so confined her. Perhaps she accused him of tearing her away from the places and people she loved. I could almost hear her words:

> Why did we have to come to this god-forsaken spot? You could have found a different job in Racine. What's worse, we're tied to this dump day in and day out with never a vacation. You still could get a job closer to Racine, you're not that old. Or, we could buy another tavern there, now that we have experience in running one.

How might Roy have responded to such an onslaught? He might have told Elsie he liked Mattoon and intended to stay right there. But would he have hung another noose in the tavern's basement and repeated his invitation for her to use it (if Clara's testimony could be believed)? Maybe Elsie and Roy had had a blow-out fight and he drove to Antigo that Sunday morning to cool off. Maybe Elsie sought her solace at the bar.

I ENVISIONED HOW THAT WEEKEND had played out for Elsie. What might I have done in her place? I turned to the notes from my 2004 hypnosis session and reconsidered the hypnotist's words, which had enabled me to look at Elsie's life from her own point of view.

When family members visited Mattoon before her death, they observed her to be fine, even upbeat. But from Elsie's perspective, everyone may have seemed fine except her. Then, when Roy left that Sunday morning, Elsie may have thought the problem she had left behind in Racine had followed her north. And if Elsie indeed swallowed a dozen Nembutal pills, she was not thinking about Grandma Green or anyone else.

"We are egocentric when we are stressed," the hypnotist had said. "Ego operates as a protection for us— as does skepticism, when we're not ready or able to deal with something."

By the end of the hypnosis session, I knew that at some point, I'd reach out to Elsie and my guide again. The time finally came at the beginning of 2016. By then, I'd lived with Elsie's story for so long she seemed more like a sister than an aunt—and I was now far older than she had been when she died. The added years had broadened my perspective and maybe I'd learned more than I fully comprehended since trying hypnosis.

In 2015, I had begun to meditate a few minutes every morning, so now easily returned to the realm beyond verbalization, a land of suspended animation and clarity. A dozen years after I had first entered the gated garden and descended the stairway to meet my guide, my central query had subtly changed, from a question of fact to one of belief. Given the research I'd done and the information I now had, did I still believe Elsie's death was accidental?

Settled in my great-grandfather's press-back rocker, feet resting on an antique, handmade stool, I closed my eyes and took three deep breaths. *Relax, relax, relax.* I looked for my spirit guide, and suddenly, there he was, with Elsie hovering in the background.

When she stepped forward, I felt her bright love beaming toward me, holding me. Elsie offered no words, yet I understood her, knew even without language that she had indeed taken those pills—not only to forget, but also to ease her pain. Like Laura and Clara, Elsie felt life deeply, but unlike her sisters, she moved inward, not outward, to express intense feelings.

Roy had paved the way for her escape, previously having suggested suicide and buying the pills that provided an easy method. Still, there was an element of accident in her death, as Elsie had not expected the pills— strengthened by the alcohol she'd consumed—to act so quickly, nor had she anticipated falling to the floor.

Elsie had never planned to leave a note. As the hypnotist had said, Elsie was not thinking about others at that moment, and anyway, what was the point? Roy would understand what had happened.

As Elsie slipped away, I nodded to my spirit guide and asked him to bring forward the essence of Barbara Mondl, the bartender who had been in the tavern that Sunday morning. When she willingly stepped forward and faced me, I sensed her tremendous strength; she had overcome many challenges before ever laying eyes on Roy and Elsie Woodson.

My mind flew to the photo of the three of them behind the bar and it seemed to me now that her expression held a hint of skepticism. Had she seen behind Roy's actor façade? Surely Barbara had stood up to Roy, her employer, when she called Pete to tell him Elsie was dead and that Roy planned to immediately bury her in Mattoon. That had taken courage and I wondered how long she had continued to work at the tavern after Elsie's death.

During this reverie, Barbara's presence in the tavern that day now seemed to exonerate Bill Johnson. As an experienced, eagle-eyed bartender, she would likely have noticed—and said something about—an attempt to add anything to Elsie's drink. On that Sunday morning, the bar was reportedly otherwise empty, there were no other customers to take her attention away from Elsie and Bill.

Roy's failure to tell the Green family of Elsie's death, combined with his plan to bury her quickly, pointed to guilt he must have felt about the role he had played in her death. For there was no doubt that he had played a role in Elsie's demise. The only questions remaining were the extent of that role and the degree of his responsibility for her passing.

After twenty-two years of marriage, Roy knew Elsie's siblings well. Did he fear what they would say—or do? Or had Roy simply wanted to provoke and put down Elsie's family?

In this meditative state, my mind sped along unhindered. Regardless of whether or not Roy was actually having an affair with Agnes, he likely had maintained a friendship with her. I recalled Mom's comment about Elsie suspecting that Roy was involved in another relationship.

On the Sunday she died, maybe Elsie had accused Roy of having an affair. Maybe Roy believed that Elsie had shared her suspicions with other Green family members. Could he trust any of them to hear his side of events?

These thoughts lined up like railroad cars and had the inevitability of an onrushing, unstoppable train. I opened my eyes, rose to sit at my computer, and quickly keyed in the new beliefs.

I finally had my answer to the question: How did Elsie die? I fully believed that Elsie took the Nembutal with her own hand, so suicide was the correct death verdict after all—as the coroner had decided at the time. At least, suicide was the correct legal ruling. Morally, I convicted Roy. He had killed Elsie as if he'd poisoned her himself. Although Elsie had in essence pulled the trigger on her life, Roy had contributed to her unhappy environment and possibly provided the Nembutal. If not first-degree murder, Roy had committed a kind of moral manslaughter.

27

ROY

*T*his search for truth came to rest slowly, a pendulum swinging widely at first, then more narrowly, finally pointing to a verdict. Once I'd settled on this conclusion, corroborating clues continued to come in, often in unlooked-for ways.

After all those years of searching, I returned to a book purchased during my novel-writing attempt. According to Serita Deborah Stevens, author of *Deadly Doses: A Writer's Guide to Poisons* (1990), most poisons have a bitter taste, so "the old trick of slipping a barbiturate into a cocktail could not work unless the victim habitually gulped drinks or was a complete innocent with no idea of how a drink should taste." Here was another reason the undertaker could never have poisoned Elsie.

Stevens' report of suicide statistics caught my attention. After World War II, barbiturate use became widespread, and the rate of suicides grew twelve times between 1938 and 1954. In 1962, a global survey of deaths by poisonings reported about seventy percent were suicides and about thirty percent were accidents; less than one percent were homicides.

Time is a wheel and current events give perspective to history. Recent headlines revealed that what was a growing problem in 1960 would expand to monstrous proportions. In 2016, the *Washington Post* ran a series, *Unnatural Causes: Sick and Dying in Small-Town America.* One part, "A River of Lost Souls Runs Through Western Colorado" (November 6), by Amy Ellis Nutt, recorded the continued increase in suicide, particularly among middle-aged white women:

> Two-and-a-half times as many people die by suicide as homicide in this country; among whites in 2014, it was nearly nine times as many, according to the Centers for Disease Control and Prevention. Although more men than women take their own lives, the rate of suicide has nearly doubled among middle-aged white women since 1999—rising from 7 per 100,000 to 12.6 in 2014—helping to explain a startling increase in their early mortality.

> The numbers are even worse for middle-aged white women with a high school diploma or less. For them, the suicide rate has more than doubled over the past fifteen years, according to a *Washington Post* analysis of federal health data. Most of the victims lived in small towns and rural areas... where social isolation can be acute.

Nutt blamed many of these deaths on a rise in the use and combinations of various psychiatric medications.

More clues about the cause of Elsie's death drifted in from Mattoon. A local historian put me in touch with Kathy Zarda, who had grown up in Mattoon, married, and moved to Milwaukee. A few months after Elsie's death, Kathy and her husband returned to their hometown so that he could join his family's business. When they still lived in Milwaukee, Kathy remembered hearing about Elsie's death. "Everyone was very surprised."

Apparently no one in Mattoon ever thought the death had been anything other than suicide. Kathy repeated a comment made by a local woman who had become Elsie's friend: "A few days before she died, Elsie said she was giving some of her clothes away 'because I won't need them where I'm going.'"

Kathy knew Bill Johnson since one of his daughters had been her friend in high school. Kathy recalled: "Bill worked nights at the mill and also ran a funeral home on County Z. It was located on the first floor of their home, with the family living upstairs." Johnson eventually closed the business and moved to Shawano.

More significant evidence came from another Mattoon contact when Kathy connected me with a former resident. He said, "Elsie was distraught because of Roy's drinking."

Bam! The comment hit like another nail in poor Elsie's coffin.

No one had mentioned that Roy might have a drinking problem, but it was certainly plausible and might explain some of his behaviors. Particularly after the move to Mattoon, Roy had ready access to alcohol. I recalled the time Roy had slapped a club into his open palm and declared that Indians weren't welcome in his tavern because they couldn't hold their liquor. Had he been drinking at the time? Maybe Roy was the one who couldn't hold his liquor. But none of my research contained any corroboration of a drinking problem—at least not then.

Roy was fortunate to have a committed wife to keep the tavern running even when he might be too drunk to function. Yet that was not the role Elsie had signed up for when she married Roy, especially a role played out in a small-town tavern far removed from her family and friends. If Roy had a drinking problem, how could Elsie not resent it?

When Roy was hospitalized with a nervous breakdown in 1958, he had fought depression fueled by job stress and anxiety about his future at Massey-Harris. Though social and outgoing, Roy clearly had a dark side, which in hindsight, may have long featured alcoholism accompanied by anxiety, depression, and secrecy. Maybe alcohol had fueled Roy's questionable behavior all along. Or, perhaps running the tavern had tipped a habit of occasional drinking into full-blown alcoholism and made Roy even more difficult to live with.

A few weeks after hearing the comment about Roy's drinking, I unearthed a previously overlooked packet of cards and letters in a box of papers at Mom's house. Slowly, the home was emptied of knickknacks, furniture, stacks of papers and books, and trinkets from long-forgotten vacations. Cleared, the rooms brightened and breathed freer, no longer tied to past attachments.

I had pulled this box, like so many before it, from its sequestered shelf, setting it aside to go through during an evening of TV watching, my eyes bouncing between twenty-first century crime dramas and scraps from the past—tidbits that might be clues or more likely, trash. Once again, information turned up as if on cue, precisely when needed to carry my quest forward. Why hadn't I noticed these notes before?

Only a month after Elsie's death, Roy had written on a plain postcard to Mom and Dad that business was good and he was busy, but *"It certainly is terribly lonesome without Elsie."* Then a year after Elsie's death, Roy wrote a longer letter:

> *It seems like it has been forever for me to get started writing a letter, but Marge and Herman, I've been so busy it's really not funny, please excuse me for not writing sooner. I've been putting in a lot of hours and I'm doing my own cooking, clean the house, make my bed, go downstairs each morning clean up the tavern and tend bar all day long until 7:00 p.m. at night and later. Besides taking care of my invoices and the books for the tavern. So I think that's quite a job for one man to do. I have a bartender coming in the evenings helping out, but for a long time I was doing it my-self....*

How's Doris and Diane, I hope they are both well and tell Doris I thank her so much for those gifts she sent me even though they were late in coming....

Don't know just when I can come down to Racine, but when I do come I want to spend about a week in and around Racine and Kenosha. It's pretty hard to get someone to take care of the business that you can trust and know that everything's going to be alright.

Please say hello to Mom Green for me and all the rest. Don't know much more to write about except I'm feeling fine and not drinking a drop haven't had anything to drink for some time.... Please write soon don't wait as long as I did, and I'm terribly sorry.

With lots of love to all, as ever,

Roy

P.S. Do you think you kids will get a chance to come up north this summer or fall[?] Sure would be glad to see you again. Try and make it and we'll all go out for a dinner.

To my amazement, not only did Roy's letter verify his drinking problem, it made clear that my parents knew about it. The letter also confirmed Barbara Mondl had not continued to work at the tavern after Elsie's death and that Roy had to hire a new bartender. I had no idea what gift I'd sent Roy—maybe cookies?

Just when I thought I had Elsie's story wrapped up, I received a letter from Bill Johnson's youngest son, Eric, (*names changed for privacy*) and learned I hadn't been the only twelve-year-old on whom Elsie's 1960 death left a deep impression. Eric wrote in response to a letter I'd sent to his sister, but since she had no longer lived at home in 1960, so she forwarded my query to him. He replied:

> *I remember ... my father sitting at the kitchen table and telling my mother what had happened. I remember him saying that Roy and Elsie were arguing about something and that Elsie got mad and went upstairs. After a little while they heard a thump on the floor, and I remember him saying ... "We all went running up there." [T]hey found her lying on the floor and ... there was an empty or partially empty bottle of aspirin there near her. I remember my dad telling my mom ... "we worked and worked on her but just couldn't bring her around[. W]e couldn't even get her to throw up. She was totally unresponsive."*
>
> *I also remember my dad saying that they all had to give a statement to the Shawano County Sheriff's Department deputy that showed up. They called the local town constable and he had called Shawano County ... I remember that this was very upsetting for my father. They were all friends and it bothered him very much.*

Many of the details Eric mentioned (the thump heard on the floor above, the efforts to revive Elsie) lined up with what I'd heard about her death. Either Eric was wrong about the aspirin bottle, or Elsie had taken aspirin in addition to Nembutal.

But one statement was glaringly different from the story of her death I had heard from Green family members. Eric reported that Roy had been present in the tavern when Elsie died—not off on some errand in Antigo. I considered his words: *If Roy had been in the tavern that Sunday morning, that one fact changed everything.*

I HAD OPENED ERIC'S LETTER ON A Friday evening and had to wait until Monday morning to phone Shawano County officials. But when I did, no luck. I called only to learn the sheriff's department keeps records no more than ten years, unless the documents figure into a court case. Nor could the Shawano County coroner locate documents from over half a century ago.

There was apparently no way to prove whether Eric remembered the event accurately and Roy had lied, yet Eric's words appeared more likably than did Roy's statement about being in Antigo that morning. If Roy's story was correct and he had not been present in the tavern at the time of Elsie's death, the decision of the undertaker and bartender (as reported by Roy) not to call for help had always struck me as odd. Even if there were no emergency services available in Mattoon at the time, surely they would have called the sheriff instead of waiting around for Roy to return. Elsie did not die immediately, and Bill and Barbara would likely have wanted all the help they could get.

Eric Johnson had no reason to dissemble and his letter completely changed my perspective on Elsie's death. I leaned back in my office chair and watched the revised scene play out in my mind.

If Elsie had retreated upstairs after arguing in the tavern with Roy, there would have been no need for a suicide note; and if by chance there had been a note, Roy would have had easy opportunity to pocket it and later destroy it.

All along, Roy's claimed absence from the tavern had made no sense. He must have lied first to Pete, stating that he had gone to Antigo that Sunday morning. But why lie about it? Roy must have feared Elsie's family would blame him for her death, especially if they learned he had been drinking and argued with Elsie. No doubt these worries were justified, but his lie backfired, magnifying his fears beyond all proportion.

The Green family viewed with suspicion both Roy's decision to bury Elsie in Mattoon and his supposed drive to Antigo on a Sunday morning, leaving Elsie alone with the undertaker and bartender in their tavern. Elsie's siblings knew Roy well enough to know he didn't leave Mattoon to attend church services. They knew Roy well enough to suspect he was lying and imagined all sorts of scenarios to explain his flight from the tavern—from a tryst with Agnes to an effort to be absent from the scene of a well-planned murder.

Roy's attempt to vindicate himself had the opposite effect. Instead of blaming him for his failure to prevent Elsie's suicide, his lie provoked Elsie's family into suspecting him of foul play. I took three deep, calming breaths. Roy's deceit had a profound impact on our family. His untruth reverberated through the years, leaving a wake of mistrust, puzzlement, and anger.

Not only did Roy's lie cause my family to view him with distrust, it pointed suspicion at Bill Johnson, an innocent man who had befriended him. Worse, it might have brought Johnson into collusion with Roy's misrepresentation of the facts. By the time they brought Elsie's body to Racine, the undertaker must have known about Roy's falsehood, and that falsehood must have affected Johnson's friendship with Roy—in subtle, if not obvious ways.

I wondered if Roy had ever fully understood the ramifications of his falsehood. Did he regret the lie and wish he could take it back? What had he learned from Elsie's death? Had he learned to stop lying?

He learned to stop drinking, I reminded myself, before another thought cut in. Even though Roy wrote my parents that he was *"not drinking a drop [and] haven't had anything to drink for some time,"* he didn't actually state that he had stopped drinking. I shook my head at my own naiveté. What were the chances that Roy stopped drinking while continuing to run the tavern for another nine years after Elsie's death? Right.

Even after *Elsie's Story* found a publishing home, added corroboration of Roy's drinking arrived in the form of a phone conversation with Barbara Mondl's son, Philip Beck, who was seventeen when Elsie died.

"Roy was a horrible drinker," Phil said. "Elsie was not a happy person. She was withdrawn and quiet," he added. "Elsie may have been verbally abused and possibly physically abused, too."

He should know. After Elsie died and Roy remarried, Phil worked weekends and summers at the tavern from 1963 to 1968. "I would tend bar for Agnes. Roy was incapacitated a majority of the time. She ran the business. He was never around or available."

Agnes had "... bruises on her arms and face," Phil said. "Roy was not a pleasant man and was worse when he was drinking."

Regardless of the abuse, Roy was a talented wood-worker, though he often left projects unfinished. One project he did complete involved cutting a window into the north wall behind the bar. Above the window, Roy hung an elaborate sunburst he created using strips and layers of different woods.

Another time, Roy planned to replace the kitchen floor of their upstairs apartment. He strung a multitude of lines in a crisscross pattern about six inches above the floor to outline the placement of tiles. Agnes "had to walk through these squares to get to the bedroom."

She showed Phil the project in progress, and they sometimes talked after closing the tavern at the end of the night. Agnes's marriage was not a happy one, according to Phil. But unlike Elsie, "she tolerated him."

Phil reviewed Elsie's death certificate and substantiated Eric's mention of a town constable. Phil also tied up another loose end: He remembered the woman whose signature had been crossed off at the bottom of Elsie's death certificate. Phil correctly deciphered the crossed-out name as "Estella" (not Mathilda after all) Schwanz, who had operated an informal clinic not far from the tavern; primarily it served as a birthing center.

Schwanz, age seventy-one in 1960, was also Bill Johnson's mother-in-law. But why she signed Elsie's death certificate in the space reserved for the registrar's signature will remain a mystery.

A few years earlier, a social worker friend had asked whether Elsie had been physically abused. I had replied that there was no evidence to suggest it. Maybe my friend had sensed the signs of an abuser in Roy's behavior before they were clear to me.

My mind went back to Beatrice. Had Roy's version of her leave-taking strayed from the truth? Maybe Beatrice had fled with her babe in arms from an abusive husband. The possibility that Elsie had been physically abused hardened my determination to tell her story, both to honor her memory and warn other women of the potential for abuse in relationships.

THANKS TO THE GENEROUS INPUT OF friends and relatives, people from Mattoon, librarians, and public officials, my understanding of Roy has changed over the decades. First, there were memories of the smiling uncle handing me a stuffed animal. Then there was the recollection of a depressed, underemployed man in an era when men were expected to be the lionhearted heads of households. Later, there was the estranged and ostracized uncle, spoken about primarily in whispers. But always, he was a large, powerful man, who, even when depressed, towered over me.

When I began this book, I was afraid to face him even in my dreams; as late as 2012, I didn't want to anger a killer, albeit a dead one. Nor did I want to one day face him in an afterlife if I'd mistakenly accused him of a murder he didn't commit.

As I began the search for answers to the cause and circumstances of Elsie's death, I sought closure, a chance to put the questions to rest. I sought acceptance of her fate, whatever the details of that fate might be. The ambiguity of Elsie's death, as Dr. Pauline Boss had explained, made the grieving process more arduous for me and the rest of the Green family.

As I learned more about Roy, my fear of him slowly disappeared. When I learned he had not killed Beatrice, had probably fathered her child, and had not outright murdered Elsie, my anger ebbed. Slowly, I saw another side to an all-too-human man who felt trapped by circumstances beyond his control. I'm not granting him any excuses; there can be none for creating an environment of supreme harm to Elsie—and possibly abusing her.

One day, I was surprised to find my verdict of Roy leaning toward compassion and sadness. The quest for truth and finding some degree of closure in the end can lead to the clarity of forgiveness.

Scholars have studied forgiveness and created various models for describing its stages. Dr. Robert Enright, professor of educational psychology at the University of Wisconsin-Madison, pioneered the study of forgiveness and theorized four phases of forgiveness— the Uncovering Phase, Decision Phase, Work Phase, and Deepening Phase.

For me, the Uncovering Phase happened in the 1980s, when I understood the long impact of Elsie's death and began to search for answers. Later, I thought I would probably decide to forgive Roy, not because of anything he had done or failed to do, but because forgiving him enabled me to move forward.

During the Work Phase, I learned about the complexities of Roy's life and came to at least partially understand his responses to challenges. Finally, once I better understood Elsie's fate, I could finally forgive Roy, without condoning his lies.

Roy rarely appears in my dreams these days, but when he does, he is smiling, though from a distance. I wave at him and he disappears.

Elsie is a different story. I see her light more clearly than ever. She often feels close at hand, a yellow star hovering in my office loft just out of reach. Not a ghost exactly, more like a benevolent presence, wanting only the best for me.

I want the best for her, too, and am wistful about the missed second half of a life that might have been. If only she'd had the advantages of age. What panoramas might she have seen as a fifty- or sixty- or seventy-year-old? What vistas might she have enjoyed in her later years?

Age can transform a black-and-white world into a full palette with shades of varied intensities. It also can provide a sort of personal scientific instrument—a combination telescope-microscope that easily zooms in and out, to look at either the broad view or the smallest detail of a life journey.

I can see a happy Elsie waving from afar, as easily as catch a glimpse of a sunny aunt knitting a maroon sweater or serving chocolate cake at a laughter-filled family gathering.

There is so much to celebrate about Elsie's life—her quick smile, generosity, and loyalty toward family, among countless other positive attributes. I'm grateful to have known her and, selfishly, for the enigma of her death, which gave me a degree of direction and a path to follow. Her light remains, and maybe one day Elsie and I will dance together along the road in some future world.

LESSONS LEARNED:
FAMILY HISTORY RESEARCH TIPS

1. **Pay deep attention.** Oral histories can accomplish more than simply confirming facts about where an ancestor attended school, married, or divorced. They can set the scene and provide context, which can point to motivations and new research avenues.

2. **Let people ramble** when conducting oral histories. This may seem obvious, but I had to remind myself that an oral history interview is different from a news interview with its more focused topic and deadline.

3. **Remember that you are not always right.** Allow new facts come to light.

4. **Beware:** you may learn more than you really wanted to know about your ancestors.

5. **Create a timeline** to help organize events and understand the impact one event might have on another. If, for example, several siblings are marrying and having children at a dizzying rate, does a younger sister feel pressure to join them?

6. **Celebrate discrepancies.** They offer clues and suppositions to test.

7. **Be thorough.** Double check every fact and rumor with a second and third source whenever possible. Be tenacious. Follow wherever your research road leads.

8. **Look at everything,** discount nothing: even your dreams may suggest a new research avenue or direction.

9. **Be patient:** new information comes to light all the time. When the house at 811 Orchard Street, Racine, became part of the National and State Orchard Street Historic District in 2016, the district's documentation suggested that Elsie may have been a live-in worker at the residence—a likelihood I'd never considered.

10. **Go in person.** The wealth of Internet sources present a temptation to forgo in-person research. But had I not visited the Wisconsin Office of Vital Statistics, I might never have found Joan Woodson's birth certificate or the penciled note on its reverse, placing her in Chicago in 1941.

11. **Relax.** After you have asked and explored and groped for answers, your questions have laid the groundwork. Often the information needed will appear on cue. (See "Be patient" above.)

ACKNOWLEDGMENTS

Steady and unyielding through the decades, Aunt Elsie inspired this work and kept it going even when I was busy with jobs and writing and publishing assignments. When I was young I did not know she would be so faithful.

I am grateful for all the cousins who shared this life journey during the late twentieth and early twenty-first centuries in a Wisconsin of family farms, North Woods vacations, and 4-H values. May they know how their kind words, reassuring nods, funny stories, or enthusiastic hugs kept me on track.

The memories they openly shared moved this research along, as did all those cards and letters written by aunts and uncles and saved by my mother. The family history work completed by Gladys Green, with help from my uncle Peter Green, served as a runway for much of my journeying into the past, pointing me to new questions to ask, new possibilities to consider.

Lisa Imhoff, Jennifer Eager Ehle, Sonja Albright, and Mary Viney—all members of our Genealogy Writers Group—suggested theories about Elsie's death, recommended research avenues, and read draft chapters. More importantly, they listened and understood when I flailed about in various quagmires of seemingly unanswerable questions. Their understanding ears fueled perseverance.

Mary Lou Santovec listened, too, and offered a continuous string of news clips as potential resources and inspiration.

Virginia Fritzsch and Lori Bessler are only two of the Wisconsin Historical Society staff who provided much-needed information. Public officials from Peoria, Illinois, to Shawano, Wisconsin, and from Iowa to Washington, D.C., often went the extra mile to respond to my queries.

Cousin Jean Makovsky located a crucial record, which led to helpful Roy Cochran and more discoveries that propelled the book forward.

Kathy Zarda, Laurel Collins, Philip Beck, and other current and former Mattoon, Wisconsin, residents provided equally critical information from that community's perspective. They helped me to better understand Elsie and Roy Woodson and their life experience Up North.

My husband Michael Knight taught me much about detailed historical research, from data mining census reports and city directories to the value of oral histories. Moreover, he never wavered: he shared my commitment to the story and read and edited every chapter.

Kira Henschel believed in *Elsie's Story* enough to publish it, designed the book's interior, and offered wise and expert answers to my publishing questions. She also guided efforts to share this work with a broad spectrum of readers, as well as fellow family history buffs.

Sincere thanks to one and all, and to those I have inadvertently omitted. You are all treasured in the box of mementos that is my heart.

ABOUT THE AUTHOR

*D*oris Green was born in Mount Pleasant, Wisconsin, to parents who grew up on farms and carried their agrarian arts and skills into their 1950s suburban neighborhood. She grew up amongst a large cohort of mostly older cousins, as well as wise-cracking uncles and laughing aunts who gathered regularly to play cards, exchange recipes, and swap stories.

Known for his reminiscences, her father was a factory worker by day, and at other times, a gardener, tinkerer, and lover of old farm equipment. Her mother, a former Western Printing worker, was a provider of books—books saved from her days at the plant, books bought for a nickel at Goodwill, and books checked out of Racine's west-side library branch.

Elsie's Story is Green's fourth nonfiction book for general audiences. She also co-wrote a CD, *2500 Business Forms and Letters*, and authored training manuals for credit union professionals. She co-founded and published *Wisconsin Community Banker* magazine for the former Community Bankers of Wisconsin and was a communications specialist with the School of Human Ecology at the University of Wisconsin-Madison.

Green lives with her husband and three distracting cats in a log house near Spring Green, Wisconsin.

Please visit Doris' website at:
www.dorisgreenbooks.wordpress.com